William of Saint-Thierry

The Meditations

with a Monastic Commentary

Translation and Commentary by Thomas X. Davis

Foreword by David N. Bell

Cistercian Publications
www.cistercianpublications.org

LITURGICAL PRESS
Collegeville, Minnesota
www.litpress.org

A Cistercian Publications title published by Liturgical Press

Cistercian Publications
Editorial Offices
161 Grosvenor Street
Athens, Ohio 45701
www.cistercianpublications.org

The works in this volume are translated from *Guillelmi a Sancto Theodorico Opera Omnia, IV: Meditationes Devotissimae*, ed. Paul Verdeyen, CCCM 89 (Turnhout: Brepols, 2005), 1–80, and from *Guillelmi a Sancto Theodorico Opera Omnia, III: De Contemplando Deo, "Meditatio Seduxisti Me,"* ed. Paul Verdeyen, CCCM 88 (Turnhout: Brepols, 2003), 171–73.

Biblical citations are translated by the author of the volume from the Vulgate Bible. All rights reserved.

1   2   3   4   5   6   7   8   9

Library of Congress Cataloging-in-Publication Data

Names: William, of Saint-Thierry, Abbot of Saint-Thierry, approximately 1085–1148? author. | Davis, Thomas X., translator.
Title: The meditations : with a monastic commentary / William of Saint-Thierry ; translation and commentary by Thomas X. Davis ; foreword by David N. Bell.
Description: Collegeville, Minnesota : Cistercian Publications/Liturgical Press, 2022. | Series: Cistercian fathers series ; ninety-one | "The works in this volume are translated from Guillelmi a Sancto Theodorico Opera Omnia, IV: Meditationes Devotissimae, ed. Paul Verdeyen, CCCM 89 (Turnhout: Brepols, 2005), 1-80, and from Guillelmi a Sancto Theodorico Opera Omnia, III: De Contemplando Deo, "Meditatio Seduxisti Me," ed. Paul Verdeyen, CCCM 88 (Turnhout: Brepols, 2003), 171-73." | Includes bibliographical references. | Summary: "This volume of The Meditations is a personal account of William of Saint-Thierry's ascent into Trinitarian intimacy. Includes commentary"— Provided by publisher.
Identifiers: LCCN 2022022463 (print) | LCCN 2022022464 (ebook) | ISBN 9780879071646 (trade paperback) | ISBN 9780879074913 (library bound) | ISBN 9780879071660 (epub) | ISBN 9780879071660 (pdf)
Subjects: LCSH: Meditations—Early works to 1800. | Spiritual life—Christianity—Early works to 1800. | William, of Saint-Thierry, Abbot of Saint-Thierry, approximately 1085–1148?
Classification: LCC BX2179 .W5513 2022 (print) | LCC BX2179 (ebook) | DDC 242/.2—dc23/eng/20220613
LC record available at https://lccn.loc.gov/2022022463
LC ebook record available at https://lccn.loc.gov/2022022464

"Thomas Davis takes his readers on an extraordinary journey through the depths and heights of William of Saint-Thierry's spirituality. The revised translation and commentary illuminate the complexity of early Cistercian thought through the lens of William's poetic imagery. Offering a guided tour through the metaphorical landscape of William's meditations, Davis provides intellectually rich insight, as well as a personal appreciation of Cistercian spiritual practice. This book is a source both for future Cistercian scholarship and for anyone who is drawn to the experiential, authentic nature of monastic prayer."

—Delphine Conzelmann, PhD, University of Basel, Switzerland

"Thomas Davis makes an invaluable contribution in his fresh translation of the *Meditations* and his insightful commentary on William's account of the contemplative ascent into God, situating the abbot of Saint-Thierry's spiritual itinerary in his broader theological vision. That ascent is motivated by ardent love and longing to see God's face, yet paradoxically necessitates a descent into the truth of a person's deepest self where one comes face to face with one's utter brokenness and the need to die to self. There one also discovers the truth of one's unimaginable beloved-ness in the eternal Word. Ascending then through the Incarnation, one's will is united with God's love—the Holy Spirit—in the *unitas spiritus* where one's life is transformed and one's spirit is enfolded in the ineffable embrace of the Divine Persons of the Trinity."

—Glenn E. Myers, PhD, Professor of Church History
and Theological Studies, Crown College

"'You have made us for yourself, O Lord, and our hearts are restless until they rest in you.' So wrote St. Augustine at the beginning of his *Confessions*, one of the most remarkable prayer-texts in the Christian tradition. Some 700 years later, a closely related insight drove William of Saint-Thierry's to pen the meditative prayers of this book. Blessed with an intimate knowledge of the Bible and the medieval interpretive tradition, a poetic sense of imagery, a refined Christian metaphysics, and an ardent personal faith, William delivered a remarkable text to guide thoughts to God. This new volume gives us a precious new portal into one of Christian history's outstanding minds."

—Fr. Joseph Van House, OCist, Our Lady of Dallas Abbey, University of Dallas

Contents

Acknowledgments

The origin of this translation and commentary is an invitation I received in 2017 to present the *Meditations of William of Saint-Thierry* during the 2018 formation program for the temporary professed nuns and monks of the US Trappist-Cistercian Region. My intent was to use the English translation by Sr. Penelope, CSMV. In preparing material for the course, I realized that a new translation of the *Meditations* would be feasible. As William's Latin at times can be more than difficult, Sr. Penelope is certainly to be recognized for blazing a trail in producing her English translation. Ironically, Fr. Cassian Russell (Monastery of the Holy Spirit in Conyers, Georgia) extended the invitation to me a week after I had decided to bring closure to studies in William and move into another patristic area. Dr. James France gave me permission to use the manuscript image of William from Zwettl, Stiftsbibliothek MS. 144, fol. 26, as part of my presentation; it now appears on the cover of this volume, by permission from Zisterzienserstift Zwettl. I am thus grateful in many ways to Sr. Penelope, Dr. France, Fr. Cassian, and the monastic participants of the formation program. I also thank Brepols Publications for permission to translate their publication of Paul Verdeyen's critical edition of William's *Meditativæ orationes*.

Sr. Grace Remington (Our Lady of the Mississippi Abbey, Iowa) kindly agreed to review my translation of William's Latin, not knowing the extensive work involved. She respected my style of translating while making helpful suggestions and calling attention to insights into William's teaching. Dr. Leo Guardado (Assistant Professor of Theology at Fordham University, New York) assisted me by making basic resources available and was instrumental in arriving at the title of my commentary on the Meditations. Both he and Fr. Duane Sisson (The Episcopal Diocese of Northern California) gave encouragement at critical times during the process of translating.

Although they were not involved in this book, my sincere appreciation belongs to E. Rozanne Elder, David N. Bell, Tyler Sergent, and the late James France for their help over the years in my studies of William. I am particularly grateful to David for his gracious Foreword to this volume. Marsha Dutton, editor of Cistercian Publications, has facilitated this publication through her familiarity with early Cistercian authors. I am ever grateful to her. Marsha's dedicated work contributes to making our great Cistercian tradition available to numerous persons.

Thomas X. Davis, OCSO
January 26, 2022
Solemnity of Robert, Alberic, and Stephen Harding,
    Founders of Citeaux

Abbreviations

CCCM	Corpus Christianorum, Continuatio Mediaevalis
CCSL	Corpus Christianorum, Series Latina
CF	Cistercian Fathers series, Cistercian Publications
CS	Cistercian Studies series, Cistercian Publications
CSEL	Corpus Scriptorum Ecclesiasticorum Latinorum
CSQ	*Cistercian Studies Quarterly*
Inst incl	Aelred of Rievaulx, *De institutione inclusarum*
Mor	Gregory I, *Moralia in Iob*
PL	J.-P. Migne, Patrologiae cursus completus, series latina
S, SS	Sermo, Sermones
SBOp	Sancti Bernardi Opera, Editiones Cistercienses
SCh	Sources Chrétiennes, Éditiones de Cerf

Works of William of Saint-Thierry

Adv Abl	*Disputatio adversus Petrum Abælardum*
Ænig	*Ænigma fidei*
Brev com	*Brevis commentatio in Cantica canticorum*
Cant	*Expositio super Cantica canticorum*
Cant Amb	*Super Cantica canticorum ex operibus sancti Ambrosii*
Cant Greg	*Super Cantica canticorum ex operibus sancti Gregorii*
Contemp	*De contemplando Deo*
Ep frat	*Epistola (aurea) ad fratres de Monte Dei*
Ep Rup	*Epistola ad Rupertum*
Er Guil	*De erroribus Guillelmi de Conchis*
Exp Rom	*Expositio super epistolam ad Romanos*
Med	*Meditativæ orationes; Meditations*

Nat am   *De natura et dignitate amoris*
Nat corp   *De natura corporis et animæ*
Orat   *Oratio domni Willelmi*
Phys an   *Physica animæ*
Phys corp   *Physica humani corporis*
Resp   *Responsio ad cardinalem Matthæum*
Sac Alt   *De sacramento altaris liber*
Spec   *Speculum fidei*
Vita Bern   *Sancti Bernardi vita prima*

Selected Works of Augustine of Hippo

Adnot in Job
              Adnotationes in Iob

Civ Dei   *City of God*
C Max Arian
              Contra Maximinium Arianum
Conf   *Confessiones*
C S Arr   *Contra sermonem Arrianorum*
En in Ps   *Enarratio in Psalmo*
Gen ad Litt
              De Genesi ad litteram
Gen ad Litt imp
              De Genesi ad litteram opus imperfectum
In Ev Ioann
              In Evangelium Ioannis tractatus
Med   *Meditationes*
Praed sanct
              De prædestinatione sanctorum
Quæst ev   *Quæstiones evangelicarum*
Sol   *Soliloquiæ*

Selected Works of Bernard of Clairvaux

Ep   *Epistulae*
Hum   *Liber de gradibus humilitatis et superbiæ*

OS	*Sermo in festivitate omnium sanctorum*
P Epi	*Sermo in dominica I post octavam Epiphaniæ*
SC	*Sermones super Cantica canticorum*
Sent	*Sententiae*

Selected Works of Origen

Com in

| Cant | *Commentary on the Canticle* |
| In Num | *Homilies on the Book of Numbers* |

Foreword

Long years ago, Fr. Thomas Davis and I were traveling from the monastery of Vina to the great medieval congress at Kalamazoo. On the flight we had been talking of this and that, including William of Saint-Thierry, when Fr. Thomas, emerging from some deep monastic reverie, turned to me and said, "You know, David, it's just as well that William died when he did. If he'd lived a little longer, he would certainly have joined the Carthusians, and then we could never have claimed him as our own."

I suspect that Fr. Thomas was right, for William was a singularly complex character with his own distinctive views, and his complexity is revealed in his writings. The work presented here—the thirteen Meditations—are complex in themselves. It is still not clear when they were written or, indeed, why they were written, though most scholars seem to think that they were composed at different times over a number of years. There is, however, no agreement as to when those times were or how long it took to produce the Meditations. There is to my mind a certain element of incompleteness about the text, of trains of thought begun but not concluded, though the main theme (as we shall see in a moment) is clear enough.

What is not in doubt is that the Meditations provide us with an important point of entry into William's mind and heart, and it is time for a new translation. The last complete English translation was by Sister Penelope Lawson, a religious of the Anglican Community of St. Mary the Virgin (CSMV) at Wantage in Oxfordshire. She was born in 1890, entered the Community in 1915, and died in 1977 at the age of eighty-seven. Her translation was published in the Cistercian Fathers Series in 1971,[1] but that translation is merely a slightly updated version of Sister Penelope's earlier translation that appeared in 1954.[2] The main changes are no more than grammatical—*thous* become *yous*, and early modern English *sayest* and *liveth* become *say* and *live*—but not all the translations are quite accurate, and there are some that are just plain wrong. In other words, it is almost seventy years since the last complete English translation of the Meditations appeared, and it certainly time for a new and more accurate version.

It should be added that translating William is not easy. One often finds oneself sailing along in the calm seas of fairly straightforward medieval Latin, heavily affected by Scripture, only to founder on a passage of almost impenetrable complexity that may have several layers of meaning. William was also well educated, widely read, and wholly familiar with the language of the Schools, and unless one is also familiar with that language, it is easy to miss the subtlety of what he is saying. One example will suffice. In the first Meditation, William tells us that God's foreknowledge and God's wisdom are one and the same (he has probably taken this from Faustus of Riez, though Hugh of Saint-Victor says much the same thing), and that in that foreknowledge/wisdom "are eternally the causes of all things that have been made temporally."[3] William is here echoing the Aristotelian idea (undoubtedly via Boethius) of formal and efficient causes, all defined by their association with the First Cause, on which everything that comes into being is existentially dependent. This is probably not immediately apparent to the modern reader, and there are many passages that are far more difficult. Many twelfth-century writers were more than happy to say in ten words what could easily be said in three. William, on

---

1. *The Works of William of St Thierry, Volume One: On Contemplating God, Prayer, Meditations*, trans. Sister Penelope [Lawson], CF 3 (Shannon: Irish University Press, 1971, with numerous re-printings).

2. *The Meditations of William of St Thierry: Meditativæ Orationes*, trans. A Religious of C.S.M.V. [Sr. Penelope Lawson] (London: A. R. Mowbray, 1954).

3. Med 1.7: *In qua sunt omnes causae aeternaliter omnium quae fiunt tempora.*

the other hand, tends to say in three what we might prefer he had said in ten.

Fr. Thomas's commentary clearly shows us that William was a fine theologian, but in saying that we must bear in mind the nature of theology before it became distorted with the logical pyrotechnics of later scholasticism. For William, and virtually everyone else up to and including Thomas Aquinas and Bonaventure, the experiential knowledge of God was the natural and logical end of the theological quest, or, if we may quote the Venerable Bede, "Theology is one thing and one thing alone: the contemplation of God."[4]

For William, this experiential contemplative knowledge was connatural knowledge. That is to say, since we are created to the image and likeness of God, *ad imaginem et similitudinem Dei*,[5] it follows that to contemplate ourselves is to contemplate our Creator. But the *ad* here is important. It implies a process, a development, whereas "*in* his image and likeness" might imply something rather more static. The *ad* implies two things: first, that we have not yet reached our goal, and second, that we need to do something about it.

Unfortunately, the image has been corrupted and stained by sin, and although the image itself can never be lost, what we see when we contemplate ourselves is a distorted image. Putting it another way, we have retained the image, but have lost the likeness. It is our responsibility, therefore, to restore the lost likeness and reveal the image in its true splendor.

How is this to be done? By following the path of virtue and avoiding the lure of vice. But in order to achieve this, we need the help of grace, and grace is none other than the Holy Spirit. William's theology, in fact, may be accurately described as pneumatocentric, Spirit-centered, for it is in and through the Holy Spirit that we become more and more virtuous, more and more like God. We can never actually *become* God—that would be a blasphemous

---

4. Bede, *In Evangelium Lucae*, III.x; PL 92:471D: *Una ergo et sola est theologia, id est, contemplatio Dei*. He says the same thing in his *Homilia LVII in die Assumptionis Mariae*; PL 94:421A.

5. Gen 1:26.

suggestion—but, by grace and only by grace, we can become "what God is," *quod Deus est*: good in his goodness, truthful in his truth, just in his justice, righteous in his righteousness, pure in his purity, and so on. But since the Holy Spirit is all that is common to Father and Son (this is pure Augustine)—their mutual love, goodness, kindness, grace, peace, fellowship, will, etc.—it is by participation in the Holy Spirit that we restore the lost likeness. But since the Holy Spirit is also one of the three Persons of the undivided Trinity, there may come a time, if God wills, that we participate in the Holy Spirit to such an extent that we find ourselves in the very midst of the Trinity itself. This is the ultimate Trinitarian intimacy of which Fr. Thomas speaks, and it is the rapture of the highest mystical experience. The clearest descriptions of this high state appear not in the Meditations, but in the letter to the Carthusian brethren of Mont-Dieu.

The customary division of the text into twelve meditations (the thirteenth was published by Dom Jean-Marie Déchanet in 1946)[6] was the work of Bertrand Tissier in 1662, but Fr. Thomas has decided to present his new translation and commentary as one uninterrupted whole. In this way, we may see more clearly William's slow ascent from unlikeness to likeness, for as he says in the letter to the brethren of Mont-Dieu, "likeness to God is the whole of human perfection. For this alone were we created and do we live: that we might be like God, for we were created to his image."[7]

Fr. Thomas's commentary is not written from the outside, but from the inside. That is to say, it is the commentary of a monk

---

6. Jean-Marie Déchanet, "Meditative oratio n°. XIII: Une page encore inédite de Guillaume de Saint-Thierry," *Collectanea O.C.R.* 7 (1946): 2–12. I have suggested elsewhere that the so-called *Oratio domni Willelmi* might also be another unfinished meditation. See David N. Bell, "The Prayer of Dom William: A Study and New Translation," in *Unity of Spirit: Studies on William of Saint-Thierry in Honor of E. Rozanne Elder*, ed. F. Tyler Sergent, Aage Rydstrøm-Poulsen, and Marsha L. Dutton, CS 268 (Collegeville, MN: Cistercian Publications, 2015), 21–36.

7. Ep frat 259; CCCM 88:281: *Propter hoc enim solum et creati sumus et uiuimus, ut Deo similes simus. Ad imaginem enim Dei creati sumus.*

writing on a monk's writing. Fr. Thomas was superior and then abbot of Vina in California for thirty-eight years, and for more than seventy years he has lived the life of a Cistercian monk of the Strict Observance. Unlike William, he has given no indication of any desire to join the Carthusians. His commentary, therefore, is, as I have said, that of an insider, one who has lived and still lives the way laid so many centuries ago by Saint Benedict, and revitalized by those giants of the twelfth century, Robert of Molesme, Alberic, Stephen Harding, Bernard of Clairvaux, and so many others, not least William of Saint-Thierry. And if William, who was always very much his own person, sometimes entertained ideas that were somewhat at variance with those of his confrères—I am thinking of the paucity of his references to the Virgin Mary, or his attitude towards meditation on the physical form of Jesus of Nazareth (dwelling on the events of Christ's humanity may actually hinder what William calls true spiritual prayer), or his views on manual labor[8]—the commentary of Fr. Thomas will provide a sure guide to the spiritual life for all those interested in realizing their true nature and experiencing the vision of God, which, as William says in the *Enigma of Faith*, is begun here below "by holiness of life and by the practice of divine contemplation," though it is perfected in heaven.[9]

David N. Bell
St. John's, NL, Canada

8. See David N. Bell, *Handmaid of the Lord: Mary, the Cistercians, and Armand-Jean de Rancé*, CS 293 (Collegeville, MN: Cistercian Publications, 2021), 96–100; Bell, "The Prayer of Dom William," 26–28; and David N. Bell, "*In manibus suis*: Guillaume de Saint-Thierry, les Pères du désert, et la spiritualité du travail manuel," in *Signy l'Abbaye, site cistercien enfoui, site de mémoire, et Guillaume de Saint-Thierry: Actes du Colloque international d'Études cisterciennes, 9, 10, 11 septembre 1998, Les Vieilles Forges (Ardennes)*, ed. Nicole Boucher (Signy l'Abbaye: Association des Amis de l'Abbaye de Signy, 2000), 475–85.
9. William, Ænig 23; CCCM 89A:143.

The Meditations

Preface

Around 1125, William of Saint-Thierry began writing a treatise usually in English titled *Meditations*, known in Latin as *Meditativæ orationes,* Meditative Prayers. He undoubtedly edited this treatise though the years; 1137 is usually accepted as a date for its completion. This treatise rises as a creation from William's life of prayer rooted in the sacraments, particularly the Eucharist, the Benedictine *Opus Dei,* the Divine Office, and *Lectio Divina,* his personal, prayerful reading. The *Meditations* reveal William's most ardent prayerful reflections, his inner conflicts, and, consequently, his intimate relationship with the Triune God.

By 1162, the *Meditativæ orationes* had been divided into twelve individual meditations. This arrangement has been handed down ever since and accepted as *The Twelve Meditations of William of Saint-Thierry.*

To have some understanding and appreciation of the inner continuity that these twelve meditations possess for showing William's intimate relationship with the triune God, this present translation of his *Meditative Prayers* presents them as one continuous treatise. Marsha Dutton, editor of this book, pointed out to me an aspect of the work: "The theology of this work is so hard that expressing it clearly [in English] is enormously difficult. . . . William is really doing narrative theology, explaining the life of a seeker in an autobiographical format." I believe this observation brings to the fore an essential value that the *Meditative Prayers* have for us. We see William using his faith in a sound theology flowing from Divine Revelation to create in his consciousness a new perspective, a new way, to seek the face of the triune God. This vision opens for us such possibilities.

In translating the *Meditations*, I used the Latin text of Paul Verdeyen, SJ, found in volume 89 of Brepols Publishers' Corpus Christianorum, Continuatio Mediaevalis (CCCM). In that volume Verdeyen titles the work *Meditationes Devotissimae,* which can be translated as *Most Ardent Reflections.* He maintains the twelvefold traditional division but has different paragraph numbering from that in previous editions and translations. I have retained his paragraph numbering.

I have translated and included as an epilogue to my translation of the *Meditations* an unknown author's brief text now generally known as Meditation Thirteen. My source for that work is the edition in CCCM 88 by Verdeyen, which he titled "Meditatio: Seduxisti Me." The Latin of that text has no paragraph numbers, but I have added them here for ease of reference.

Scriptural references throughout the volume come from the Vulgate translation of Saint Jerome.

A thoughtful and contemplative reading of these most ardent reflections offers a penetrating insight into William's participation in and intimate relationship with the triune God, for whom he lived and for whom he longed. He writes in his *Golden Letter* to Carthusian monks that his reflections can form minds to prayer. My commentary on William's *Most Ardent Reflections* endeavors to offer my personal reflections and explanations as a guide through his meditations.

Thomas X. Davis
Abbey of New Clairvaux

The Meditations[1]

1.1 *O the depth of the riches of the Wisdom and Knowledge of God! How unfathomable are his judgments, and how incomprehensible are his ways! For who has known the thought of the Lord, or who has been his counselor?*[2] *For you show compassion, Lord, to whom you show compassion. Lord, you offer mercy on whom you will have compassion. In fact, it is not because of the one who wills, or the one who runs, but of you,* Our God, *having compassion.*[3]

1.2 At this, the earthen vessel recoils from the hand of the one who shaped it, the one who says through the prophet, *I made, and I will carry.*[4] It recoils from the hand holding and carrying it. About to fall, about to break, about to crumble, it shrieks, *What more does He want? For who resists His will?*[5] And it adds, *Why have you made me this way?*[6] The earthen and good-for-nothing

---

1. This translation presents the meditations as an unbroken text, apparently their original format (see above, page 3). However, numbered paragraphs in the translation indicate the numbering of 12 meditations following the paragraphing in Paul Verdeyen's edition: *Guillelmi a Sancto Theodorico Opera Omnia*, Pars IV, *Meditationes Devotissimae*, ed. Paul Verdeyen, CCCM 89 (Turnhout: Brepols Publishers, 2005): (e.g., 1.1= Meditation 1, paragraph 1). When I further divide those paragraphs I do not add numbers.

2. Rom 11:32-34

3. Rom 9:15-16

4. Isa 46:4

5. Rom 9:19

6. *this way = sic.* This Latin word appears significant in the *Meditations*; William uses it 79 times, 15 times alone in the first meditation. For William in the *Meditations, sic* expresses a definite manner of existing, being rooted in the here and now but with consequences in eternity. This *sic* is integral to his teaching about the profound bonding between what is in time (*sic*) and what is in eternity. Because of the word's importance in the work, I note it each time it appears to indicate its

vessel, *a vessel of* reproach and *anger*, fit for destruction,[7] speaks to you this way,[8] O eternal Wisdom. It ought rather to tremble before you and to pray to you, who *have the power to make from the same lump of clay one vessel for honor and another for reproach.*[9]

1.3 But vessels of honor and choice endure. *Vessels of mercy, which you have prepared for glory,*[10] do not speak like this. Rather, they acknowledge you as their creator and potter.[11] Indeed, they are the clay molded in your hand, and woe to them if they fall from this hand. They will be broken, crushed, and reduced to nothing! They know this and do not forsake your grace.

1.4 Have mercy, Lord, have mercy! You are our potter,[12] and we are the clay. Somehow or other, we have held together until now! Until now, your powerful hand carries us. And until now, we hang on to your three fingers—faith, hope, and charity—on which *you weigh the massive bulk of the earth,*[13] the strength of your holy church. Have mercy, Lord! Hold us lest we fall from your hand. Fire *our inner depths and our heart*[14] by the fire of your Holy Spirit, and *strengthen the work you have accomplished in us,*[15] lest we fall apart and be reduced into our clay, or into nothingness.

1.5 We are created for you by you, and our turning is completely[16] towards you. We acknowledge you our Maker and the one who formed us. We adore and invoke your wisdom in arranging [all things for us] and your goodness and mercy in holding us together and sustaining us. Bring us to completion, you who have made us! Bring to completion the all-embracing form of your image and likeness, according to which you formed us![17]

---

relevance to the meaning of the sentence. This relationship becomes clearer as the *Meditations* develop and is a foundational element of William's ascent into contemplative intimacy.

7. Rom 9:22

8. *Sic*

9. Rom 9:21

10. Rom 9:23

11. *Figulus*

12. *Plastes*

13. Isa 40:12

14. Ps 25:2

15. Ps 67:29

16. Song 7:10

17. Gen 1:26

1.6 The clay vessel, destined to be clay, speaks to you, the voice of one who is falling and bursting out, *Why have you made me this way?*[18] But the vessel destined for honor does not speak like this. *For with the heart it believes for righteousness, and with the mouth it confesses for salvation*[19] that you are good and have done all things well.[20]

You have done well; well have you made one for honor and another for disgrace, giving free will to both, so that each one does what that one does, not forced by necessity but with a spontaneous will, and each should have his own due merit for virtue. For virtue is the spontaneous assent of a will to good.

1.7 O eternal Wisdom, having knowledge of everything, you knew beforehand concerning both options, how one would use freedom to decide what kind of judge it would be of itself and its circumstances, and which one would not receive in vain the grace prepared for it.[21] But your foreknowledge does not force them to be what they will be, as if they had to be this way[22] because you foreknew they would be this way.[23] Rather, because they would be this way,[24] and you know all things before they happen, you knew this is how it would be, and your foreknowledge is never mistaken.

This, God, is your foreknowledge—your wisdom itself that coexists with you eternally and would do so even if not a single creature existed. In your wisdom eternally exist all causes of everything that happens in time, as well as the very foreknowledge of a creature to be created in its own time.

1.8 For you, this creature was not something in the future, because in your very Word, consubstantial with you and through whom whatever was made was made, was life![25] Life was already existing this way[26] in the Word just as it was going to be, exactly the way[27] it was going to be, because in him *was life*. However, it is not that life was forcing things to be so, but what would come to be this way[28] existed already this way[29] in him.

18. *Sic;* Rom 9:20	22. *Sic*	26. *Sic*
19. Rom 10:10	23. *Sic*	27. *Sic*
20. Mark 7:37	24. *Sic*	28. *Sic*
21. 2 Cor 6:1	25. John 1:3-4	29. *Sic*

What then? Does the way something will come to be in time cause what exists to exist in God? Is it the cause of eternity? After all, if the thing were to end up not being this way[30] in time, it appears impossible to be able to exist eternally in the Word of God. But your knowledge, or rather foreknowledge, God, is your truth itself that declares, *I am the truth.*[31] And just as you, God, do not force a thing to be as it is going to be by foreknowing what it will be, so in this same way,[32] you cannot be forced by it to foreknow what it will be. Yes, for you nothing is past, nothing is future, but you are always what you are. But in whatever way a thing may exist, either past, present, or future, it is life in Your Word!

1.9 *The wicked walk around in a circle.*[33] Whoever you are, take yourself to the center of truth, away from the circle of error! In such a circle,[34] the clay vessel is reduced to its own clay. Divine foreknowledge does not force the vessel to this fate, because it does not hide this future[35] from it. Nevertheless, because God foreknew that the vessel would be this way,[36] God predetermined it to destruction.

1.10 God's foreknowledge is his goodness, which from eternity has been prepared for all, although not accepted by all. About those who will accept it and those who will not, this also is not foreign to God's foreknowledge, which, as is said, was prepared for everyone from eternity because of God's goodness, even had nothing been created.

For this goodness of God is the Holy Spirit, coeternal with the Father and the Son. Therefore it is written that at the creation of the world *the Spirit* of the Lord *was moving upon the waters.*[37] That is to say, he was offering himself to all and manifesting himself to all by being generous and providing things needful for their use, as is proper to the Holy Spirit, and simultaneously fleeing from an ill-willed soul, in whom wisdom cannot enter.[38]

1.11 Therefore, God's foreknowledge about creatures is foreknowledge on the part of God and predestination on the part of

---

30. *Sic*
31. John 14:6
32. *Sic*

33. Ps 11:9
34. *Sic*
35. *Sic*

36. *Sic*
37. Gen 1:2
38. Wis 1:4

humans. This is election or rejection. Thus that saying, *You have not chosen me, but I have chosen you.*[39] Predestination, however, is the preparation for grace. Grace is indeed the effect itself. Concerning this—why one person should be taken into grace and another rejected[40]—do not ask unless you wish to go wrong.

1.12 If you are proud, this is not hidden from the foreknowledge of God. Nor do you escape his providence whereby you are predestined to punishment prepared for the proud. For *God resists the proud but gives grace to the humble.*[41] Therefore, pride is both what is deserved and a sign of rejection, just as humility is both what is deserved and a sign of election.

The clay vessel then says, *Why have you made me this way?*[42] That is to say, Why have you predestined me to destruction? Truth responds to it: That I may speak in your own terms, it was because I knew beforehand that you would be a future vessel of wrath suitable for destruction, a future fool, you, who would neither know nor desire to be saved, a proud vessel who would scorn to be humbled. Therefore I look for nothing more than that you will go irrevocably to destruction.

In fact, you are not resisting my will, since my will is with the poor; that is, may my mercy be near to those who know themselves as poor. *However, persons powerful in iniquity ought to suffer powerful torments.*[43] I wish to have compassion only on the humble. Indeed, *I have compassion on whom I have compassion.*[44]

1.13 Continue to ask: Why have you not given me humility? Because I gave you what is greater—the freedom to decide. And by its use, you are, as it were, *powerful in iniquity. You have loved malice over and above goodness.*[45] What is more, you have made me responsible for your bad deeds. And, in this way,[46] you are so determined to

---

39. John 15:16
40. Luke 17:34
41. Jas 4:6
42. *Sic*; Rom 9:20
43. Ps 51:3; Wis 6:7

44. Rom 9:15 with indirect reference
    to Exod 33:19
45. Ps 51:3, 5
46. *Sic*

excuse yourself from them that you wish to accuse me! You are not willing *that your iniquity, bordering upon hatefulness, be discovered.*[47] Therefore you shall go to your own place, a vessel fit for destruction.[48]

2.1 *Go to Him and be enlightened, and your faces shall not be ashamed.*[49] I am ashamed, Lord God, I am ashamed with a hideous and horrible confusion as often as I go to you and find the door of your vision shut before me. I almost seem to hear that terrible voice: *Amen, I tell you, I do not know you.*[50] And, indeed, I desired to be enlightened by you! As things are now,[51] because of my grief of heart and perplexity of thought, all of me grows dark so that it almost seems to me that it would have been better if I had not gone.

For who will comfort me if you have wished me to be left desolate? May all my consolations that are not you or do not come from you flee and perish! *Woe to the person who is alone,*[52] says Solomon. Indeed, woe to me if I am alone, if you have not been with me, or I with you.

2.2 Lord, I believe myself blessed, yes, most highly blessed, if I am conscious that you are with me. But I am wearisome to myself; yes, I hate myself as often as I am conscious that I am not with you. As long as I am with you, I am also with myself. I am no longer with myself as long as I am not with you. Yes, woe to me however often I am not with you, for without you I cannot possibly exist. I could not remain alive, remaining alive anywhere in any way, either in body or in soul, save by your ever-present power. I could not desire you or seek you save by your ever-present grace. I could never find you were not your mercy and your truth running to meet me.

2.3 But when I am with you in all these ways, and I am conscious of your grace working in me, it is good for me that I exist, that I am alive. *My soul will exult in the Lord.*[53] But if I am myself absent from you in thought and ardent devotedness when you are present to me bestowing your favors, then in this situation[54]

47. Ps 35:3

48. Acts 1:25; Rom 9:22

49. Ps 33:6

50. Matt 25:12

51. *Sic*

52. Eccl 4:10

53. Ps 33:3

54. *Sic*

these benefits of your grace shown me appear as a devoted and meticulous burial rite shown to a dead body.

2.4 If sometime or other I am conscious of you passing by, you do not stop for me but pass me by as I cry out after you like that Canaanite woman.[55] And when you seem wearied with the importunate cries of my need, you throw before my shameful conscience a dog's past impurity and present thoughtlessness. Either you drive the dog from your table unfed, famished, and beaten by floggings of his conscience, or you just let him go. Should I then not draw nearer again? Yes, surely, Lord. For the pups that are chased out from their master's house with beatings return immediately and, watching closely about the house, receive their *daily bread.*[56] Driven out, I come again. Shut out, I howl. Flogged, I beg. A dog does not know how to live without intimate companionship, nor can my soul be without the Lord her God.

2.5 Therefore, open to me, Lord, that I may go to you and be enlightened by you. *You dwell in your heaven,*[57] *but you have made darkness your secret place, even the dark waters amid the clouds of the air.*[58] As the prophet says, *And you have set a cloud so that prayer may not pass through.*[59]

But, as for me, I have rotted on earth.[60] *I have added to the heavy clay weighing upon me and to the shield covering my heart.*[61] Your heavenly stars do not shine for me. *The sun is darkened. The moon does not give its light.*[62] I hear of your mighty acts in *psalms and hymns and spiritual songs.*[63] In the gospels your words and deeds shine forth before me. Your servants' examples beat unceasingly upon my eyes and ears. They strike me with terrors and taunt me with the promises of the truth of your Scripture that impose themselves persistently before my eyes and pummel the deafness of my ears with their clamor.

55. Matt 15:22; Mark 7:24   58. Ps 17:12   61. Hab 2:6; Lam 3:65
56. Matt 6:11   59. Lam 3:44   62. Matt 24:29
57. Ps 122:1   60. Exod 8:14   63. Eph 5:19

In fact, I have become hardened by perverse habits and extreme dullness.[64] I have learned and have become accustomed to sleep in the splendor of the sun, not seeing what is taking place. Placed in the sea, I do not hear the roaring of the waves or the thundering in the sky. *I am dead at heart.*[65]

2.6 *How long, Lord,* how long? How long until *you* do not *burst through the heavens and come down,*[66] and not strike my hardness in the wrath of your bringing things to an end so that I may no longer be what I am, but may be conscious that it is you who rules Jacob and the utmost bounds of the earth. And *may I return,* at least *at eventide, and hungering like a dog, seek through* your *city,*[67] a part of which is still traveling on earth but is in its greater part already rejoicing in heaven. Perhaps I may find some who will receive me in to their tabernacle-tents,[68] me who faint and have no couch of my own *on which to lay my head.*[69]

2.7 At any rate, sometimes I hear your Spirit's voice, though passing by like *the whistling of a breath of gentle air.*[70] I understand it saying, *Go to him and be enlightened.*[71] I hear, and I am struck. And arising as from sleep and shaking myself awake, I am somewhat astounded. *I open my mouth, and I draw in this Spirit.*[72] I stretch out my soul's thoughts that they might be a little less sluggish. I come forth from the depths of my nocturnal conscience and go forth into the light of the one rising for me, the Sun of Righteousness. But when I wish to focus my sleepy eyes on him, they, unaccustomed to light and accustomed to darkness, react violently. And while the pupil of reason blinks and shudders at the unaccustomed brightness, I wipe away the rheum of a long sleepiness from them as best I can, with the hand of exercise.

2.8 If by your gift I find *a fount of tears*[73] that is accustomed to spring up rapidly in humility and in the valleys of a contrite soul, I cleanse my hands for work and my face for devotion. In fact, as

64. Acts 22:17

65. Ps 30:13

66. Ps 12:1; Isa 64:1

67. Ps 58:15

68. Luke 16:9

69. Matt 8:20

70. 1 Kgs 19:12

71. Ps 33:6

72. Ps 118:131

73. Jer 9:1

a falcon spreads its wings towards the south[74] to make its feathers grow, *I stretch out my hands to you, Lord. My soul is like soil without water in your sight.*[75] Like *desert land, both inaccessible and parched, in this manner*[76] *I appear before you in the holy place to see your power and your glory.*[77]

2.9 And when I lift up to you, O Sun of Righteousness, the mind's eyes or reason's thought, what happens to me is what usually happens to people drunk from sleep or with weak eyes. Seeing one thing, they think they are seeing two or three things, until in the process of seeing they begin to understand that the problem is with their sight, not with the thing seen.

For when the soul awakens from the use or enjoyment of the senses and sensory things, the imagination is the first to greet it. It muddles the soul, which is accustomed to sensory things, so that just as the soul used to be wholly given over to the senses, now[78] it does not know how to think or understand anything except by images of sensory things.

2.10 For this reason, when I have awakened from a sleep of negligence, I suddenly turn my gaze to God, about whom the divine law instructs me, saying, *Listen, Israel! The Lord your God is one God.*[79] When I ought to direct my mind's insight entirely to him by whom I am about to be enlightened and whom I am about to worship or pray to, God as Trinity looms before me—[the mystery] that the catholic faith demonstrates to me, that faith repeated over and over to me through my forebears, impressed on me through use itself, and that you yourself and your learned ones commended to me.

2.11 But the foolish imagination of my soul accepts and perceives it in this manner: she fancies the number of Trinity to be in that singleness of the substance of divinity, which, existing without any number, created everything existing *with weight and measure and number.*[80] As it were, she assigns to each single Person of the Trinity his own place[81] so that in this way[82] she prays to the Father through

74. Job 39:26	77. Ps 62:3	80. Wis 11:21
75. Ps 142:6	78. *Sic*	81. *Locus*
76. *Sic*	79. Deut 6:4	82. *Sic*

the Son and in the Holy Spirit, as though she sees herself as passing from one to the other through the third. With this approach,[83] the mind, clouded by oneness, is scattered among the three, as if it insists on discerning three bodies, or on making them into one.

When this imagination, that is, the mind imagining, imagines such a thing—even unwittingly—or receives the unwelcome image despite its protests, faith comes and censures it. Then reason through faith judges, authority condemns, and together all these within me cry out,[84] as was said above, *Listen, Israel! The Lord your God is one God.*[85]

2.12 For although faith, reason, and authority teach me to think of the Father by himself, the Son by himself, and the Holy Spirit by himself, yet they judge that nothing be allowed about the holy Trinity that makes division of substance in time or place[86] or number, or that may be seen to sound like a confusion of Persons. In this way[87] they emphasize the unity of the Trinity so as to eliminate solitariness, yet in regard[88] to the trinity of the Unity in the substance of deity, they do not accept plurality of number. Truly, your grace, Lord, coming to us in advance of any merit, any carefulness of expertise and virtue, gives us however small the degree of knowledge we have of ourselves and of you.

2.13 Actually, grace submits us to humility, humility to authority, and authority to faith. Faith equips reason. Reason, by means of faith, either educates or destroys and casts out imagination. Reason, however, does not equip faith by means of understanding. Rather, through faith it looks for an understanding to come from above, from you, the Father of lights, from whom is *every good and perfect gift.*[89]

This understanding is not acquired from reason or formed by reasoning. In fact, it comes from *the abode of your greatness,*[90] drawn into faith and formed by your wisdom, thoroughly like its origin.

---

83. *Sic*

84. Ps 102:1

85. Deut 6:4

86. *Locus*

87. *Sic*

88. *Sic*

89. Jas 1:17

90. Wis 9:10

For coming into the mind of the believer, it gathers reason to itself and makes it like itself. Indeed, it vivifies and illumines faith.

2.14 A soul stands frightened and bewildered when about to pray to her God. Always she carries herself in her hands[91] as if always about to offer herself to you, fearful of the familiar and startled at the unusual, bringing the seal of her faith for finding you, not yet finding the one for whom she may open it—your countenance, Lord, seeking your countenance,[92] yet not knowing but also not wholly ignorant of what she is seeking.

She hates as idols the phantasms of her heart concerning you. She loves you as her faith describes you to her, but her mind is not sufficient to see you. Aflame with longing for your face, to which she would offer her sacrifice of devotion and righteousness, her *oblations and burnt offerings,*[93] she is more troubled when she is prevented.

And when she does not so quickly achieve the illuminating light of faith from you in whom she trusted, sometimes she grows so unsettled that she can hardly believe she believes in you at all. In fact, she hates herself because, it seems to her, she has no love for you! Far be it, however, that she does not believe in you, she who is thus so[94] tormented by desire for you! Far be it that she does not love you, she who desires you even to the point of disregarding herself and all that exists!

2.15 *How long, O Lord,*[95] how long! If you do not *light my oil lamp,* if you do not *light my darkness, I shall* not *be rescued from this trial.* Nor, unless *in you, my God, shall I pass through this wall.*[96]

3.1 Lord, I dare not now look intently upon your face, which I desire even to the point of death. For you said to Moses, *No person will see me and live.*[97] Although I truly desire to die that I may see you, or to see you that I may die, nevertheless, I cover my countenance as Moses did, not daring to look upon you directly,

91. Ps 118:109

92. Ps 26:8

93. Ps 50:21

94. *Sic*

95. Ps 12:1

96. Ps 17:29-30

97. Exod 33:20

as it is written there: *Moreover, Moses covered his countenance, as he did not dare to gaze directly upon the Lord.*[98]

3.2 For perhaps he might have turned his gaze directly upon the Lord if he had been desiring not to gaze upon who God is, but what God is. For he had already heard who God is: *I am the God of Abraham, the God of Isaac, the God of Jacob.*[99] Nevertheless, you responded to this same Moses, who heard of his death yet was still burning with this same desire and praying that your glory be revealed to him, *I will reveal to you all good.*[100] And, O Lord, where is all good if not in your countenance? That is why David, burning with this same desire, said, *You will fill me with the joy of your countenance.*[101]

3.3 Forgive, Lord, forgive. My heart is impatient for you. *I search for your countenance, I seek out your face*[102] always by means of your very self, *lest* in the end *you avert your face from me.*

In fact, I know and am certain[103] that those who *walk in the light of your countenance*[104] do not blunder, but walk securely. Their every discernment *proceeds from your countenance.*[105] They are the ones who live because they live according to what[106] they read and comprehend within the paradigm of your countenance. Lord, I do not dare to turn my gaze directly to you lest I be turned to stone. However, I stand before you as a poor person, both beggar and blind so that you see me not seeing you. My breast is full with longing for you. All that I am capable of being, whatever I know, and this very fact, that I so languish and faint for you, I offer you. But where I may find you I do not find.

3.4 Where are you, Lord, where are you? And where, Lord, are you not? Of course, I know, and of course I am conscious, that you are with me in this way, *in whom we move and exist,*[107] and because of this most beneficial presence, *my soul is aflame and faints for your salvation.*[108] Of course I know, and I am most truly

---

98. Exod 3:6
99. Exod 3:6
100. Exod 33:19
101. Ps 15:11

102. Ps 26:8-9
103. 2 Tim 1:12
104. Ps 88:16
105. Ps 16:2

106. *Sic*
107. Acts 17:28
108. Ps 118:81

aware, that you are with me most beneficially. I know, and I am aware! I adore, and I thank you.

Yet since you are with me, why am I not with you? What stands in the way? What hinders it? What blocks it? If you are with me, doing good for me, then why am I not also with you enjoying you, the Good of all my good? Is it on account of my sins? Where is he who did away with them and *nailed them to his cross*?[109] Is it because I do not love him? Would I not be willing to die a hundred and a thousand times for you, Lord Jesus? If this does not suffice for you, neither does it suffice for me. For nothing suffices for my soul, nor does she seem to herself to love you completely unless she may enjoy you.

On the other hand, she will not be able to enjoy you unless it is by your gift and according to her own manner that she will be able to see and understand you. But why does she not see you? I, who now love you until death, would then love you unto life eternal!

3.5 Lord, already your fragrance—I know not what it is—breathes on me. At least if it were perfected in me, I would now in the meantime no longer seek it. In fact, you sometimes send me as it were mouthfuls of your consolation. Yet what is this compared to the longing of my hunger? I plead, O you who are her salvation, *tell my soul*[110] why you have breathed into her a longing for you! Surely it is not merely to torture me, tear me apart, and kill me? O, would that it had killed me! I implore you, Lord, is this my hell? So be it then! May it never cease torturing me, may I never cease to burn in it, may it never be permitted to subside at all, even for one day, one hour, or one moment, until I appear in your sight[111] and your glory[112] appear to me, and the eternal festivity of your face will have illumined my soul.

3.6 Lord, that Moses of old may have covered his countenance and veiled his face before you,[113] bearing the form of your people whom he was leading, who were always fleeing from the face of the Lord. Your Paul, who is also all ours because he is all yours, the trumpet of the New Testament, speaking for himself and for

---

109. 1 Cor 5:2; Col 2:14   111. Ps 41:3; Deut 31:11   113. Exod 34:35
110. Ps 34:3   112. Lev 9:6

his disciples, in longing and in your love, says, *All of us with face unveiled, looking intently into the glory of the Lord, are transformed into the same image from brightness to brightness.*[114] That man of yours was fleeing not away from your face, but to your face.

3.7 Forgive, O Lord, forgive my audacity and persistence. We dare till now because we are on fire! Your fire, *which you have sent upon the earth,*[115] urges us on, and you have vehemently desired that it be kindled. I beseech you by your most powerful goodness and most meek patience that are always upon us, be patient with me as I am yet seeking something more. And tell my soul what it is that she longs for when she longs for your face. For she is so[116] blind and *so disturbed within herself*[117] that she both languishes with longing and forgets what she longs for. Does she wish *to see you as you are*?[118] And what does it mean: "as you are"? Does it mean quality, or quantity? In fact, you are neither quality nor quantity. Neither quality nor quantity is in you, because you are what you are. What, therefore, is "as you are"? To see this is beyond us, because to see what you are—this is to be what you are.

3.8 For *no one sees the Father except the Son, and the Son the Father,*[119] for this it is to be the Father, that he sees the Son, and this it is to be the Son, that he sees the Father. It continues, *and to whom the Son wishes to reveal him.*[120] However, there is not one will for the Father and another one for the Son. For they have one and the same will, who is the Holy Spirit. Thus the Trinity-God reveals himself through the Holy Spirit to any friend of God whom God would significantly will to honor.[121]

Yet does a person ever see God as the Father sees the Son, or as the Son sees the Father? For them, as was said, to see one another is not to be two different things but to be one God. Absolutely, yet not exactly in the same way.

3.9 To make this somewhat clearer for us: we must look at what belongs to ordinary understanding by looking at sight and its

114. 2 Cor 3:18

115. Luke 12:49

116. *Sic . . . sic*

117. Ps 41:7

118. 1 John 3:2

119. Matt 11:27

120. Matt 11:27

121. Esth 6:6, 9

natural capacity. Every bodily sense, in order to be a sense and to sense, needs in some way to be changed into what it senses by a certain sense stimulation. For example, sight [changes] into what is visible to it, hearing [changes] into what is heard, and so on with the other senses. Otherwise, it neither senses nor is a sense.

Unless, of course, this sense reports back to reason the object sensed, and the soul of the person sensing is changed into the object sensed by a certain transformation of itself into the object or into the quality of the thing sensed, it is not a sense, nor can it sense. Therefore if by love, which is its own particular sense, a soul senses that God is good, and loves God because God is good, this can only be because, participating in the good itself by an ardent devotedness, the soul itself is made good.

3.10 Let us return to the sense of the soul. Is it not about this that Paul says, *Looking intently at the glory of God, we are changed into the same image?*[122] This is the way with the sense of the soul. The soul's sense is love. It is by this that the soul senses whatever it senses when it is delighted or when it is offended. What it senses, it senses. When the soul reaches out to any object by this, it is changed into what it loves by its own type of transformation, not that it might be identical in nature but that it may be conformed by an ardent devotedness to the object loved. For it cannot love a good person because the person is good unless it is itself made good by that very same goodness. Is this not the meaning for *Be aware of the Lord in goodness?*[123] And Wisdom: *For in knowing you, awareness*[124] *is perfected.*[125] And the Apostle: *Have this awareness*[126] *in you, which was also in Christ Jesus.*[127] This is the charity by which one who loves *remains in God, and God in him.*[128]

3.11 O Charity, Charity, you have brought us to this point, that by loving God and the Son of God, *we are called and we are gods and the children of God.*[129] And if *it does not yet appear what we shall be, when he will have appeared we shall be like him, because we shall see*

---

122. 2 Cor 3:18

123. Wis 1:1

124. *Sensus*

125. Wis 6:16

126. *Sentite*

127. Phil 2:5

128. 1 John 4:16

129. Ps 81:6

him as he is.[130] *Lord, it is good for us to be here.*[131] It is delightful to stay here! O, would that it be permitted to die here! However, I beg, give to those meditating and speaking and writing about you a balanced understanding, concise and orderly words, and a heart on fire for you, O Jesus, when they open the Scriptures that are from you.[132]

3.12 Forgive, Lord, forgive; the love of your love drives me. You know; you see! I am no *scrutinizer of* your *majesty*[133] but a poor person [in need] of your grace. I implore you, Lord, through the sweetness of your most sweet gentleness, that your majesty not overwhelm me, but your grace lift me up. Forgive, I say, for the vision of God is faith's proper desire—here *in mystery*, there indeed *face to face.*[134] Do not presume or be over-confident, O man![135] Do not stand here, whoever is a man of desire, as Daniel was![136] Do not say, "It is enough"! Whatever is your consciousness of God at this moment, whatever you see, whatever faith teaches you here about God, it is mystery. At times it is indeed more obscure, at other times, however, more distinct. Yet those who are conscious of it know how sweet the vision is when present, how desirable it appears when absent. Here it is the stone having *a name written on it, which no one knows except the one who receives it.*[137]

3.13 Moreover, concerning the vision that will be face to face, it is said, *No person shall see me and live.*[138] For that person who sees does not live, but says, *Unhappy person that I am, who will free me from this body of death?*[139] One hopes, then at last, to be truly victorious when one sees perfectly.

What use are physical senses[140] here? What use is imagination? What can reason accomplish? What can rational understanding do?

---

130. 1 John 3:1-2
131. Matt 17:4
132. Luke 24:32
133. Prov 25:27
134. 1 Cor 13:12
135. *O homo. Homo* implies a human being, whereas *vir* means a man in gender, but in this case *man* seems more appropriate for the context as William is speaking to himself.
136. Dan 9:23
137. Rev 2:17
138. Exod 33:20
139. Rom 7:24
140. *Sensus*

For although reason sends us to you, God, by itself it cannot attain you. Nor by the same token can understanding, which consists of reason's inferior insights, pass beyond the limits of reason. Nor does it have the capacity of reaching all the way to you. But *what is truly from above*[141] has the fragrance that is from on high. Nothing human is present; all is divine. Where it infuses itself, it confers reasons proper to itself that do not communicate with inferior reason except insofar as they have it in subjection by means of obedience to faith.

3.14 This [understanding from above] divides nothing, blends nothing together in the Holy Trinity. For the Holy Spirit gently touches a faithful consciousness when and as and in what manner he wills, so that people praying to you or contemplating all that you are not have sometimes gone beyond. Through this very contemplation of all that you are not, they may see to some extent who you are, although they may not see you as you are.

Nevertheless, this intermediate insight may soothe something in the devoted mind. For it is evident that it is not from those things that you are not, and even if it is not entirely all that you are, it is nevertheless not foreign to what you are.

3.15 For in this way[142] the Spirit of the Lord suddenly clothes[143] the serene and humble person upon whom he rests and *changes that person into another person*,[144] so that the Trinity does not divide and Unity does not confound the sense of one contemplating. The Trinity of Persons does not upset the devotedness of the one seeking the one God, and Unity of substance does not darken the charity of the person rejoicing in the delightful love between the Father and Son. In neither case does solitariness or plurality lead into confusion. And besides that, Unity of Trinity and Trinity of Unity so influence one that, with a devoted and realistic understanding, by not comprehending, one may comprehend the majesty of divine incomprehensibility.

---

141. Jas 3:17

142. *Sic*

143. Acts 2:2

144. 1 Sam 10:6

3.16 And in this way,[145] *tasting and seeing how gracious the Lord is,*[146] all of a sudden a person's whole being becomes sweet by tasting sweetness and illumined by seeing the light of his truth. Suddenly, from the fullness of the highest good, the person is so delighted with the joy of the Holy Spirit that if it is brought to perfection in him, he will be confident of having obtained eternal life. As it is said, *this is eternal life, that they know you as the only true God, and Jesus Christ whom you have sent.*[147] *Therefore, go to him and be enlightened, and your faces will not be ashamed.*[148]

4.1 *Lord, compassionate and merciful, patient and most gracious, you, Lord, are amiable to all, and your compassionate graces cover all your works.*[149]

4.2 You exhort us, Lord, both you and your Holy Spirit, that *we pray and be vigilant*[150] in prayer. Just as you are devoted and merciful and desiring to be compassionate, so you encourage and teach us. You prepare the case for us, *giving* us *judgment and justice,*[151] so that when we pray we ought to pray as if you had a just cause for being merciful.

Indeed, you yourself have composed for us a form of praying,[152] lest in any way you fail us in our case: yourself our judge, yourself our advocate. You have commanded us to petition confidently in your name and to believe that whatever things we will have petitioned for, we will achieve. Yes, they will be done for us.[153]

4.3 Lord, your goodness prompts you to do this. A grave need, on the other hand, lies heavily upon us. Yet while you are encouraging, we grow sluggish. While you are constantly reiterating, we are negligent. While you are promising, we do not believe. Yet in your abundant mercy and compassion, you arouse the slothful and negligent. In your patience, you overlook the skeptical.[154] Furthermore, when we do not know or are unable to pray in the way that

145. *Sicque*
146. Ps 33:9
147. John 17:3
148. Ps 33:6
149. Ps 144:8-9
150. Matt 26:42
151. Ps 118:121
152. Matt 6:9; Luke 11:2
153. Mark 11:24
154. Wis 11:24

behooves us, you send us your Holy Spirit, *who helps our weakness and interposes for us with inexpressible sighs.*[155]

4.4 Therefore, we pray because you encourage. We ask confidently because you promise. Immediately, you run and listen intently to us as persons praying, finding what you are doing so that you may be gracious to us. *You are a gracious Lord to all.* You multiply your graciousness for us. *Your acts of compassion upon all your works*[156] begin to appear to us. For you, God, approach and do not distance yourself. When you begin to approach us and *your consolations gladden our souls,*[157] immediately the dead soul's senses revive at the fragrance and touch of your healing presence. Faith leaps up, confidence rejoices, the heart is set on fire, and tears flow that do not extinguish this flaming fire but rather inflame it all the more.

And when your Spirit helps our weakness, we copiously weep rich, sweet tears from the ardent devotedness of your sweetness. When you wipe them away with a devoted hand of consolation, they flow more copiously. They become for us *by day and by night bread,*[158] a refreshment, both strong and pleasant because we consider it sweet to weep in your loving presence, our Lord God, who made us, we who are *your people and the sheep of your pasture.*[159]

4.5 *I, I am*, as your prophet[160] says to you, Lord, *a person looking at my poverty. I am poor and in hardships from my youth. Exalted, on the other hand, I am humbled and thrown into disorder.*[161] *For you have shown me many harmful troubles. Yet you have turned toward me and given me life and once again have led me out from the depths of the earth. You have multiplied your greatness, and, having turned to me, you have consoled me.*[162]

4.6 For at that time when you created me in your Paradise and gave me the very tree of life for my possession in perpetual right, you willed or permitted that I would also reach out my hand to the tree of knowing good and evil. Thus, as if tired of my inner

---

155. Gal 4:6; Rom 8:26   158. Ps 41:4   160. Lam 3:1
156. Ps 144:9   159. Ps 94:7 (Gallican   161. Ps 87:16
157. Ps 93:19   Psalter)   162. Ps 70:20-21

blessings, I might discover, with the consent of my Eve, my flesh, to see what I could do outwardly. I tasted and saw[163] not your graciousness, but my disorder, and I saw myself to be a person whose deformity needed a covering, whose nakedness was terrified at your encounter, and whose freedom had need of the restraining discipline of laws. In your eyes, I was found nude[164] without all those things people thought were within me. Repulsive in my own eyes, I was able to lie hidden neither from myself nor from you. I, needing a director, had undertaken the office of directing others.

For this reason, Lord, I hid myself among the trees of Paradise. For this reason, I took refuge in my darkness. *Fleeing, I went far away*, yet not from you but to you, and *I dwelt in solitude. I wait* for you there, *you who have made me safe from faintheartedness of spirit and from tempest.*[165]

4.7 *I have put my mouth in the dust, if perhaps there may be hope,*[166] *like a solitary wild ass breathing in the scent of my beloved.*[167] And when I have completely returned to myself, *I sit alone and silent,*[168] *hearing neither the voice of one demanding*[169] nor the noise of a hostile encounter. Seeing that time benefits me, and that I have time to be undisturbed, I shake myself up: Who am I? From where have I come? Where am I going?

4.8 I recognize myself as one of the children of Adam, *a child of wrath by nature,*[170] but a child of your handmaid holy church by grace, one of the exiles from Paradise, living and working in the land of the accursed, which you have cursed through the works of Adam.[171] When I have worked it, it does not yield its fruits but *produces for me thorns and thistles. In the sweat of my brow I eat my bread,*[172] according to the most severe sentence of your just judgment, by which *you have rebuked the proud and accursed those who have turned aside from your commandments.*[173]

163. Ps 33:9

164. Gen 3:7

165. Ps 54:8-9

166. Lam 3:1

167. Jer 2:24

168. Lam 3:28

169. Job 39:7

170. Eph 2:3

171. Gen 3:17

172. Gen 3:18-19

173. Ps 118:21

4.9 O good Creator! How well had you created me! How gloriously had you fashioned me! How happily had you placed me! For you had created me, as your apostle says,[174] *among the good works you had prepared so that I might walk in them;* you formed me *to* your *image and likeness*[175] *and had placed me in the paradise of* your *delight, so that I might work and guard it,*[176] that I might work, exercising good enthusiasm, and might be on guard, lest the serpent steal in. The serpent did steal in. It seduced my Eve and *established me as guilty in collusion*[177] through her. On account of this, I have been expelled from the paradise of a good conscience; I am made an exile *in a foreign land,*[178] in a region of unlikeness.

4.10 But, O Lord, you who have created all things and *have seen all you have created, that they are very good,*[179] will you destroy your good work through my evil work? In fact, you did not create me for Paradise, but Paradise for me when you made me a human upon the earth.

4.11 O Creator, *may you not regret having made me a human upon the earth,*[180] but command, as in the beginning, that I be a reasonable person having power over my earth, so that my body may be subject to the spirit, and the spirit to you. May you not regret the dignity bestowed upon this human, so that I may have dominion over the beasts of my earth, the fierce and untamed movements of my soul's affections, and over the reptiles on the ground, those sudden, unexpected thoughts both harmful and deadly with poison from the earth to which they unendingly cling fast, over fish of the sea and birds of the air, namely, thoughts of the spirit of this world that are scrutinizing and persistent in pursuing curiosities of the world and greatness of its day, over even the beasts of burden, those bodily senses created simultaneously with us for this purpose: to serve us, as their name implies.

174. Eph 2:10

175. Gen 1:26

176. Gen 2:15

177. Gal 2:18

178. Ps 136:4; Bar 3:16

179. Gen 1:31

180. Gen 6:6

You who have given them to us, grant us that they may submit to the bridle of reason, the prod of good zeal, and the stall of discipline, where they may feed and be nourished with their food, to be brought forth and put to use as necessity requires. However, may they not be allowed to grow wild in wide-open ranges of unrestricted wandering. The day will come, it will come, says the one who promises, when the lion and the lamb will lie down together, when whatever in any way harms *will not harm on all your holy mountain.*[181] The beasts of burden also *will feed in the most luscious pastures,*[182] no longer as beasts for our weakness, but instruments for blessed happiness.

4.12 In the meantime, Lord, *listen attentively to the heavens, and may the heavens listen attentively to the earth, and the earth listen attentively to the wine and oil and corn. And may these listen attentively to Jezreel,*[183] that is, to the seed of God that you have sown in us. For as the prophet says, *you have tricked me,* Lord, *and led me into solitude,*[184] promising that there you would speak to your servant. And now, thanks to you who have spoken, once and again, many times, to my soul, which says to you, *you are my God,*[185] you sometimes answer gently and graciously, *I am your salvation.*[186]

4.13 And now, O Desire of my soul,[187] my soul itself desires to be free for you for a time, and *to taste and see how gracious you are, Lord.*[188] She prays for your most lavish mercy, that you would make all that is exterior and interior peaceful and silent within me, so that you might preserve within me the authority over all that is within me, which you have given me, but that outwardly you might *strike a treaty with the beast of the field, the reptile of the earth,*[189] *and the bird of the air, and that you might wipe out bow and sword and war from* my *earth,* so that my *entire place may be in peace and my dwelling be in Sion.*[190]

---

181. Isa 11:9

182. Ezek 34:14

183. Hos 2:21-22

184. Hos 2:14

185. Ps 15:2; Hos 2:24

186. Ps 34:3

187. Isa 26:9

188. Ps 33:9

189. Hos 2:18

190. Ps 75:3

4.14 Give me, Lord, the consolation of my solitude, a solitary heart and frequent conversation with you. For I will not be alone as long as you are with me, my God. But if you leave me, *woe to the person who is alone.*[191] For if I fall asleep, there will be no one to keep me warm while I am sleeping. If *I fall, there will be no one to pick me up.*[192]

4.15 But now, *O my refuge and strength,*[193] lead me *into* your *inner desert*[194] just as you led your servant, Moses. [Lead me] where *the bush burns but is unconsumed,*[195] where the holy soul that has won admittance into this place is all aflame, just as the Seraphim is all aflame with the full fire of the Holy Spirit and is not consumed but cleansed. Only then can she withstand the better sight, the miracle of all your miracles and the vision of visions.

[Lead me] to where the place is holy, where none can stand or advance unless the shoe straps of their fleshly encumbrances have been removed and they approach with bare feet,[196] namely, with clean and pure affections. [Lead me] where the One who is, even though he cannot be seen as he is, is nonetheless heard saying, *I am who am,*[197] where at present one's face must be covered *lest one see God face to face,*[198] but where with the humility of obedience one's listening is focused with attention so that he may *hear what* his *Lord God is saying within him.*[199]

4.16 *In the meantime,* Lord, *hide me in the secret place of your tabernacle-tent,*[200] *during the day of* these *evils,*[201] *in the secret place of your face far from the strife of tongues.*[202] Indeed, *you have placed upon me your gentle yoke and light burden.*[203] And when you show me the difference between your service and service of the world, you question me charmingly and gently about whether it is better to serve you, the living God, or strange gods.[204]

---

191. Eccl 4:10-11
192. Eccl 4:10
193. Ps 45:2
194. Exod 3:1
195. Exod 3:2

196. Exod 3:5
197. Exod 3:14
198. Exod 3:6-7
199. Ps 84:9
200. *Tabernaculum*

201. Ps 26:5
202. Ps 30:21
203. Matt 11:30
204. Deut 7:4

I adore your hand laying the yoke that I warmly kiss. I embrace the burden, and it is very gentle for me to sweat under it. For many *masters other than you have possessed me*[205] for a long time. Their yoke is neither gentle nor their burden light. I desire to be under your law. I acknowledge your yoke and the light burden that supports and does not crush me.

4.17 But upon entering into the new discipline of your service,[206] I seem to see *new heavens and a new earth,*[207] and *behold, you make all things new*[208] for me. Teach me, Lord, for I am a countryman coming from the countryside of the world into the well-ordered life of your city and to the charming refinement of your court. Take away my form, the form of the world, according to which I had formed myself. Form me like your citizens, lest I appear among them as deformed. Also, teach me *the language that I do not know, that I began to hear coming out of the land of Egypt*[209] but do not understand, *having been for a long time in a foreign land,*[210] that language of course in which you speak with your sons and daughters and they with you. Make me too understand the nods you use to make intelligent persons understand *what is your good, pleasing, and perfect will.*[211]

4.18 And already my soul gives you thanks, gracious Father. When you start to speak to her, she begins to recognize your voice, although she does not adequately understand what you are telling her and what you want her to do. Since your voice, like your grace, does not sound outwardly but works effectively and graciously inwardly, your voice never comes empty.[212] Actually, when I speak with you, I concentrate on you, and this too is beneficial for me. Whatever happens to be my prayer, I never pray or worship you in vain, since even in praying, *a significant reward*[213] comes to me.

4.19 Therefore, Holy Spirit, teach me *to pray without ceasing*[214] so that you may grant me to rejoice in you without ceasing.[215] For

205. Isa 26:13
206. RB Prol.
207. Rev 21:1
208. Rev 21:5

209. Ps 80:6
210. Bar 3:11
211. Rom 12:2
212. Isa 55:11

213. Ps 18:12
214. 1 Thess 5:17
215. 1 Thess 5:16

although your poor person, *poor in spirit*,[216] laments when praying, either remembering his sins or finding himself in dire straits, the more intensely he suffers, the more intensely he rejoices.

On the other hand, the person who rejoices in the world, the more intensely he rejoices, the more intensely—if he has any sense—he is tormented and grieved by the secrets of his conscience. Consequently, devout and pure prayer is never without joy.

5.1 When I desire to stimulate, exercise, and accustom my heart for praying continually and effectively, I prefer to be instructed by no one in this schooling other than you, O Lord Jesus, Wisdom of God the Father.[217] Consequently, I call to mind the ways of prayer that you used, praying in the presence of people on this earth. You were giving us a pattern for an all-embracing prayer. For instance, I find you sometimes praying alone,[218] sometimes in the midst of a crowd,[219] sometimes in exultation of spirit,[220] once in a bloody sweat,[221] and once exalted on the cross.[222]

5.2 Exultation of spirit and praying in solitude are most delightful for me to imitate. But unless *you come in advance to me with the blessings of your delight*,[223] though indeed I easily find a place, I do not so easily find a solitary heart. Undoubtedly, exultation of spirit rises out of a purity of conscience that I am not conscious of in myself, or from an abundance of your grace of which I am unworthy.

5.3 To be able to pray in the midst of a crowd was yours, to whom nothing was lacking. Nevertheless, when you demand this, neither do we shrink from it.

5.4 I know, Lord, I know this way of bloody prayer and prayer on the cross would be absolutely necessary for me. For when I am conscious of what there is in me that prayer needs to sweat out and the cross crucify, indeed I do not have a bloody sweat, although my heart sweats bloody tears before your eyes. Nor does my body

216. Matt 5:3

217. 1 Cor 1:24

218. Matt 14:23

219. John 11:41; 12:27

220. Luke 10:21

221. Luke 22:42

222. Luke 23:43, 46

223. Ps 20:4

find a cross on which to be crucified, although my unhappy soul is crucified in itself beyond every sorrow of a cross.

5.5 All the same, I am crucified with you,[224] Lord Jesus, though on the cross of profession, which by your gift I daily and continually offer you, for these are your given gifts. But as I contemplate from my cross with its pleasures the passion of your cross, pierced through with the nails of fear of you,[225] I am confounded and totally lose courage, not from the pain of my cross, that because of your grace is nothing to me now, but from the pain of my heart, where I meditate upon your work, *vivified through the years,*[226] and made clear in all these years, both before and after redemption's accomplishment. No one can compensate for it; no death, no life suffices to be equivalent to it. Yet the world, having been redeemed by it, despises it.

5.6 Because of habit itself, we are desensitized when seeing you crucified, thinking of you as dead and buried. What should pierce through further into the heart and more penetratingly is this: struck on the face with blows, scourged, mocked, spat upon, pierced by nails and the lance, crowned with thorns, given gall and vinegar to drink, you on your cross were thirsting[227] for nothing but our salvation. *The earth trembled*[228] when you were crucified;[229] we laugh. Heaven with its lights was obscured;[230] we burn to shine in the world. *Rocks were rent;*[231] we harden our hearts. *Graves broken open*[232] gave up their dead; we, luxuriously resting upon beds of lewd playfulness,[233] are the dead burying our dead.[234]

5.7 Lord, if I have remembered this correctly, during the time of your passion, you offered three prayers to God the Father. It is well known that they embraced everything that would be accomplished by the price of your blood in your passion itself: for yourself,[235] for your friends,[236] and for your enemies.[237] It is true that when

224. Gal 2:19

225. Ps 118:120; Gal 2:19

226. Hab 3:2

227. John 19:28

228. Ps 75:9

229. Matt 27:51

230. Luke 23:45; Matt 27:45; Mark 15:33

231. Matt 27:51

232. Matt 27:52

233. Amos 6:4

234. Matt 8:22

235. Mark 14:36

236. John 17:9

237. Luke 23:34

you prayed for yourself, you did not labor, for as the apostle says, *you were heard by reason of your reverence.*[238] You prayed also for your friends *who persevered with you in your times of trials,*[239] and for your enemies who were crucifying you, but not knowing what they might be doing.[240]

5.8 Where is the prayer for those persons who sin knowingly? As long as they are this way,[241] they are outside of the embrace of the crucified one, who with his arms outstretched on the cross seemed to embrace in the very form of a gibbet all for whom he was suffering. Therefore, the Apostle says, *no sacrifice for sins is left for us who sin willingly.*[242] Unless repentance removes these sins, unless a bloody sweat expels them and the cross crucifies them, I do not find persons sinning willingly and knowingly to have a share in the prayer of the one sweating blood or hanging in sacrifice on the cross.

5.9 Woe to me whom conscience accuses, whom truth does not excuse, so that I might be able to say, "I did not know what I did! Therefore, Lord, forgive, by the price of your precious blood, all my sins that I have incurred, knowingly or unknowingly. And speak to your sinner; whisper to your poor one what he may do to atone for them, and especially for those that I have committed knowingly." For if you appear to have excluded all who sin know-ingly, woe to the entire world, because you may appear to have embraced a very, very few persons.

The Apostle says, *no offering is left for those persons sinning voluntarily. Anyone who makes null the Law of Moses dies without any mercy, because of the testimony of two or three witnesses. How much more, do you think, has one deserved worse punishments who will have trodden underfoot the Son of God, who will have treated the blood of the testament as polluted, and who will have abused the grace of the Spirit whereby he has been sanctified? Indeed, we know who said, "Vengeance is mine; I will repay!"*[243]

238. Heb 5:7

239. Luke 22:28

240. Luke 23:34

241. *Sic*

242. Heb 10:26

243. Heb 10:26-30

5.10 Truly, Lord, I have sinned *willingly and greatly after having received the knowledge of truth,*[244] *and I have abused the Spirit of grace,*[245] from whom I have freely received the washing away of sins in baptism. And after receiving the knowledge of truth, I have returned to sin *as a dog to* its *vomit.*[246] But have I trampled you underfoot, Son of God? I have trampled you underfoot if I have denied you, although I do not allege Peter to have trampled you underfoot, he who, as it happened, denied you. He loved you most ardently even as he was denying you once, twice, and a third time.[247] Have I treated the blood of the testament as polluted? Whosoever is conscious of such a thing, may he be anathema! God forbid that my heart has even been conscious of this! God forbid that such a declaration ever pass through my lips!

5.11 Not that sometimes *Satan* hasn't *attacked* my faith *to sift it like wheat!*[248] Yet your prayer has reached even to me, *so that my faith* in you *may never be lacking.*[249] Virtue is the willing assent of the mind to good. You know, my Lord, how I have always kept my willing assent in fidelity to you. Keep it in me until the end! I have always believed in you. I have never denied you. I have always loved you, even when I have sinned against you. I am sorry for my sin until my death, but I am not sorry for your love. I am only sorry that even then I did not love you to the extent[250] that I should have. For if I had loved you to that extent, I would not have sinned.

5.12 Yet alas, how I fear lest the fact that I have loved you may bring me forth into Judgment, because if it is so serious to sin *after having received the knowledge of truth,*[251] how much more serious is it after the most sweet tasting of your good, after having received the sweetness of your delightful love? For even in my childhood itself, I, an unclean child, already loved you because of your grace. And yet I did not sin against you in a childish manner. From then until now I have never stopped sinning, nor have you stopped

---

244. Heb 10:26   247. Mark 14:66-69   250. *Sic . . . sic*
245. Heb 10:29   248. Luke 22:31-32   251. Heb 10:26
246. Prov 26:11; 2 Pet 2:22   249. Heb 10:26

being gracious to me. What remains unless it may be said to me, *"You have received good things in your life"*?[252]

5.13 But, Lord, transform your judgment into mercy, and *condemn sin by sin.*[253] As you have justly condemned me for the so-little love with which I loved you then, now having received from your grace the fullness of your love, may I come before your Judgment and *appear in your holy place,*[254] and before the eyes of your mercy, by the same reason by which that sinful woman appeared of whom you said, *Many sins are forgiven her for she has loved much.*[255]

5.14 But first of all, deign to let the fire of your perfect love set my heart on fire. Let its great ardor well up within me and boil away all poison of sin. Let it search out and wash away with the tears of my eyes all the infection of my conscience. May your cross crucify whatever has been collected through *concupiscence of the flesh, concupiscence of the eyes, and pride of life,*[256] in the vast expanse of my negligence. May whatever *has been singed and undermined*[257] by *the flesh's will*[258] and the mind's consent be destroyed at the rebuke of your countenance.

5.15 Lord, anyone who wishes may listen and ridicule me confessing![259] Anyone may see me prostrate along with your sinful woman at the feet of your mercy, washing them with heartfelt tears and anointing them with the ointment of conscientious devotedness. This is my whole substance, however small it is, either in body or in soul, as the price of an ointment pleasing to you, which I will pour out upon your head—*whose head is God*[260]—and over your feet, the lowest part of our humble nature.

5.16 *Let the Pharisee murmur.*[261] You, my *God, have mercy on me. Let the thief holding the moneybag* complain and *gnash his teeth at me;*[262] as long as I am pleasing you, I care very little about whom I may displease. O love of my heart, daily, yes, even continually, may

252. Luke 16:25

253. Rom 8:3

254. Ps 62:3

255. Luke 7:47

256. 1 John 2:16

257. Ps 79:17

258. John 1:13

259. Ps 79:17

260. 1 Cor 11:3

261. Luke 15:2

262. Mark 14:5; John 12:6

this my anointing be yours, because when I anoint you, I anoint myself also. Of course, my nature of long-standing wickedness has hardness, *has become like a leather pouch in hoarfrost.*[263] Unless it is softened with the loveliness of this ointment, it stiffens, hardens, cracks, and spills out whatever of your goodness it is shown to have held within, if anything. In fact, you have said, *She did what she could do.*[264] Grant to me, Lord, faithfully to do for you whatever I am capable of doing, whatever I have skill in, whatever I am, whatever I am able to be. Let me keep nothing for myself.

5.17 I present my case before you and not before anyone else. I lie at the feet of your mercy. There I will lie, there I will lament until you make me hear your kind voice, the judgment of your mouth, the verdict of your justice and mine also, for you have given it to me: *since she has loved much, many sins are forgiven her.*[265]

Lord, because the Father has handed over to you every judgment,[266] today, come to me in advance with kindness. And judge me with this judgment. For because of the love of your love, I prefer to be justified and saved by this judgment than to be magnified and glorified in any other way. Lord, do not exclude me from the embrace of your redemption. For in everything I desire to share in your cross.

5.18 You have said, *Vengeance is mine, I will repay.*[267] No! No! Most Kind One! But let vengeance be mine so that I may repent. *It is a horrible thing to fall into the hands of the living God.*[268] Command whatever you wish, but grant me to understand and to be able to do what you command, you who have given me a *heart prepared*[269] for this so that neither my heart nor my body may withdraw in anything from doing your will.

5.19 *You have known my sitting and my rising, and all my most recent and former thoughts.*[270] Unform me from a world to which I have conformed myself, and conform me to [Christ,] the form of your grace, from whom I have fled. And give to my heart a form of

---

263. Ps 118:83
264. Mark 14:8
265. Luke 7:47

266. John 5:27
267. Rom 12:19; Deut 32:35; Heb 10:30

268. Heb 10:31
269. Ps 111:7
270. Ps 138:3, 5

penitence pleasing to you. Furthermore, grant to me, Lord, a faith unadulterated and devoted, conscientious, strong, and unshaken, so that, giving grace for grace,[271] you can also say to me, *Go, for your faith has made you alive![272]*

6.1 *I saw a door opened in heaven,* says John, *and the first voice which I heard was like a trumpet speaking to me, saying: "Ascend to here."*[273]

6.2 O Lord, you have created heaven and earth.[274] Yet you have cursed the earth in the sin and work of Adam,[275] and you have deputed it to be inhabited by his children. Those who live in it *are under the curse,*[276] since they both bear the ongoing punishments of the ancient curse and, by turning away from your commandments, daily accumulate new punishments. It is said about them, *They are cursed who turn away from your commandments.*[277]

I am weary of so many old and new curses. On account of these, *what I never took* I am forced *to pay,*[278] and what I did take, I am forced to reimburse with high interest. How willingly, how desirously I would flee from our earth into your heaven, which you have kept for yourself, if I would find the ascent to the opened door. For once for all, [heaven] has been cleansed from pride, as the proud one has been cast from there.[279]

6.3 I am told that nothing of all the misfortunes that we endure here is there. In that place there is no morning and evening; the morning's joy does not pass away, and the evening's tears do not last.[280] You know how much their passing would delight me. But *there only one day exists,*[281] a festive one with the continuous vision of your glory, a holiday from all that could possibly interrupt the festival of your countenance.

6.4 I am told that not *fire, hail, snow, ice, or winds from hurricanes* ascend upwards to there. However, here these events constantly

271. John 1:16
272. Luke 7:50
273. Rev 4:1
274. Gen 1:1
275. Gen 3:17
276. Gal 3:10
277. Ps 118:21
278. Ps 68:5
279. Luke 10:18
280. Ps 29:6
281. Zech 14:7

descend upon us in order to trouble us while *fulfilling your word.*[282] Neither death nor corruption of body or soul is there. A plague of any kind of inner disturbance is utterly removed. There is only virtue, only happiness and joy, and your charity, ecstatic in its own good, without an inkling of squandering.

6.5 Still, I am told that that festival day is magnificent with the rejoicing and praises of the angels, glorious with the crowns of the apostles, martyrs, and all the good persons who have pleased you from the beginning of the world: the church gathered together in that celebration has arranged everlasting dwellings for this festival day.

When on occasion we see *two or three* of these gathered together here on earth *in your name, with you* present *in their midst,*[283] and we see *how good and how joyful their dwelling together*, how full with the anointing of the Holy Spirit, it is apparent to all that *there* your *commandment is a blessing.*[284] Then how much greater is it where *you have gathered together your saints, who have preferred your testament over and above sacrifices and, having become heaven, now proclaim your justice?*[285]

6.6 In fact, that beloved disciple of yours was not the only one to have found the ascent, nor was the open door to heaven[286] shown to him alone. Yes, you have proclaimed it openly to everyone, and not just through a herald, nor any prophet, but through your own very self. You have said, *I am the door. If anyone enters through me, that person will be saved.*[287] You are the door, then. And when you say, *If anyone enters through me,* you are seen to be open to all who wish to enter!

6.7 But if we who are on this earth see the door in heaven lying open, what does it profit us who are not able to ascend there? Paul replies, *The one who ascends, he it is who descends.*[288] Who is this? Love. For the love in us ascends to there, into you, Lord, because

282. Ps 148:8   285. Ps 49:5-6   288. Eph 4:10

283. Matt 18:20   286. Rev 4:1

284. Ps 132:1-3   287. John 10:9

the love in you descends here to us. Truly, because you have loved us, you have descended here to us. By loving you, we ascend there into you. You yourself are the one who said, *I am the door.*[289] I implore you, by your very self, *open to us*[290] your very self, so you can show us more clearly what house you are the door to, and when and to whom you are open.

6.8 Well then, isn't the house whose door you are, as has already been said, heaven, where the Father dwells, and about whom it is said, *The Lord, his seat is in heaven*?[291] Indeed, no one comes to the Father except through you, who are the door.[292] Yet a certain servant of yours says that those who are still delighted in visible beauty are not able to think any spiritual thing about God. They do not prefer heaven to earth.[293] Their opinion would be more tolerable if they were to believe that God, whom they still think about in a bodily way, were in heaven rather than on earth.

For, O Maker of all places and times, you neither move in time nor occupy a place. You are not supported by a material heaven lest you fall. Neither do you inhabit it in this way,[294] *that you fill heaven and earth.*[295] You are present everywhere if being "in a place" can be said about you. You are entirely everywhere, if *entirely* is a word that can be established in you or about you, in whom there is no division.

6.9 Nevertheless, you yourself have taught us to say, *Our Father who are in heaven.*[296] And so[297] all persons, both Jews and Gentiles, accept this belief, affirming God to dwell in heaven.

But the belief of those forming an opinion from what is false is one thing. It is another thing for those who set forth what is true, using similar words, so that intelligent people are capable of understanding this truth. People who form an opinion because they cannot grasp or understand things as they are, are allowed to form an opinion that is a little more tolerable from such words.

---

289. John 10:9

290. Matt 25:11

291. Ps 10:5

292. John 14:6

293. Jer 23:24

294. *Sic*

295. Jer 23:24

296. Matt 6:9

297. *Et . . . sic*

For this reason, the prophet says, *Our God, however, is in heaven,*[298] and a little later, *who dwells in Jerusalem.*[299]

6.10 I plead, reply to people reaching out for you, thirsting after you, *Master, where do you live?*[300] You respond immediately, saying, *I am in the Father, and the Father is in me.*[301] And in another place: *On that day you will know that I am in my Father, and you in me and I in you.*[302] Furthermore, *I in them and you in me, so that they may be brought to perfection in oneness.*[303] Consequently, your place is the Father and you are the Father's place. Nor is that all: we are also your place, and you are ours.

6.11 Therefore, O Lord Jesus, since you are in the Father and the Father is in you, O Highest and Undivided Trinity, you are your own place, indeed, you are your own heaven. Just as you have no exterior source, in this way[304] you have no need of a place in which to subsist except from yourself and in yourself.

However, when you dwell in us, we are your heaven, indeed! Yet you are not supported here so as to have a dwelling place. Rather, you support this place so that it may be habitable, and also, you exist as our heaven, into whom we can ascend and dwell. And so, as I see it, our dwelling is in you. Or rather, your dwelling in us is our heaven.

But for you, your eternity is *the heaven of heaven*[305] whereby you are what you are in your very self: the Father in the Son, and the Son in the Father, and the Unity whereby the Father and Son are one— this is the Holy Spirit, not as if coming from somewhere else to be in the middle but existing in the middle by sharing their existence.

6.12 Indeed the source and organizing of this unity, whereby we are one among ourselves and in you, is the same Holy Spirit, making us children of God by grace, we, *who by nature were children of wrath.*[306] As the Apostle says, *Behold the manner of charity the Father has given us that we may be called and are children of*

298. Ps 113:11	301. John 14:10-11	304. *Sic*
299. Ps 124:1-2	302. John 14:20	305. Ps 113:24
300. John 1:38	303. John 17:23	306. Eph 2:3

God.[307] Indeed it is by this gift, who is the Holy Spirit. And a little later in the text: *Most beloved, now we are children of God, but it does not yet appear what we shall be. We know that when he appears, we will be like him for we will see him as he is.*[308]

6.13 Certainly the birth of the Son from the Father is of eternal nature. Our birth is adoption by grace. The former birth is not something that happens, nor does it effect unity, for this very unity itself is in the Holy Spirit. The latter birth does not simply exist but comes about through the Holy Spirit to the degree that it is imprinted by the likeness of God. Surely this birth is beyond the manner of human nature, yet it falls short of the essence of divinity. The seed of this birth is said to be the Holy Spirit, about whom the same Apostle says, *Anyone who is born of God does not sin, for his seed remains in him, and consequently he cannot sin.*[309] The vision of God bestows on us the likeness of God, whereby we will see God, not what God is, but as he is! Yes, that likeness whereby we will be like God! For the Father to see the Son, this is to be what the Son is, and vice versa. However, for us to see God, this is to be like God.

6.14 The unity, this likeness, is itself heaven, where God dwells in us and we in God. But you, O Highest Truth, are *the heaven of heaven,*[310] you who are what you are, you who have being from yourself, you who belong to yourself, you who are sufficient for yourself: to whom nothing is lacking, nothing is superfluous, with whom there is no discrepancy, no disorder, no change, *no rearrangement, no shadow of alternation,*[311] no indigence, and no death. But in you is the highest harmony, highest clarity, highest plenitude, and fullness of life.

6.15 Moreover, no repulsiveness in your creature is repulsive to you, nor does malice harm, nor does error lead astray. You have preordained for individuals their own dwellings of virtues or happiness. All must arrive at them, whatever necessity may impede or

307. 1 John 3:1
308. 1 John 3:2
309. 1 John 3:9
310. Ps 113:24
311. Jas 1:17

detain. As for evil persons, you have predetermined boundaries for them in their evil activities. They do not have the power to go beyond even if the will to do so is present.[312]

O Lord, this height, this depth, this wisdom, this power[313]—are they the heaven whose door you are? Yes, this is certain! Yes, it is so![314]

6.16 So it is! The door has been opened, and *the ark of the testament is seen in heaven,*[315] as the same John says. What is the ark of the testament recognized in heaven if not, as the Apostle says, *the administering of the mystery hidden from the ages in God who created all things?*[316] Indeed, you are the true ark of the testament. In you has been hidden from eternity and fulfilled in these latter times everything that has been testified to by all the holy ones and prophets, by the law, prophecies, signs, and prodigies. *You are the ark covered over on every part with* pure *gold,*[317] for the fullness of wisdom has resided in you and, having embraced you completely, is glorifying you.

6.17 In you is *the golden vessel containing manna,*[318] the holy and immaculate soul, in which *the fullness of divinity dwelt corporally.*[319] In you is *the rod of Aaron that blossomed*[320] with the dignity of the eternal priesthood.[321] In you are *the tablets of the testament* that establish the world as heir of your grace, and nations destined as *coheirs both as united in a single body and participants in your promise.*[322]

The glorious cherubim,[323] the fullness of knowledge, *are above all these.* Yet they are not above as if because of a preeminent dignity, but because these things need to be carried and supported by them. *Their overshadowing of the Mercy Seat*[324] is witness to the incomprehensibility of the mysteries of your forgiving grace.

6.18 You have revealed to a desiring world at these end times these good things hidden through the ages in your secret heaven,

---

312. Job 14:5

313. Rom 11:33; Eph 3:18

314. *Sic est plane, sic es.*

315. Rev 11:19

316. Eph 3:9

317. Heb 9:4

318. Heb 9:4

319. Col 2:9

320. Heb 9:4

321. Ps 109:4

322. Eph 3:6

323. Heb 9:5

324. Heb 9:5

when you opened in heaven the door that is your very self. Yes, you opened yourself when *your grace appeared to all humanity to teach us,*[325] *when your graciousness and kindness appeared, saving us, not because of the works of justice that we have done, but according to your mercy.*[326]

Then, with heaven opened, every good, every glory, every charm of heaven poured itself out upon the earth. Then it was made known in the sight of all how great was the kindness toward us dwelling within you, O God, you *who did not spare your own Son, but handed him over for us all!*[327] *It was made known when you made known* to the world *your salvation* and *revealed your justice in the sight of all nations,*[328] which you have accomplished for us with the blood of your Only-Begotten, when he himself rendered to you a most pure obedience of charity[329] for our salvation, and to us the charity of his obedience.

6.19 *Since you have blessed your earth,*[330] our nature, it subsequently began *to bear its fruits.*[331] As a result, a public road has reached into your heaven, well worn by the footprints of the apostles, martyrs, and all the saints who, by the example and grace of charity received from you, have loved you to the extreme of disregarding themselves. In fact, they did not fear *to lay down their lives*[332] for you.

6.20 Lord, the riches of your grace that are in your possession and not to be discovered were hidden in the heaven of your secret until the soldier's lance opened the side of your Son, our Lord and Redeemer, on the cross. The mysteries of our redemption flowed out,[333] so that *into his side,* yes, *we may thrust,* like Thomas, not just *a finger or hand,*[334] but may enter completely into that open door, and then proceed all the way into your heart, Jesus, the sure seat of mercy, even proceed all the way into your holy soul, filled

325. Titus 2:11-12
326. Titus 3:4-5
327. Rom 8:32
328. Ps 97:2

329. 1 Pet 1:22
330. Ps 84:2
331. Pss 66:7; 84:13
332. John 15:13

333. John 19:34
334. John 20:27

with all the fullness of God,[335] *filled with grace and truth,*[336] our salvation and consolation.

6.21 Lord, open the door of your side, the ark,[337] so that all of your own to be saved may enter before the face of this deluge, flooding over the earth.[338] Open to us the side of your body so that those who desire to behold the secrets of your Son may enter and may receive the mysteries that flow from it, yes, and *the price of their redemption.*[339] Open the door of your heaven, so that your redeemed *may behold the good things of the Lord in the land of the living.*[340] As yet they toil in the land of the dying. Let them behold and long, ardently desire and run. You have become for them the way through which they journey there, the truth to which they journey, the life for which they journey. This way is the exemplum of humility, the truth of innocence, life, eternal life!

6.22 Merciful Father, Charming Lord, Delightful Brother, You have become all this for us, who are your little children. You said to us, *My little children, I am with you a little while yet.*[341] We are your servants, for you told us, *You call me Teacher and Lord, and you speak correctly, for so I am.*[342] For we are your brothers, whom you commanded to go where they would see you.[343] O Good Father, Delightful Brother, Charming Lord, you are whatever is good, delightful, and gentle, in whom so much goodness abounds. Open yourself to us that your charm, coming from you all the way into us, may remain and fill us.

6.23 Open yourself to me, you who are the door, so that through you, by an ardent devotedness, although I do not yet deserve its full effect,[344] *I may enter on occasion*[345] *into the place of your wonderful tabernacle-tent, even as far as into the house of God.*[346] For once *you revealed to the ear of your servant*[347] that at some time or

---

335. Col 2:9
336. John 1:14
337. Gen 6:16
338. Gen 7:6
339. Ps 48:9

340. Ps 26:13
341. John 13:33
342. John 13:13
343. Matt 28:7
344. *Effectus*

345. *Aliquotiens*
346. Ps 41:5
347. 1 Chr 17:25

other he will have heard to some extent *the voice of exultation and praise, the sound of feasting,*[348] but he is not permitted to enter. My soul, because of this, you have reason to be sad. You have reason to be *disturbed within me.* But *hope in God, for I praise him still, the salvation of my countenance and my God.*[349]

6.24 Open to me, Lord, so that because I am an alien and am still not a worthy citizen to be enrolled there, yet by your gift, I may be permitted to travel there on some occasions,[350] or on very few occasions,[351] so that I, beholding, may see your glory[352] and not leave unless expelled.

If I deserve to ascend there more often, if to linger there for a considerable time,[353] if to return later, may I become known to your citizens, not those rejoicing here, but *like all those rejoicing*[354] and dwelling there. No words can express their joy, *for their sharing embraces all.*[355] They will not consider me an alien if sometimes[356] you command me to rest among them in some part of your house.

6.25 Lord, my heart is restless and impatient for you.[357] I find no rest for it apart from you. Therefore, when I am expelled from heaven, I am so tired of my life that at some time or another it is pleasing to me to descend alive into hell[358]—may it never happen to me that I descend there dead—to see what is going on there. But when I find written on its first threshold that there is no one *in hell who will praise you,*[359] I flee from there while saying to it, "anathema!" Inside there, I hear eyes *weeping and teeth gnashing,*[360] but, Lord, may it not happen to me to descend all the way down there.

6.26 Lord, my eyes are always looking *to you, who dwell in the heavens,*[361] to your home, to the city Jerusalem, from where you have come down to us, and whose wonderful pattern you have

---

348. Ps 41:5

349. Ps 41:6-7

350. *Aliquotiens*

351. *Aliquantulum*

352. Ps 62:3

353. *Aliquamdiu*

354. Ps 86:7

355. Ps 121:3

356. *Aliquando*

357. Ps 41:6

358. Ps 54:16

359. Ps 6:6

360. Matt 8:12

361. Ps 122:1

brought with you for us. Set on fire by that, I am ardently and desirously running back to there. If I find you, the opened door, I enter in, and as long as this is permitted, it is fortunate for me. If I find the door closed, I return dismayed. In fact, prohibited from seeing your glory, I am sent back wretched to my home. Furthermore, I am forced to endure my personal and well-known poverty.

6.27 O, if I will see, O, if I will persevere, O, if at any time or other, I will have heard, *Enter into the joy of your Lord,*[362] may I so[363] enter as never to come out from there. *Lord, you are mighty, and your truth surrounds you.*[364] Bring to perfection what you have made! Give what you have promised!

7.1 *My heart has spoken to you; My face has sought you. Lord, I will search for your face. Do not turn away your face from me. Do not avoid your servant in anger.*[365]

7.2 Indeed, it seems exceedingly rash and insolent to compare your face to my face, Lord God, evaluator and judge of hearts,[366] because *if you have entered into judgment with your servant,*[367] the face of my unjust face has no choice but to flee from the face of your justice.

If, by your gift, an ardent charity would excuse and devoted humility would help my poverty, then *let those persons flee who hate.*[368] I would not flee from your face. The one anticipates; the other fosters confidence.[369] *I am not conscious of these in myself.*[370] Yet I profess myself to be a friend. In fact, if you ask me as you asked Peter, *Do you love me?*[371] I would say clearly, I would say confidently, "Lord, you know all things; you know that I want to love you."[372] If you question me a thousand times, I will respond a thousand times with nothing other than, "You know that I want to love you." In fact, my heart so[373] wants this that it wants nothing so much as to love you.

---

362. Matt 25:21

363. *Sic*

364. Ps 88:9

365. Ps 26:8-9

366. Prov 24:12

367. Ps 142:2

368. Ps 67:2

369. The first of these is charity, the second is humility.

370. 1 Cor 4:4

371. John 21:15

372. John 21:16

373. *Sic . . . sic*

7.3 I also embrace humility, which those making distinctions define as contempt of one's own excellence. But as long as I still sometimes unwittingly pursue trivial honors, or when I do not shake myself free of them quickly enough when they are offered to me, then I know very well that I am not humble.

7.4 There is another kind of humility, namely, self-knowledge. In this, if I am judged according to what I know about myself, then it is all over with me, and, as they say, it is under an evil omen that I have put out my foot into the justice of your judgment. On the other hand, if you judge this to be virtue, and *if my sin is always present to me*,[374] I consider myself not at all lacking in this virtue, since even when I do not want to, and when I am focused on better things, the filthy face of my sins thrusts itself before the eyes of my mind in such a way[375] that frequently I loathe myself on account of them.

7.5 O Lord, what more can I say about the ignominious face of my conscience? Whatever form, howsoever it may be, its entire face so[376] desires your face that it loathes and despises all the things of this life, even life itself, for the sake of its love. It does not care at all what it sees, so long as it can see you.

Yes,[377] in the meantime, O desired vision, *my face searches for you, I seek for your face. I implore you, do not turn it away from me*.[378] But, in the meantime, O Eternal Wisdom, teach me by the illumination of your countenance what is that face of yours and what is my face, because I am wasting away with desire to see you face to face. Nevertheless, I do not know either adequately. In fact, I know that if it was not granted to the Apostle Paul to see you face to face in this life, and to your beloved disciple to see you as you are,[379] what is not granted to one who is so[380] loving and so loved is hoped or sought for only by someone who is not of sound mind.

374. Ps 50:5
375. *Sic*
376. *Sic*
377. *Sic*
378. Ps 26:8-9
379. 1 John 3:2
380. *Sic*

7.6 At the same time, when I hear *face to face* in David's psalms I cannot despair, because I hear of someone else hoping for this from you. This is not because I have forgotten who I am, but I am hoping in the tenderness of your mercy, and although I am making miserable progress in this, I do not want to love you less than any other person loving you. For although it seems that Moses is denied[381] what David had in no way despaired of, David himself sings and chants concerning this same Moses along with other fathers, *they did not take possession of the land by their own sword, and neither did their own arm save them. Rather it was your right hand, your arm, and the illumination of your countenance.*[382] He says about himself, *At your will, Lord, you have provided strength to my beauty. You turned your face from me, and I have become confused.*[383]

7.7 Consequently, Most Loving One, turn to me that face that on occasion you turned from David, and he was troubled.[384] *Turn to me, and I will be consoled,*[385] that face with which before you turned away from him *you provided strength to his beauty according to your will.*[386] May your right hand, your arm, and the illumination of your countenance, which occupied the land of the Fathers in whom you were well pleased, also occupy my land.

For I hear of no one other than David who treats and speaks so frequently and so familiarly concerning your countenance and your face. And we should not believe that he had no experience with your countenance! *He implores that every one of his decisions come forth from it,*[387] and he anticipates that he will *be filled with joy from your face,*[388] actually pronouncing a blessing on the *blessed people who know rejoicing.* He declares, *Lord, they will walk in the light of your countenance.*[389]

7.8 *O God of my heart,*[390] how much more attentive can I be in asking advice from your very countenance, so that my deci-

---

381. Exod 33:20

382. Ps 43:4

383. Ps 29:8

384. Ps 29:8

385. Ps 170:21

386. Ps 29:8

387. Ps 16:2

388. Ps 15:11

389. Ps 88:16

390. Ps 72:26

sion may flow forth from it with all the assent of my conscience shouting it? This your countenance and your face I find to be the knowledge of your truth. Your happy people show to it their face of good will. They exult in the joy of the Holy Spirit and in the festival of the great year of Jubilee[391] by contemplating and enjoying your truth itself. Yes, they walk in its light, *arranging their steps* and all their dealings *according to the declarations of your justice.*[392]

7.9 In fact, there is another face and another countenance of your knowledge. Moses was told concerning this, *You will not be able to see my face, for no person will see me and live.*[393] In this life, sight or knowledge of your divine majesty is better known by not knowing, and to know something by knowing the ways in which one does not know it, this is the highest summit of knowledge in this life.

7.10 However, O Lord, although *you made the darkness* of our ignorance and human blindness *the hiding place* of this face, still *your tabernacle-tent surrounds you*[394]—those resplendent saints of yours who once lived. Sharing the intimate companionship of your own light and fire, they blazed and shone, *enlightening and setting others ablaze*[395] by their word and example. And they declared to us the festal joy of this knowledge of you, coming unexpectedly in the life to come where we will see you as you are, or face to face.

7.11 In the meantime, indeed, the flashing splendor of your truth has illumined the earth's orb through them, and *flashes scintillated.*[396] Persons who have healthy eyes rejoice at them. On the other hand, those *who love darkness more than light*[397] are shaken up and thrown into confusion.

In this way[398] the manifestation of this your truth, through whomever it is made, is like *your sun, which you have made to rise upon the just and unjust.*[399] The sun remains in the clarity of

391. Lev 25:13

392. Ps 118:133, 160

393. Exod 33:20

394. Ps 17:12

395. John 5:35

396. Ps 76:19

397. John 3:19

398. *Sic*

399. Matt 5:45

its own nature. It uses material things as it finds them, drying up mud, melting wax, enlightening every eye of both those who see and the blind: of those who see, so that they can see more clearly, of the blind, so that they remain in their darkness.

And so[400] it is with you, O Wisdom of God and Light of Truth, when you came into the world, through whom the world was made, *you enlightened every good person coming into this world, yet the darkness has not embraced you. On the other hand, to as many who have received you* and the light of your truth, *you gave them the power to become the children of God.*[401]

8.1 For this reason, *O Sun of Justice,*[402] you, illuminating all with *the light of your countenance*[403] and the splendor of your truth, you invite your spouse, whoever she may be, saying, *Show me your face, my sister, my spouse.*[404] And immediately, a person of good will to whom is announced the peace from heaven[405]—who is the brother of Christ, whose soul is designated his sister—desires just as she is *to appear this way*[406] *before you in your holy place,*[407] *and to see light in your light.*[408]

If he is a sinner, he shows you the face of his misery, searching for the face of your mercy. If he is holy, he runs to meet you with the face of his justice, and he finds in you a face resembling its own because, *Just Lord, you love justice.*[409] On the other hand, if his brow is that *of a harlot,* who *does not choose to blush,*[410] then he, fleeing the truth, rushes headlong into your most furious justice.

8.2 Facing you, the human soul shows you as many faces as it has affections. Yet you, O Truth, entertain all of them, adapting yourself to all of them while you yourself remain unchanged. Devoted humility finds in you an intimate grace. Flaming love finds a sweet-scented source of fuel. A humble heart's repentance finds a justice you prepared for it. The harlot's brow finds its own confusion.

---

400. *Sic et tu*
401. John 1:5-12
402. Mal 4:2
403. Ps 4:7

404. Song 2:14
405. Luke 2:13-14
406. *Sic*
407. Ps 62:3

408. Ps 35:10
409. Ps 10:8
410. Jer 3:3

8.3 In this way,[411] O Supreme Justice, mercy and truth meet in you[412] when in a just soul the truth of human justice humbly confesses and the truth of your own justice rightly has mercy on the soul confessing truth. And while the soul offers the kiss of a just confession, you receive it with the kiss of peace.

8.4 This is a kiss of a bridegroom and bride. That her face may be found worthy of your kiss, O Lord, your face was spat upon. That hers may appear lovely and beautiful, your face is made black and blue by being slapped with human hands and blows from rods.[413] That hers may appear exquisite and beautiful before your eyes,[414] your face was *drenched with disgrace*[415] before human eyes. Why not? For over and above all this, you have prepared for her a bath in your most precious blood,[416] wherein she may be cleansed. Son of God, you suffered horrible things for us who have done horrible things. For these, a face of any kind of repentance could not have atoned before the face of utmost justice, had not your innocence been added to what you suffered for us, and moreover since *you are the Son, who is listened to because of your reverence.*[417]

8.5 Lord, your hands were pierced with nails on behalf of my hands, which have done what they ought not to have done, your feet on behalf of my feet, your eyes for my inappropriate gaze, your ears for my hearing: all these have fallen asleep in death on my behalf. *The soldier's spear opened* your *side,*[418] so that through your wound there would flow from my impure heart everything whatever in it that by a long decay had been *dug deeply and burned by a fire*[419] for some time. Last, you died that I might live, were buried that I might rise.

This is the kiss of your sweetness to your spouse. This is the embrace of delight for your friend. Woe to the person who will not have participated in this kiss. Woe to the person who will

411. *Sic*
412. Ps 84:11
413. Lam 3:30
414. Song 2:13-14
415. Lam 3:30
416. Eph 5:26
417. Heb 5:8
418. John 19:34
419. Ps 79:17

have fallen from this embrace. The confession of the thief on the cross received this kiss.[420] Peter received it when the Lord looked at him in his denial, *and he went out and wept bitterly.*[421] And many of those who crucified you, and then converted to you after your passion, are bonded to you in this kiss. That Mary who was once the possession of seven devils[422] rejoiced in that embrace from which the wickedness of Judas the traitor fell.[423] Publicans and sinners, whose fellow dinner guest and friend you became,[424] were drawn tightly together in this embrace. Present there are the converted harlot *Rahab, Babylon that knows you, strangers, Tyre,* and the black *Ethiopians.*[425]

8.6 On the other hand, Lord, where do you draw those whom you embrace and clasp close to you if not to your heart? Your affectionate heart is that manna of your divinity, O Jesus, that you possess within you, in the *golden urn*[426] of the overflowing wisdom of your soul. Blessed are they whom your embrace has drawn close to your soul. Blessed are they *whom you have hidden in the hiding place* of that hidden place, *in the depths of your heart,*[427] *that they may be covered over with your embrace from human turmoil, and may hope only in your* protecting and nurturing *wings.*[428]

For *they are covered with the embrace* of your power, those who *are hidden in the secret place* of your heart, charmingly sleeping and rejoicing in affectionate anticipation *in the midst of the chosen lots,*[429] the merits of a holy conscience and anticipation of your promised reward, neither lacking because of faintheartedness nor grumbling because of impatience.

8.7 However, those who more affectionately kiss one another more affectionately mingle their spirits with one another. They are filled affectionately with each other's fragrance. Take to yourself, Lord, and do not reject my entire spirit, which I pour completely

420. Luke 23:43	424. Matt 9:10	428. Pss 90:4; 16:8; 30:21
421. Luke 22:62	425. Ps 86:4	429. Ps 67:14
422. Luke 8:2	426. Heb 9:4	
423. Matt 27:5	427. Pss 30:21; 39:9	

into you, which is entirely foul. Yes, pour into me your entire spirit, which is entirely fragrant, so that because of your charm and your sweetness, my spirit may no longer be foul smelling. O Most Affectionate Lord, may it always penetrate more deeply into me.

This is what happens when we do what you commanded us *to do in remembrance of* you.[430] There is nothing more affectionate for the salvation of your sons and daughters. Nothing more powerful can be provided than when we eat and drink the incorruptible banquet of your Body and Blood.

Like your clean animals,[431] we bring it up again from the depths of memory into our mouths, so to speak. Always ruminating with a new intensity of ardent devotedness in a new and unending service of our own salvation, we sweetly store up again in this same memory what you did for us, what you suffered.

8.8 When you say to a soul who desires, *Open wide your mouth and I will fill it,*[432] she both tastes and sees your charm[433] in the great and incomprehensible sacrament. Here is accomplished what the soul consumes, *bone of your bone and flesh of your flesh.*[434] Just as you prayed to the Father when about to enter into your passion, this the Holy Spirit accomplishes in us by grace what is by nature in the Father and in you, his Son, from all eternity, namely, *that as you are one, so we may be one in you.*[435]

8.9 Lord, this is your face turned to the face of a person longing for you. This is *the kiss of your mouth*[436] upon the mouth of a person loving you. This is the embrace of your delightful love, reaching for the embrace of your spouse, who yearns for you, saying, *My beloved is mine and I am his. He shall dwell between my breasts.*[437] Again, *my heart said to you, My face has searched for you.*[438] For if our soul's face does not look for your face, its face is not natural. Rather, it has put on some mask, that of a beast.

430. Luke 22:19; 1 Cor 11:25
431. Lev 11:2-8; Ps 67:11
432. Ps 80:11
433. Ps 33:9
434. Gen 2:23
435. John 17:21
436. Song 1:1
437. Song 2:16
438. Song 1:12; Ps 26:8

8.10 Who would not seek it? Who will not spend all of his strength for it? Who will not languish for it? Who will not faint for it? Who will not die for it? Have mercy, Lord. I would already have died—by what manner of death I do not know—had not *your visitation guarded my spirit*.[439]

On the contrary, when you show your face, an enemy finds *a furnace of fire*[440] in you; a sinner finds *traps, fire, sulfur, and stormy winds*[441] *as his share of the cup*; a proud person finds the power with which *you resist the proud*;[442] hypocrites find the light of truth that they hate. And all of these *have consciences branded* with a face of their own individual evils,[443] as if they had a general face of unrepentant meanness. Yes, you welcome this face with the face of justice that judges justly, and you greet those who hate justice with your loathing for iniquity.

8.11 Because they have *proved themselves to have no knowledge of God, you, God, have given them over to a degenerate thinking to do those things that are not proper,*[444] things that are shameful to be recounted in your presence.[445] Yet they perform them imprudently and irreverently in your presence. From their lusts, that is, from their daughters, and from their sins, that is, from their sons and their grandchildren, they forge for themselves from a multitude of sins that strong, that tearful, long chain whose iron links make a charmingly clanking sound for the time being.[446] Painfully pulled tight, it drags its makers down into hell, where no one will evermore *praise you,*[447] O God, where there is no hope, from where there is no exit.

8.12 I wonder about these persons, if having been placed in hell it will be given to them to know in some way how good it is to enjoy you. For if it is given to them to know in some manner, I do not believe there is in hell a greater torment than to be without the vision of you.

---

439. Job 10:12
440. Ps 20:10
441. Ps 10:7
442. 1 Pet 5:5
443. 1 Tim 4:2

444. Rom 1:28
445. Eph 5:12
446. their lusts = *concupiscentiis suis*; their sins = *peccatis suis*; multitude of sins = *multitudine peccatorum*
447. Ps 6:6

But, alas, alas, those who have been guilty of such horrible deeds also suffer horrible consequences, because your blood, Christ, will not come to the assistance of the unrepentant. Rather, they will be judged culpable of your blood,[448] which they have trampled underfoot[449] by sinning and not repenting. This is the *face of your fury*,[450] which terrified the prophet, and he trembled in the presence of the face of those whom it awaits. As the Apostle says, *a certain terrible anticipation of a judgment and fiery indignation that is about to consume its adversaries.*[451]

8.13 Lord God, judge of the living and the dead,[452] are these the two flocks of your right hand and left hand, on the day of your Judgment?[453] Between these two lots[454]—the destiny of death and life, of damnation and redemption, of anger and grace—*where will I be found?*[455]

O Truth, Truth, by reason of the glory and majesty of your face, *do not hide it from me.*[456] But shine all its *brilliant rays* upon me,[457] *so that I may see light in its light*,[458] that is, what my face is before your face and what yours is before mine, whether truth is in me, Jesus, in the same way[459] as it is in you, *to rid me of everything from my former way of life*,[460] *the old man, who is corrupted according to the desires of error.*[461] To be sure, O Truth, I know that I am seeking you, but whether I am truly seeking you, I do not know.

8.14 This is my face in your presence, a face of my great misery and of my great need. For although *your consolations* sometimes *rejoice my soul*,[462] nevertheless, I know who I have been. Still, I do not know what shape I may be in now. *One thing I have asked the Lord, this I seek,*[463] that as the face of my misery cringes before you, so in this way[464] may the face of your mercy itself shine upon me

---

448. 1 Cor 11:2
449. Heb 10:29
450. Isa 51:13; Jer 4:26; 25:37
451. Heb 10:27
452. 2 Tim 4:1

453. Matt 25:31-33
454. Ps 67:14
455. 1 Pet 4:18
456. Ps 26:9
457. Ps 143:6
458. Ps 35:10

459. *Sic*
460. *Conversatio*
461. Eph 4:22
462. Ps 93:19
463. Ps 26:4
464. *Sic*

more and more, to the point of an utter destruction of my misery and darkness.

9.1 Lord, there is such a density and immensity of my misery in me that I am not qualified either to divide and analyze it or to survey the enormous face of its entirety. For behold, as is its custom, its darkness has enveloped me. And also, my unencumbered view and hearing is not focused on you, my Lord God, with whom I desire to speak and whom I desire to hear. This is how[465] it always happens to me, that my own house, my conscience, drives me away from you.[466] Is this not so: *Let the wicked person be taken away so as not to see the glory of God?*[467]

And with the eyes of my mind blinded, I press forward, somehow groping to where I was heading, with intent of an ardent desire that is fatigued and shattered. I fall back into my depths from your heights. I fall from you, back into myself, and from myself, I fall below myself. And with every strategy of my endeavor exhausted, I am, like some particle of dust, *aimlessly blown from the face of the earth,*[468] made a plaything of the winds, because of the fancies of my thoughts, my desires, my affections, that are just so many human faces, as there are minutes in many hours, or as many things or issues that have come and gone.

9.2 Therefore, although the face of your goodness always turns toward me to do me good, the face of my misery is always looking down upon the stupid earth. In this way[469] it is wrapped up in the fog of its own blindness, so that it neither knows nor is able to appear before you except inasmuch as the face of your truth sees through everything that is unable to escape notice in any possible manner. Because of this, *I leave my gift before* your *altar,*[470] disgusted with myself and shaking myself up; I rise within my very self, and lighting the lamp of the Word of God, I enter into the gloomy house of my conscience *with indignation* and bitterness *of*

---

465. *Sic . . . sic*
466. Isa 26:10 (Vetus Latina)
467. Isa 26:10 (Vetus Latina)
468. Ps 1:4
469. *Sic*
470. Matt 5:24

my spirit,[471] so to speak, ready to discern the source of this darkness and the source of this hateful fog that is making a separation between me and the light of my heart.

9.3 And look! It is as if a sort of plague of flies rushes into my eyes and utterly drives me out from the house of my own conscience. Yet I enter, as if into something belonging to me by right, and look, there is a crowd of thoughts so insolent, so uncontrolled, so wide-ranging, so confused that the human heart, which gave birth to them, is not adequate to discern them.

9.4 Nevertheless, I sit down as if I were about to judge them. I command them to stand before me so that I may analyze the face and families of each one, and then, for I am going to assign each one its own place within me, before I can examine them closely, before I can analyze them, they scatter. And some presenting themselves in place of others, they seem to mock the person who is judging them.

9.5 I am furious and angry with myself. I stand up, about to deal more severely with them in the name of authority, as if in my own kingdom. I gather together in my presence, as if I were forming my council to assist me, those thoughts that at some time or another I have experienced as reliable and stable, those *drawn from the fonts of the Savior.*[472] He is their judge. He is their accuser, and he is their witness.

9.6 I dissociate myself from the unclean and worst thoughts as not worth being heard and, without any judgment, to be damned and punished with appropriate penalties of chastisement. I drive away idle and hateful thoughts as if they were annoying flies. In the meantime, I admit thoughts about business and jobs, reasonably listening and processing them, and assigning them their proper time and place. Those that are condemned by the judgment of my own conscience receive their sentence without murmuring. Idle ones, seeing this sorting out to be seriously in progress, and fearing to interrupt what is happening, disperse or become weaker. Those

471. Ezek 3:14   472. Isa 12:3

concerning business, seeing themselves ignored and of little value since their purpose has come to an end, are now embarrassed to be nearly numbered among the idle thoughts, so withdraw.

9.7 Therefore, in this way,[473] the fog of my thoughts having been dispersed for a time, I direct myself to their origin, mainly to regulate the self-control of my affections. And I find that their comings and goings have been blocked with regard to things of the flesh because of the requirement of the solitude into which I have fled. If the affections were to find them unguarded, I would not—I confess my wretchedness—trust my frailty at all.

But also, thanks to the grace of him *who comforts me,*[474] love, the most distinguished of affections, devotes itself to the one thing that *I* continuously *ask and need from the Lord.*[475] It *brings* the entire crowd of them *back into bondage.*[476] It gives them standards. It shapes their performance. It sets up in advance *limits beyond which they are not permitted to go.*[477]

9.8 So, with the fog of them all now dispersed, again I turn healthier eyes upon you, O Light of Truth. With everything else shut out, I can shut myself away with you, O Truth, *hiding myself in the hiding place of your face.*[478] There I can speak with you more secretly and more intimately, opening to you all the deep places of my conscience; casting off Adam's garments of skin that you made for him to cover the disgrace of his confusion,[479] I show myself to you as naked as when you created me.[480] Behold, here I am, Lord, not such as you made me, but such as I have made myself ever since I fell away from you, from the way you made me. Behold my wounds, both recent and old. I eliminate nothing, I expose all to you, both your good deeds and my evil deeds.

9.9 *You have created me in your image.*[481] You have placed me in your Paradise.[482] You gave me by name a place in the midst of the

---

473. *Sic*
474. Phil 4:13
475. Ps 26:4
476. 1 Cor 9:27
477. Job 14:5
478. Ps 30:21 (Vetus Latina)
479. Gen 3:21; Mark 10:50
480. Gen 2:25
481. Gen 1:27
482. Gen 2:15

community of your children. From the very time of my impure childhood, *you have imprinted, like a seal upon me, the light of your countenance.*[483] I fled from your Paradise, and instead of the place you had given me, I found a sewer and concealed myself in it. Always I held on to the seal of your countenance in faith and intention, but I rejected it in my behavior. For by following my concupiscence and my heart's vanities, I squandered my adolescence and almost engaged in the way of the flesh.

9.10 But my spirit has always loved you, even when my flesh neglected you. When I fled from these sins, *I fled to you* for help.[484] You pulled me out from the world's abyss. I worked out a treaty with you. *I swore and determined to observe the judgments of your justice.*[485] And opening to me the deep, secret hiding-place[486] of your mercy, you gathered me into it. When I was gently resting there, I saw and longed for the Day of Man. Yes, you sent me away when I was indecisively willing and not willing. But you have not abandoned me.

9.11 If sometimes I was forgetful of my God, and I was stretching out my hands where I shouldn't have, immediately the secret tormentors of my conscience broke into pieces all the bones of my soul's interior, using the rod of your discipline. On the outside, yes, *the sinners plowed upon my back.*[487] For a long time, you have supported me and upheld me in this way[488] as I was falling and rising, dying and coming back to life.

When finally I was utterly exhausted both physically and mentally, and *I was crying to you from the belly of hell,*[489] immediately you came to me. You stretched out your hand[490] and *led me forth from the lake of misery.*[491] *You* reinstated me in my former state and *restored to me the joy of your salvation*[492] more fully than previously.

9.12 So I was, Lord, and so I am now.[493] I am present before you in all that I am. All my evil deeds, which are manifest, are not hidden

483. Ps 4:7	487. Ps 128:3	491. Ps 39:3
484. Ps 142:9	488. *Sic*	492. Ps 50:14
485. Ps 118:106	489. Jonah 2:3	493. *Sic . . . sic*
486. *Sinus*	490. Ps 137:7	

from you or from me. In fact, many others, which are hidden from me through my blindness and forgetfulness, are nevertheless manifest to you. If any good is in me, nothing of it is uncorrupted, for the enemy early on stole abundantly from me. Or if this enemy had not been able to do this, then in some way or other he corrupted me. Even so, I have harmed myself far more than my enemy has.

9.13 Behold, my face is before you. Present before your face, its name is misery, O Supreme Mercy. I do not hide its hidden corners and recesses from you. You know this, O Truth! I implore you that this may be the truth present before you. I fear no one in such a way as I fear myself,[494] lest I deceive myself.

9.14 Do I not believe you? Do I not believe because of you? Do I not believe in you, my God? Let not those who set restricting boundaries and limits to my faith ridicule me. Along with heart, mouth, hand, and writings, of course, I offer to you, Light of Truth, my free and full assent to believe all things that the catholic church believes concerning you. If these limits of my faith are adequate, fill them! If they are less than adequate, make up for them!

9.15 Nevertheless, I say confidently regarding hope that I do not truly believe if I hope for something other than that in which I believe. I believe in you! I hope in you! Give yourself to me! I seek nothing else! Yet I do not hope if I do not love. Nor do I love if I do not hope. Therefore, Father, because I love miserably, I hope halfheartedly. And this being my situation,[495] while what has sprung up from the root of faith[496] is wilting away, even the root itself grows weak. Yet I still believe in you, I hope in you, and I love you, O Life Eternal.

9.16 O Fatherland, O Fatherland, where there is no evil, where all is good! Yes, it is from a great distance that I see and greet you. I know about evil things, [that][497] there evil things do not exist, those evil things that a long and wearisome experience has taught me all too well. But about good things that are there, then to the

---

494. *Sic . . . sicut*
495. *Sicque*

496. 2 Thess 1:3

497. that] CCCM 88 *quia*, with variant *quod.*

extent that my knowledge about them is a stranger, to that degree is my experience far off.

Have mercy, Lord. Look, *I have run and aimed straight towards you! Arise to meet me and see!*[498] Lord, *make my end known to me and what are the number of my days, so that I may know what it is that I lack.*[499]

9.17 I stand in your faith.[500] I go forward in hope. Indigent and mendicant, I stand waiting for *your love.*[501] O Love, O Fire, O Charity, come to us! Be our Leader and Light, the Fire burning and consuming in the repentance of sinners. Be our Paraclete, Comforter, Advocate, and Helper in the petitions of our prayers. Show us what we believe! Whisper within us that for which we hope! Give us a face like the face of God! Let us bring them together so that we can say, *My heart has said to you, "My face has sought you!"*[502]

10.1 *May it be far from me to glory save in the cross of Our Lord Jesus Christ.*[503] My entire way of life is toward my Crucified One.[504] His cross is my glory. My forehead is signed with it. My mind rejoices in it. My life is oriented by it. My death is lovingly blessed by it.

10.2 Lord, may they not look down upon me because of this, those who merit to see you *sitting upon the high and lofty throne of your divinity*[505] and filling the whole earth with your majesty. For those things that are under you, the mysteries of your human dispensation, fill to overflowing the temple of all contemplation, whatever its greatness may be.

May your holy angels have their glory in the heavens, but also let them sometimes communicate their grace to us on earth, since their joyful perfection still loves to profit us in ours and finds it pleasant to do so. As the Apostle says, *The manifold wisdom of God is made known to the principalities and powers in the heavens through the church.*[506] Therefore, may they pardon us, Lord, even

498. Ps 58:5-6   501. Ps 39:18   504. Song 7:10
499. Ps 38:5   502. Ps 26:8   505. Isa 6:1
500. I Cor 16:13   503. Gal 6:14   506. Eph 3:10

in this: if your love sometimes leads us to the point that we desire to see with them what we love with them. We rejoice with perfect charity with those seeing what we do not as yet merit to see.

10.3 May they delightfully contemplate in your wisdom the majesty of your divinity, which beheld what was before and after our epoch and which inserts all this past and future into the now of your eternity. *This wisdom reaches from end to end mightily*[507] and has strewn our epoch, a time of the human dispensation, with your selfless *love charmingly arranging all things*[508] on behalf of the daughters of Jerusalem, souls devoted yet still weak. They do not yet *have senses trained*[509] and suited for contemplating such loftiness. They love to be deeply moved[510] and set free by your lowliness that is so similar to their own.

Sometime or other, Lord, you will also teach my spirit, aligned among them, *to adore you in spirit and in truth,*[511] you who are spirit, when my fleshly desires will not work against my spirit or pamper it more gently.[512]

10.4 But now, in the meantime, since [my spirit] is not able to be resolutely free in this way[513] for those things that are yours, as is expedient for it, you so charmingly dispose its own things for it as is agreeable. For as I have not yet gone beyond the basics of my sensual imagination, you allow and will be pleased that my soul continues to exercise its weak character with its mental imagination itself vis-à-vis your lowliness, that is, to embrace the manger of the one being born and to adore your holy infancy, to lick the feet of the one hanging on the cross, to hold on to and kiss affectionately the feet of the one rising, to insert a hand into the place of the nails and exclaim, *My Lord and My God.*[514]

10.5 And in all of this, as Job says, *visiting my treasured one,*[515] *I shall not sin*[516] when I pray and will worship what I will see in my

507. Wis 8:1

508. Song 3:10

509. Heb 5:14

510. *Affici*

511. John 4:24

512. Gal 5:17

513. *Sic*

514. John 20:28

515. treasured one]
Lat. *speciem* (see
Med. 10.12)

516. Job 5:24

imagining, what I will hear, and *what my hands will touch concerning the Word of Life*.[517] For boldly I will say that in a delightful arrangement of your Wisdom this grace is prepared for us from eternity.

With you, it has not been the least of the foremost reasons for your incarnation that the little ones in your church, nourished with milk, *are still in need of milk and not solid food*.[518] As they are unable to think of you spiritually, according to your own manner, they might have in you a form not unfamiliar to them, or a face they could set before themselves without any scandal of faith in the sacrificial offering of their prayer. For as yet they are not able to gaze into that brightness of your divine majesty.

10.6 Therefore, *although we have* no longer *known you according to the flesh*,[519] all the same we know you accordingly as you now sit, glorified at the right hand of the Father in the heavens, *made so much better than the angels as you have inherited a more distinctive name than they*.[520] We pray to, we adore, and we implore that very flesh of ours that you have not cast off but have glorified, which is *the footstool of your feet*.[521] David exhorts us to do this: *Adore the footstool of his feet, for it is holy*.[522]

10.7 Blessed is that temple of the Holy Spirit from which no forgetfulness banishes Christ exalted on the cross and the blood flows down always fresh for the salvation of the person believing and loving. What the Prophet claims is always taking place: *Deliver me and be merciful to me*.[523] As often as the loving ardent devotedness of a person at prayer contemplates this, just so often is the effect of our redemption celebrated within us. Because we cannot do this as we desire, this is why we still mentally depict for ourselves, with even greater daring, a form of your passion so that the eyes of our flesh may also have something to look upon, something to cleave to, not adoring the picture's image but the truth contained in the

517. 1 John 1:1
518. Heb 5:12
519. 2 Cor 5:16
520. Heb 1:4
521. Ps 109:1
522. Ps 98:5
523. Ps 25:11

image of your passion. For when we look more attentively upon the image of your passion while it is silent, you are seen to say to us from the cross, *When I loved you, I loved you to the end.*[524] Let death and hell clutch me in their own death! *But you, my friends, eat, and you, my most beloved, drink abundantly* unto eternal life![525]

10.8 And in this way[526] your cross becomes that linen sheet *let down from heaven by four corners*[527] and shown to Blessed Peter, in which all animals, both clean and unclean, are present.[528] We give thanks as it lifts us up into heaven, where we who are unclean are likewise cleansed. For by means of an image of your passion, Christ, your goodness towards us, having been contemplated by us, suddenly carries us into an ardent devotedness for the highest good. You allow us to see that face in the work of your salvation, not now as from an understanding forced by human endeavor and with eyes of the mind, trembling and shrinking away from your light, but with a tranquil experience of love and good use of vision, enjoying gentleness while your wisdom is gently arranging for those things that concern us.

10.9 For the person who *ascends by some other way*[529] exerts effort. But in fact the person who enters through you, O Door, walks on level ground and comes to the Father, *to whom no one comes unless through you.*[530] Such a person no longer works for an understanding surpassing knowledge.[531] Rather, this person is set thoroughly free by the charm of a most ardently devoted consciousness.

And with a more abundant rush of a river joyfully flooding that soul,[532] it seems to her that she *sees you as you are.*[533] From the sweetness of thinking about the wonderful sacrament of your passion, she ponders the good you've done for us that is as great as you yourself are, since it is your very self. She seems to herself to see you *face to face,*[534] the face of the highest good, as you appear to her on your cross and in the work of her salvation. The cross

---

524. John 13:1

525. Song 5:1

526. *Sicque*

527. Acts 10:11-12

528. present] CCCM 88: *intrantes*

529. John 10:1-2

530. John 14:6

531. Eph 3:19

532. Ps 45:5

533. 1 John 3:2

534. 1 Cor 13:12

itself becomes for her the face of a mind exceptional in ardent devotedness to God.

10.10 For what better preparation, what more tender disposition is there possible for people about to ascend to their God so as *to offer gifts and sacrifices*[535] according to the precept of the law, than *ascending not by steps to his altar,*[536] but across the level ground of likeness, smoothly and with no stumbling: that is, a human walking toward a human like himself, who says to him at the very threshold of the entrance, *I and the Father are one.*[537] And immediately, with his ardent devotedness assumed into God through the power of the Holy Spirit, he can take into himself *the God coming and dwelling with him,*[538] not only spiritually but also corporeally, through the mystery of the holy and life-giving Body and Blood of Our Lord Jesus Christ.

10.11 Lord, this is your Face toward us and our face toward you, full of good hope. Lord, clothe me in this by your salvation, and form this face of your Christ in me, for it is impossible for you to turn it away however often *it will have appeared before you in the Holy Place.*[539]

10.12 O, whoever you are! Go, and you will find this treasure hidden in the field of your heart. *Sell all that you have,*[540] even your very self as a perpetual slave so that you may possess it by the right of a hereditary possession.[541] Yes, you will be happy, and *all will be well with you!*[542]

The treasure in your possession is Christ in your consciousness.

11.1 *God of heavenly powers, turn toward us and show your face, and we will be saved.*[543]

Because of the gift of your grace, Lord, I do not have the face of my heart turned toward things that are fleshly. Since you have put them behind me,[544] and have put both the world and all things that

---

535. Heb 5:1
536. Exod 20:26
537. John 10:30
538. John 14:23

539. Ps 62:3
540. Matt 13:44; 19:23
541. Lev 25:46
542. Ps 127:2

543. Ps 79:8
544. Ps 20:13

belong to it below me, why, I ask, when I search for you with all my heart, and rejoice that I have captured your face, which my face desires only, do I suddenly find myself estranged from you? *Why do you hide your face? Do you think of me as your enemy? Surely you are not willing to devour me for the sins of my youth?*[545] Is it that I am not turned to you, or perhaps you are still turned away from me?

11.2 If I am not turned to you, God of heavenly powers, turn me back[546] towards myself. If you are turned away, *God of heavenly powers, turn back!* You have said, *If you are turned away, Israel, turn back.*[547] And again: *Be turned towards me, and I will be turned to you.*[548] You know the gift of your grace in the heart of your poor one: *My heart is ready, God, my heart is ready!*[549] Command what you will! Make me understand what you command! Grant me the power, you who gave the power to will. And whatever you will, let it be accomplished in me or from me. *I have willed that I may do your will, my God. And in the depths of my heart, I embrace your law* with its commands.[550]

11.3 In fact, there is another, *your perfect law, converting souls,*[551] but I do not know it, Lord. It is hidden *in the secret hiding place of your countenance,*[552] where I do not deserve to enter. If just once you should so[553] grant me entrance there that I might see it, then, *with the pen of that scribe who writes rapidly,*[554] the Holy Spirit, I would transcribe it two or three times upon my heart to have a place where I might return, and, understanding what I am doing from then on, I might walk straight ahead simply and confidently.[555]

11.4 Now, however, I am like *a blind person groping around*[556] *in midday.* Wherever I put a foot forward for my ascent, I fear a pitfall and debris. And, like a blind person, I am told to go hither or thither, this way or that. But like a person who does not see, I know neither here or there, nor this way or that way.

545. Job 13:24, 26	549. Ps 56:8	553. *Sic*
546. Ps 79:8	550. Ps 39:9	554. Ps 44:2
547. Jer 4:1	551. Ps 18:8	555. Prov 10:9
548. Zech 1:3	552. Ps 30:21	556. Deut 28:29

11.5 *Send forth* to me, Lord, *your light and your truth. They have led me forth and brought me to your holy mountain and into your tabernacle-tents.*[557] You tell me, *I am the Way* by which you will go. I am *the Truth* to which you will go. I am *the Life* for whose sake you will go.[558] And you know where to go; *you know the way,*[559] also. But Lord, *I do not know where I am going, and how then am I to know the way?*[560] *You have held my hand and led me in your will.*[561] You held my hand when you stretched out your right hand to your blind one, who was crying out to you and weeping. And you said, *Come to me, all you who labor and are burdened, and I will refresh you.*[562]

11.6 Once I heard this, *I ran in the way of your commandments, for you have expanded my heart.*[563] I came to you, offering to you *my ready heart*[564]—God, yes, my heart is ready—and saying, *Lord, what do you wish me to do?*[565] You responded to me, *Go, sell all that you have, and give to the poor, then come and follow me.*[566] I went, I ran, I sold all that I had, even my very body, my very soul. I gave nothing to the poor, because I had nothing. And, Lord, I sold you whatever I had. And you are my reward. You know that I retained nothing for myself. Or, if anything has escaped me and is still hidden in some secret hiding place of my conscience, I will search it out and faithfully offer it to you.

11.7 But when I looked for payment from you, you charged me *for the sins of my youth,*[567] a long-ago debt. I implore you, Lord, *have patience with me,*[568] for I have no means with which I may repay you.

11.8 I have come to this moment. Here I stand. It is not permitted to advance further.[569] Therefore, blind and poor, a beggar, I sit alongside the road where you are passing by. I cry out to you, *Son*

557. Ps 42:3
558. John 14:6
559. John 14:4
560. John 14:5
561. Ps 72:24

562. Matt 11:28
563. Ps 118:32
564. Ps 56:8
565. Acts 9:6
566. Matt 19:21

567. Ps 24:7
568. Matt 18:26
569. Job 38:11

of David, have pity on me.[570] And the crowds close in against my face and chide me to be silent. But I cry out so much the more. *Have pity on me, Son of David.*[571] *I exerted myself, clamoring; my throat is hoarse, my eyes failing while I hope in my God.*[572] But you pass by the one clamoring.[573]

11.9 Sometimes you stop for me, but just for a little while. You command me to come to you, and you say to me, *What do you wish that I do for you?*[574] In all truth, *with all my bones,* I reply to you,[575] *Lord, that I may see!*[576] Yet you pass on!

11.10 *Have pity, have pity on me, Son of David.*[577] I cannot follow you, for I am blind. Have pity on me. I have from you the reason—however trifling—that drew me to you. I do not have the strength that would enable me to run after you. *Have pity on me, Son of David.*[578] *At least you, friends*[579] of my Lord, servants of my God, have pity on me and say to him, *Send him away, for he clamors after us.*[580] *Woe to me that my sojourning is prolonged. My soul has been a sojourner*[581] in the house of darkness too long. What have I done? What have I accomplished? *It is the Lord. He will do what is good in his sight.*[582]

11.11 I will sit by the roadside. I will not desert the road.[583] Perhaps at some time or other he will come back without the crowds and will see me, who is unable to see, and will have pity on me. His good word is present in my heart, saying, *Wait for the Lord, behave manfully, and let your heart be encouraged, and hold fast to the Lord.*[584]

11.12 In the meantime, *my soul and everything that is within me,*[588] be gathered together before me.[586] For *the Word of God is living and efficacious, more piercing than a two-edged sword, reaching*

---

570. Luke 18:38

571. Luke 18:38

572. Ps 68:4

573. Luke 18:41

574. Mark 10:51

575. Ps 34:10

576. Luke 18:41

577. Luke 18:40

578. Mark 10:47

579. Job 19:21

580. Matt 15:23

581. Ps 119:5-6

582. 1 Sam 3:18

583. 2 Pet 2:15

584. Ps 26:14

585. Ps 102:1

586. Gen 49:1

all the way in until it even divides soul and spirit, and even joints and marrow. It is the discerner of thoughts and intentions of the heart. No creature may be invisible in his sight. Everything about me may be naked and open to his eyes. Even our speaking is in his presence.[587]

11.13 *I have told the Lord: You are my God. My destiny is in your hands.*[588] *Let us cast lots* to know by whose sin this evil has fallen upon us[589] *so that God might turn his face from his child.*[590] The decision of my destiny is the discovering of your truth, O God. *As the Lord lives,*[591] *if my* right *hand, my eye, or my foot has become a stumbling block for me*, I will not spare it, but will cut it off and *will cast it away from me.*[592]

11.14 Tell me, O Word of God, can it be that I have not done well in believing in you, even to the point of *having left all things so that I am following you?*[593] All the thoughts and intentions of my heart, my soul and spirit, joints and marrow answer that it is good.[594] I add further to enquire, was *this good act not done well?* My *thoughts* are murmuring softly, and when they have received permission to speak, they recall what the Lord said to Peter: *Peter, do you love me? He replied, You know that I love you. Feed my sheep!* And three times this was said,[595] *like a threefold cord* whose significance suggests something *not to be easily broken,*[596] for the proof of love is shepherding of the flock![597]

11.15 *Intentions:* A shepherd who is in fact not a hireling, even though he will *have laid down his soul for the sheep,* scarcely provides for them.[598] But it is most grave for him to be in command when he is not able to lead them. There was a time when King David was so[599] weak in body that he lay on his bed, so[600] sensible of the cold from old age that *he was not able to get warm with*

---

587. Heb 4:12-13 (Vetus
    Latina)
588. Ps 30:15-16
589. Jonah 1:7
590. Ps 68:18
591. 1 Sam 14:45

592. Matt 18:8-9
593. Luke 5:11
594. Heb 4:12
595. John 21:17
596. Eccl 4:12
597. RB 64.23

598. John 10:11; 15:13;
    1 John 3:16
599. *Sic*
600. *Sic*

blankets.[601] He was governing the people of God from his bed, and by royal word alone, with *the eyes of all Israel looking toward him* for everything. *Fascination with frivolous things was not yet obscuring the good.*[602] The hardened indifference of a world grown old had not yet reached so[603] intense a degree that its respect for aged seniors was not preserved.

11.16 Now indeed, while it is the duty of the shepherds of the church to feed the Lord's flock in body and soul simultaneously, God is nevertheless concerned especially for the soul, saying, *First, seek the kingdom of God.* Furthermore, about the body, which is secondary, as if wanting to put them at ease, he adds, *all these things shall be added to you.*[604]

Today, who would listen to anyone preaching this? Who would allow someone to do this? Who would spare the old man? Who would ignore human weakness? Prudence of the flesh, the spirit of this world, curiosity, refinement, and other things of this nature are required by ecclesiastical superiors. Simplicity is mocked, religion is despised, and humility is of no importance. And yet, if it seems to suffice in one way or another for a person in command to provide for the interior life, who is sufficient for this today, except people who prosper, even with plenty of those exterior goods? Would that they would adequately know their limitations!

11.17 Because of this, *Woe to us, for we have sinned.*[605] Because of this, as the Prophet says, *we have extended the hand to Egypt and the Assyrians, so as to have our fill of bread.*[606] For, contrary to the Apostle, *we have become slaves of human masters,*[607] thieves, usurers, and children of strangers[608] prospering abundantly in this world. Today, if one who is in command does not acquiesce to such people, if one does not conform to a world shaped in this manner,[609] if a person [does not] flatter those set over him[610] or

601. 1 Kgs 1:1-20	605. Lam 5:16	609. *Sic*
602. Wis 4:12	606. Lam 5:6	610. Ps 65:12
603. *Sic*	607. 1 Cor 7:23	
604. Matt 6:33; RB 2	608. Ps 143:7, 10	

does not charm his subjects with many things, by misrepresenting much and masquerading even more, what will he do? What will he be able do? Where will he find himself?

11.18 Even today, it is obvious that compliance scarcely procures even a few friends, and these are unsteady and fleeting. Truth procures public enemies, and these are cruel and persistent. All the same, this may be the way *to lay down one's life for one's brothers,*[611] even if only an exterior mantle of *goat's hair*[612] may endure the buffeting of this wind, so that on the inside the house of God remains in its beauty.

O that *the sword may* not *reach all the way to the soul!*[613] For we have been numbed by *fascination with things of no importance*[614] and by fickleness of concupiscence. *Our hearts are hardened.*[615] We are made like *Ephraim, a heifer taught to love to thresh.*[616] In this way[617] we have withdrawn out of ourselves. In this way,[618] through an ardent devotedness of the heart, we have passed over into things, albeit those that are necessary. It was our duty to deal with them, with the consequence that we were delighted in accomplishing things that ought to be experienced with shame and revulsion. Besides, some persons actually hanker after these things when this duty is not imposed on them.

11.19 Today, where is Martha's complaint that she *alone* is left *to serve?*[619] Today, is it not rather Mary's grumble that is heard all over the house, because she is permitted *to sit at the Lord's feet?*[620]

On account of this, we run a risk to both our body and our soul because of lengthy service[621] and exhaustion from a prolonged use of our strength. It is lawful, as I see it, for us now to catch our breath at the hands of royal munificence, so that our old age may be allowed to be called *emeritus* and to have lavished upon it something better than what it is itself conscious of deserving.

611. John 5:13; 1 John 3:16
612. Exod 26:7
613. Jer 4:10
614. Wis 4:12
615. Exod 7:13
616. Hos 10:11
617. *Sic*
618. *Sic*
619. Luke 10:40
620. Luke 10:39
621. *militiam*

In fact, the ancient law and custom of the Roman military is that sixty-year-old persons are to accept a discharge.

11.20 Will Jacob always have to endure his bleary-eyed Leah? Will he always have to work for Rachel and never acquire her? When even everything *that was lost was being exacted from him,* while *his wages were changed from day to day,* so that he had to accept the black for the white? Inside he put up with jealous wives, and outside, Laban quarreling with his sons.[622] At some point, Jacob ought *to provide for his house,*[623] and it seems just that at least in his old age and decline he be permitted to return to his father's house.

11.21 *Joints*: If a situation begins to unfold in a certain way,[624] so it ends. For instance, a joint in the whole body is dislocated, with its unity lost: it necessarily follows that there are parts. And *a divided kingdom is left desolate; house falls upon house.*[625]

11.22 A wise father of a family, *setting out for abroad* and arranging his house in order, *and having given to each one of his servants authority for that one's task,*[626] sets a doorkeeper at the entrance. For a house without a doorkeeper is like a public rest stop along the road. Anyone who wishes can enter and leave, carry things in and carry them out. The church is a house. The doorkeeper himself is the door, Christ Jesus. *Whoever does not enter* or exit *through him is a thief,* who *climbs in* or climbs out *by some other way.*[627]

11.23 *He was made obedient* to the Father *until death.*[628] The person who does not master this rule of obedience has withdrawn from Christ. For as the Apostle says, *Reflect on him who endured such contradiction from sinners against himself, so that you do not become exhausted, growing dispirited. For you have not yet resisted unto blood.*[629]

11.24 Old age excuses no one. Sickness excuses no one, until the one who led a person in leads that person out. Otherwise, if the door be without a doorkeeper and open to all, what is left except

---

622. Gen 31:39-41

623. Gen 30:30

624. *Sic*

625. Luke 11:17

626. Mark 13:34

627. John 10:1

628. Phil 2:8

629. Heb 12:3-4

that just[630] as in the case of exiting, there is an equal and impartial permit for entering?

11.25 *Marrow*: Alas, alas, *the wicked are walking in circles*, O God, *you have multiplied the children of men according to your height*.[631] For led around in circles of error, we are paralyzed by a certain heady dizziness so that we cannot attain to the center of truth and a still point of unity that, while remaining stable, gives movement to everything else. This is truth. This is he who said, *I am the truth*,[632] and *you will know the truth and the truth will set you free*.[633] Especially from the circle of error!

11.26 Therefore, let us reflect on the center of truth, whether the circle within which we are circling is guided by it and through it. If a circle is guided undeviatingly, that is, correctly according to its own laws, it will align with itself. If not, then deviation is obvious.

11.27 Ardent devotedness and activity need to be reflected upon. Let ardent devotedness be attached to the center of truth. Exterior activity, having orbited around it, will respond appropriately to it. Indeed, an entire ardent devotedness is due to God. When God is adhered to faithfully, whatever way the circle of movement is revolving, it cannot err in circling correctly. Rather, it runs smoothly so that every part of its radius relates equally to the center of truth. It is possible to have a point of reference without a circle, but in no way can a circle be drawn without a point of reference.

If circumstances do not require an activity to be performed, or the possibility for it is absent, a wholesome ardent devotedness is sufficient. But when the demands of charity require activity, then the truth of charity owes that activity either to God or to one's neighbor. If no need is present, the charity of truth requires us to keep ourselves free for such need.

And so just as unreserved ardent devotedness is due to God, so[634] all one's activity is also due to God when one is free. Moreover, when the needs of our neighbor are not demanding, the

630. *Sic*　　　　632. John 14:6　　　　634. *Sic*
631. Ps 11:9　　　　633. John 8:32

person who dissipates elsewhere anything of ardent devotedness or activity due to God commits a sacrilege.

11.28 In fact, whatever necessity urgently demands, people must not be so[635] quick to volunteer that their ability is questioned. For indeed, the center of truth must be consulted as to whether or not one is capable. If one is not capable yet presumes so, that one does not cling to the center. Consequently, one throws into disarray the perfection of the circle's circumference. For there are persons who never love to cling to this center-point of stability but are always orbiting outside of it. These are wicked persons, who walk in circles. These are children of men.[636] When the unfathomable judgment of God disseminates them in this world, or allows them to be disseminated, they become enemies of unity and truth.

11.29 In the last analysis, if it is indeed possible, let those from whom this is urgently demanded fix their ardent devotedness on truth and not refuse this act of service. If this consultation of truth responds that they are not capable or fit, let them devote themselves internally to the stability of truth, *lest placed externally, as it were, on the rim of a wheel,*[637] they be hurled into the precipice of error. Nevertheless, if in a pressing urgent need, truth once consulted has freed a person who in turn judges in favor of his own will without serious concern about his capability, he has been encircled by a great error. For if people err knowingly, they are guilty both of negligence toward neighbors and of deceit in respect to truth, so that now they have neither activity nor ardent devotedness. Consequently, one does not err if he errs unknowingly, but he errs altogether if he is untroubled. However, no one is entirely a stranger to truth who does not dread the tribunal of truth.

11.30 Because we are about to enter into the tribunal of truth, let us avoid all the twisted turnings of errors by a short and faithful declaration. Conceivably, we wish not to be able to do this so that we will not be found to be liars in the tribunal of truth. Let

635. *Sic*   636. "Children of men"   637. Ps 82:14
= *filii hominum*

us acknowledge ourselves as liars, according to the tribunal of our own will. And in addition to this, asking pardon by both our ardent devotedness and our activity, we will appear all the more truthful before the tribunal of truth. For we must not do anything deceitfully in the sight of truth, *lest our iniquity be discovered as hateful.*[638]

11.31 *Spirit*: I agree. And, indeed, here is the marrow and center of truth—not to pamper disease, but to force out the poison of inner wickedness.

11.32 *Soul*: So[639] it is. Just as formerly I took delight in command, so now my will is to acquiesce. And my own choice brings about the welcome excuse of my own needs and does not allow me to attend to the needs of the brothers.

11.33 *Spirit*: Although, O Soul, compassion for the needs of the brothers is not lacking, yet in this situation,[640] as you say, your loving care is. Therefore, nothing stands firm unless it is a humble confession and a striving for every virtue, so that howsoever we may appear unfruitful and useless externally, internally we may be found not entirely empty and sterile. And although the crowds may drown out our voice, let us cry out with our whole heart and entire mind, *Jesus, Son of David, have mercy on me!*[641]

12.1 *Lord, hear my prayer! Grasp with your ears my supplication! Hear me clearly in your truth and in your justice,*[642] *Lord,* you who *are near to all calling upon you in truth.*[643] Just as the Scripture of your truth promises us, just as truth is before you, it is my will to call upon you in truth today; so[644] hear me, O Truth, *in the abundance of your mercy, and in the truth of your salvation.*[645] For I have said: Now I have begun! May this change be yours from the right hand of the Most High, O Right Hand of the Most High!*[646]

12.2 I am made vile and contemptible to myself, for I have grown old in my past evils and sins, which are great and innumerable. In

638. Ps 35:3

639. *Sic*

640. *Sic*

641. Luke 18:38

642. Ps 142:1

643. Ps 144:18

644. *Sicut . . . sicut . . . sic*

645. Ps 68:14

646. Ps 76:11

the case of good acts (if any have been perceived to have been in me), I myself am most uneasy about them. Therefore, today I come to you, O Source of new life, as if my entire past life were dead, as one about to make a new beginning in you. If I have done any good things, they are yours! I consign them to you! You will return them to me *in time acceptable*[647] to you. The evil things that I have borne are mine. Alas, how many and how great they are! For their most part, they have perished from my memory.

12.3 And would that a suitable atonement would delete from your presence those sins that because of their awfulness have been long implanted in my memory, from where no forgetfulness can ever eradicate them. All the same, I so[648] hate their memory that often I wish that I had completely forgotten all of them. But you, Lord, *have not remembered the sins of my youth.*[649] These were the first-born of Egypt,[650] which you killed in Egypt. And what I did in Egypt, I left behind in Egypt when I departed from there. Then *you led me wandering around in the desert for a long time. You taught and guarded me as the apple of your eye.*[651] You reproached me sinning. You are consolation in my sorrow. You taught my ignorance until you have led me right up to the threshold of the Promised Land.

12.4 When I stand there, contemplating the delights of the land of the living ones that you are showing me, and I remember what was said to Moses, *You will see it but you will not enter,*[652] I am completely shattered by terror. For if he deserved to hear this because of the excess of a single sin, what am I about to hear, I who am about to lay out my sins before you today, so great and numerous, completely laid out before you?

12.5 However, today, everything—both what I hold in my memory and what I have forgotten, my past evils and what they deserve—is not past; in fact, just as they are in your presence, O

647. Ps 68:14
648. *Sic*
649. Ps 24:7
650. Ps 134:8
651. Deut 32:10
652. Deut 32:52

Truth, when I am silent, so[653] let them come into your presence today as I make my confession.

Let them be brought forward as if gathered *into a little bundle to be burned*[654]—no, rather in a great bundle, enormous and unmovable *if there is no one present to help.*[655] I don't sort them out. I don't count them out (nor am I able to). It is true, O Truth, that I have sinned in your presence as much as ever and in whatever way I might. Just as you know that I have sinned, so I acknowledge myself to be.

Let no one make light of them to me. Let no one exaggerate them. Let no one diminish them. Let no one multiply them. Let me not do this to myself! For in your presence, God, the hearing takes place. I will not spare myself. You, Lord, spare me. Nevertheless, may you not spare to the extent that from this day on *you bear witness that I am your enemy,*[656] and *write bitter things against me for the sake of destroying me, amid the sins*[657] of my past life.

12.6 *O Protector of humankind, do not put me in a place further against you,*[658] for there *I have become an excessive burden to myself.*[659] But take away the sin of mine that separates me from you and myself. If you forgive, Lord, forgive! If it pleases you to punish, I will punish alongside you! Nevertheless, do not wipe me out with *a blow proper for an enemy.*[660] *For I am prepared for the scourges* of your hand, *and my sorrow will always be in my sight. For I will proclaim my iniquity and will ponder* that I suffer *for my sin.*[661] Truly, I do not believe that I am in the hands of an enemy. Rather, with complete trust, I give myself into your hands, which I have repeatedly experienced. When one of these strikes me, the other caresses. When one throws me down, the other catches, lest I be bruised.

12.7 But sometimes you even *stretch out your hand, surpassing the anger of enemies,*[662] bearing down heavier than any enemy, and, angry, *you turn your face from us.*[663] Then *heaven becomes as bronze*

653. *Sicut . . . sic*

654. Matt 13:30

655. Ps 21:12

656. Job 13:24

657. Job 13:26

658. Job 7:20

659. Isa 59:2

660. Jer 30:14

661. Ps 37:18-19

662. Ps 137:7

663. Ps 87:15

and earth as iron[664] for us, and everything is hard and everything is evil. This is usually what happens when your countenance is turned. For the sake of your name, Lord, spare your servant in this fate. Flog as much as you wish, while always *illuminating your countenance upon us. And may you be merciful to us.*[665]

12.8 Nevertheless, *you are the Lord of vengeance.*[666] *You act freely* in remitting or alleviating them. For *you have deflected* our *evils to yourself,*[667] and *paying* in your passion *for what you have not appropriated,*[668] *you have prepared your throne for judgment,*[669] so that you yourself, having been judged unjustly, may in your justice acquit those who have been judged justly. Therefore, Lord, *your judgments will help me.*[670] You will look on me *according to the judgment of those who love your name,*[671] as on one occasion you judged the sinner who loved you: *Many sins are forgiven her, for she has loved much.*[672]

12.9 Today, may your love itself be the advocate in my cause; if I have denied your love on this earth, I fear lest love itself may deny me in heaven.[673] *If I have been ashamed,* I fear lest *it may be ashamed of me.*[674] I am really ashamed that I do not have the love I ought to have. And because today is the day for my judgment, O Judge of my heart, today *judge me* in this matter as well, *and scrutinize my cause*[675] to see whether in fact I have the advocate I claim to have.

For in this matter my mental insight is so[676] darkened that deep down within I hesitate whether I seem to myself to see something I do not see, or not to see what I see. For in fact I am absolutely certain in my own eyes that I am always loving your love insofar as I am moved with affection whenever I am reminded or remember it.

Always, on the other hand, when I ponder or am reminded of you, and I am not changed, not affected, I fear that, perhaps, this

664. Deut 28:23

665. Ps 66:2

666. Ps 93:1

667. Ps 20:12

668. Ps 68:5

669. Ps 9:8

670. Ps 118:175

671. Ps 118:132

672. Luke 7:47

673. Matt 10:33

674. Luke 9:26

675. Ps 42:1

676. *Sic*

being the case, I am convicted of not having always loved you when everywhere and on all sides the signs of your very present power and goodness beat so as to arouse my senselessness in this.

12.10 O Light of Truth, today scatter from me these shadows and dispel the darkness. In this, *feed me with the bread of life and understanding, and give me to drink of the water of saving wisdom.*[677] Yes, to understand the things that are yours is both food and drink. For there are things that are yours that we persist in and work at because they need to be broken down, chewed up like food. But there are some things that just pass through us like drink, refreshing us in their own way. Since, however, we seek your love through understanding and sometimes find it, it is *the bread of life itself, strengthening the human heart,*[678] which we often seek with great effort before we have it, since, because of Adam's sin, *we eat in the sweat of our countenance.*[679]

12.11 But sometimes your *Spirit blows where it wills, and when it wills.*[680] And it breathes on us the grace of your love. In fact, we hear its voice because we receive the experience of love. *Yet we do not know* from what judgment of your mercy it comes, or by what judgment of your justice, having greeted us, sometimes more sweetly and sometimes more lightly, it passes on. The Spirit itself is our drink.

12.12 Today, Lord, feed me with your bread *that gives life to the world,*[681] so that I may be given a firmer and more solid understanding of those things that I seek [to know] concerning your love. May the sweetness of your grace as a wholesome drink arrange and soften the food itself, lest a more solid food hurt rather than strengthen my less capable experience.

12.13 Lord, I ask whether I have your love. If I discover that I have, it is *in this* alone that *my soul is praised.*[682] This pleases me. If it is otherwise, it is hateful to me, and there is nothing that I love, for I will have hated even myself. I am conscious of and proclaim

---

677. Sir 15:3

678. Ps 103:15

679. Gen 3:19

680. John 3:8

681. John 6:33

682. Ps 33:3

that I have a love for your love, insofar as I am willing to love absolutely nothing, not even myself, except in it and on account of it. Deep down, I would not care how I spent myself for it, whether in death or in life, so that I might merit to look fully on its face and walk openly in its light and enjoy its delights.

12.14 This is my conscience, called forth and spread forth before you, in the light of your truth. It seems to me to respond without any anxiety about the love of your love. However, regarding you, whether it always loves you and loves you enough, it is disturbed in responding in the presence of your judgment. Yes, wherever and in whomever I see your love and its obvious signs, it makes me completely happy. And yet, since all things speak to me all the time of the presence of your goodness and power, I am sometimes scarcely moved by them. If then today you would ask me as in time past you asked the blessed apostle, *Do you love me?* I answer hesitatingly, *You know that I love you.*[683] Yet I respond with a joyful and carefree mind, "You know that I want to love you!"

12.15 Lord, *open my eyes, and I will reflect upon the marvels of your law* and of the law of your love.[684] Thus perhaps I seem to myself to love your love because on occasions when I have thought about you and about it, to some extent I experience, see, and taste it. But you I do not experience, or scarcely experience, or see, or scarcely see, or taste most rarely and most meagerly.

In fact, a thing is loved with difficulty that is not known to its lover through its very self. For your numerous and great benefits, and your love itself, which I most definitely love, send me to you. But when I do not find you, I fall back on it, and I rest in it, not without hope.[685] For when I delightfully experience your love with ardent devotedness, then I seek you with an understanding of love itself. I love what I experience, I desire what I seek, and, languishing in desiring, I fail.

For sometimes understanding itself is deeply affected by your gift, yet according to my capacity. Understanding is not allowed

683. John 21:17   684. Ps 118:18   685. Ps 15:9

to swallow all the saliva contained in this good taste. For this is, so to speak, snatched out of its mouth, and it falls back into its hunger and ignorance. It is not allowed to stand in the light of your countenance until it discerns and puts an end to the annoyance of this uncertainty.

12.16 Whenever *fire blazes up in my meditation*[686] and I work to know what I have and *what I do not have,*[687] I inaugurate for myself a way of ascending to you. I ask help from you in this undertaking. *Therefore, I arrange* these *ascending steps for myself in my heart.*[688] First, a great will is seen as necessary, then an enlightened will, and then an ardently devoted will. In everyone who is ascending, the will is to be as great as it is able to be, enlightened according to your gift, and finally ardently devoted according to its own nature: a will as great as you have created it, as enlightened as you have made it worthy, as ardently devoted as you have formed it.

12.17 You have formed, however, without form since you are neither form nor something that has been formed. Nor can any form of your love be possible to exist so as to be formed in anything as something formed. Yes, love is the wisdom about which it is said, *It is the breath of the power of God, and an obvious genuine emanation of the splendor of God omnipotent. Consequently, nothing defiled is involved in it. Yes, it is the brilliance of eternal light, the mirror without blemish of God's majesty, an image of his goodness.*[689] Therefore we cannot take hold of it when we wish. And unless it first comes to us, and unless its grace anticipates us, any kind of attempt of our understanding does very little or nothing in moving us forward.

12.18 For as the Apostle says, you are *in the form of God.*[690] The form of your deity is the very simplicity of your nature and substance. Your love must be like it. For as a certain wise person says concerning faith due to you, "We ought to strive so[691] to form our faith about a thing as that thing actually is."[692] So[693] it follows

---

686. Ps 38:4
687. Ps 38:5
688. Ps 83:6

689. Wis 7:25-26
690. Phil 2:6
691. *Sic*

692. Boethius, *De Trinitate;* PL 64:1250A
693. *Sic*

that this must be understood all the more concerning your love, insofar as charity is more preeminent than faith. However, ardent devotedness alone discerns this.

12.19 I keep my will for your purpose or for you. I can have no greater will, and I would rather not exist than not to have it. If the protection of this *shield* had not previously encircled me,[694] when *men were rising up against us, they would perhaps have swallowed us alive.*[695] Indeed, at times I am conscious of some gentle urgings of illuminating grace and ardently affecting grace, but the experience of their fullness is far from me.

Furthermore, since my will, of whatever size you gave me, is illumined only rarely and meagerly because of my sins, and, alas, since it is affected even more rarely because of my inclinations and merits, which go along with them, I do not know if it should be called love.

12.20 Love, it is true, is usually defined by those formulating definitions as an intense will. But people who formulate this definition have not taken it into account in declaring limits for your love. If it is called desire, I do not disagree. For truly, I desire you. But as long as my profession appears before you so poor, so miserable, my conscience is not able to rejoice. Let the one who wishes laugh and ridicule me. I know what I suffer in this matter. And I know that there is no one to suffer with me in this, no one who has suffered or is suffering the same. *Truly, my tears were bread to me day and night. How long will a person say to me: Where is your God?*[696] That is, how long will there be any place in my soul's ardent devotedness where my God is not present in his own way? And in love most of all, which should be God's own dwelling place in me?

12.21 He will not relieve me of this sorrow until he reveals himself to me, when I will see what I will love, and with an absolute joy of mind will love what I will see. But, in the meantime, what I

694. Ps 5:13   695. Ps 123:2-3   696. Ps 41:4

experience partially I love partially, because if I did not experience it to some small extent, I should in no way love it.[697]

12.22 For when I see your children feasting amid the delights of your love at your table, I, starving, vehemently love your love in them. And in the depths of my heart I affectionately embrace those persons loving you. Also, I see them rejoicing in my joy that I have from their joy. They desire to express the measure of their joy but are not able to. For the ardent devotedness they enjoy by loving you can certainly be experienced by a sensible tenderness in a sort of spiritual or divine joy. As the savor of any sort of food can gently penetrate none unless they taste it, so[698] this savor cannot be analyzed by reason, nor declared by words, nor perceived by the senses. It is something divine, *a guarantee and a betrothal pledge of the Holy Spirit,*[699] with which you rejoice and nourish your poor one in this life, *lest he faint on the way.*[700] As Job says, *You proclaim* the joy of eternal life *to your friend that it may be his possession and that he can attain it.*[701]

12.23 In fact, a holy soul is reshaped to the image of the Trinity, *the image of the One*[702] who created it, and in the very manner of the Trinity's blessedness. For the enlightened and ardently devoted will—that is, intellect and love and the state of enjoyment—just as is said and believed of the Trinity, are three persons of loving relationships but one substance of blessedness. For what is loved is only loved by being understood, only understood by being loved, and only enjoyed by being loved and understood by the one who is worthy of enjoying it. In fact, in that place[703] this is what it is to have and to enjoy: the ability to understand and to love.

12.24 Happy the conscience whose ardent devotedness maintains the way of ordered charity. With uninterrupted steadiness, it thus[704] makes progress by advancing toward you. With your grace cooperating with it, it thus[705] prospers in its advancing forward,

697. 1 Cor 13:9
698. *Sic*
699. 2 Cor 1:22
700. Matt 15:32
701. Job 36:33
702. Gen 1:27
703. I.e., heaven
704. *Sic*
705. *Sic*

so that it does not faint until you perfect it. *With a lavishness of your sweetness, which you hide from persons afraid of you,*[706] you perfect persons hoping in you, especially those whose works shine out in the sight of the children of men and women to your glory, *O Father, who are in heaven.*[707]

12.25 These are the ones who love you. When I see such as these and do not find myself among them, it is loathsome for me to live. Their wisdom is not from the spirit of this world, nor from the prudence of this era. In fact, *because they were not well educated, they entered into the power of the Lord, and poor in spirit, they think only of your justice.*[708] Because of this, you have taught them, so that by their life and manners *they may publicly declare your marvelous deeds.*[709]

12.26 These are your unpretentious servants, *with whom you are accustomed to have familiar conversation,* who in approaching you do not have trust *in chariots* of their own natural talents,[710] or *in horses* of their own strength, but only *in the name of the Lord.*[711] As a result, *your wisdom charmingly arranges all things*[712] for them. They attain their destination by a brief shortcut and lightly burdened, where chariots and horsemen fail. They do not form or conform your love to themselves by investigating with subtleties. Rather, your love itself, finding unpretentious substance in them, forms and conforms them to itself in both effect and ardent devotedness.

The result is that *besides what is hidden within, namely, glory and riches in a house*[713] of a good conscience, with no artificial effort but as with a clear natural complexion, the inner light shines forth in their outer countenance to such an extent that from their countenance and behavior with its evident charm and simplicity, a kind of appeal comes forth from your charity. By its appearance alone, it challenges rude and sometimes barbarous souls toward your love.

706. Ps 30:20

707. Matt 3:16

708. Ps 70:15-16; Matt 5:3

709. Ps 70:17

710. Prov 3:32

711. Ps 19:8

712. Wis 8:1

713. Song 4:1; Ps 111:3

Indeed nature returns to its original source, and without a human teacher, they become people ready to be taught by God.[714] And when their spirits, *with the Holy Spirit helping their weakness,*[715] pass over into divine affections, their bodily senses assume a definite spiritual discipline. Even their bodies put on an evident spiritual appearance, and their faces assume a more than human aspect, with a certain extraordinary grace.

12.27 But their flesh, *sown in corruption,*[716] even now begins *to rise in glory* through their diligent dedication in good discipline, so that *heart and flesh,* equally, *may rejoice in the living God,*[717] and *with the soul thirsting after you, the flesh, too, may thirst in ever so many ways.*[718] *For the blessed meek possess the land* of their body,[719] which is made fertile by discipline of spiritual exercises. Even though it has been uncultivated and forsaken, yet by good use it bears fruit in fasts, in vigils, in labors, ready for any good work, and without inconsistency or sluggishness.

12.28 When I see these people, I am entirely, ardently, devoted to the love of your love, which is operative in them and which I perceive in them because of a clear definite experience that is known to lovers. Consequently, I love them because they love you. I love them very much, just as I love the love with which you are loved, the same love that I love in them. And if I love them in this way, it is because I love nothing else except you in them, and in their natural ardent devotedness. Since I love that same ardent devotedness to such an extent, for it is full of you, I never love my own ardent devotedness in myself unless in it I find myself to be ardently devoted to you.

In these persons whom I love in you and in myself, what do I want to love, unless it is you? What else do I love except you? Nothing from deep down within me! For if I experience myself loving either them or myself in any other way whatever, I hate myself more in this than I love myself.

714. John 6:45

715. Rom 8:26

716. 1 Cor 15:42-43

717. Ps 83:3

718. Ps 62:2

719. Matt 5:4

12.29 Accordingly, I find you, Lord, in my love, but would that I always find you! For as my love is not love unless it loves, and yet your will is always passionate in me, that is, your love urging me towards you, why then am I not always ardently devoted to you?

Is love one thing, and the ardent devotedness of this love something else? As I look at it, love belongs to nature; to love you belongs to grace. And ardent devotedness is its manifestation. The Apostle says about this, *The manifestation of the Spirit is given to each one for its effectiveness.*[720] For as long as *the body, which is corrupted, aggravates the soul, and earthly dwelling presses down on a mind thinking about many things,*[721] there must be a regress or progress of the soul, however loving it is. If ardent devotedness were not comforting the one and restraining the other, it would fall into every sort of ruin, from which no progress could lift it up.

12.30 Therefore, God, your love is always in the soul of your poor one, but hidden like fire under ashes, until *the Spirit, who blows where it wills,*[722] pleases to manifest itself in the measure it wills for our usefulness. Be present, therefore; be present, O Holy Love! Be present, Sacred Fire; *burn up* the pleasures *of our inner depths and* the thoughts of *our hearts.*[723] As extensively as you wish, bring forth a greater abundance of humble material for the flame of your appearance. As you please, appear to make clear *the glory* of a good conscience *and the riches* it possesses *in its house.*[724] Make it clear that you act carefully to safeguard. Hide, lest you act thoughtlessly to scatter, until God, *who has begun this good work*, brings it to completion,[725] he who lives and reigns through all ages of ages. Amen.

Meditation Thirteen

13.1 [William speaks:] *Lord, you seduced me and I am seduced.*[726] You have been the stronger one, and you have prevailed.

720. 1 Cor 12:7
721. Wis 9:15
722. John 3:8

723. Ps 25:2
724. Ps 111:3
725. Phil 1:6

726. Jer 20:7

I heard your voice, saying, *Come to me, all you who labor, and are burdened, and I will refresh you.*[727] I came to you. I believed what you said. Where have you refreshed me? I was not laboring, and I labor now. And now I am completely exhausted with work. I was not overburdened then, but now I am ready to drop under the burden. You have said, *My yoke is gentle and my burden light.*[728] Where is that gentleness? Where is that lightness? Already I am growing weary under the yoke. Already I am fainting under the burden. *I have looked all around, and there is no one to help. I have sought; there was no one who could assist me.*[729] Lord, what is this? *Have mercy on me, for I am weak.*[730] *Where are your mercies of old?*[731] Our fathers, who have gone before us on this way, have they possessed the land by their own sword? Was it their own arm that saved them? By no means! *It was your arm and the light of your countenance.*[732] Why? For you have been well pleased with them. *You yourself are my king and God, you who command Jacob's well-being.*[733] And in me, Lord, what has displeased you?[734] Why do you not judge your servant? You said concerning the humble service of the sinful woman, *What she could do, this she has done.*[735] Have I not also done everything I could? And, what is more, I seem to have done more than I appear to have been capable of doing.

13.2 *The Lord's response: My son, do not disregard the discipline of your father, and do not be wearied when you are reproved by him. For the Lord chastises whom he loves. He thrashes every son he receives.*[736] *Indeed, who is the son whom the father does not correct?*[737] If you are beyond discipline, you are not a son, but illegitimate.[738] Son, I have not seduced you, but gently I have brought you to this moment. What I have told you, what has been proclaimed to you, "Come to me," is proclaimed to all, but it is not given to all that they come.[739] This is given to you, in preference to many great people

727. Matt 11:28

728. Matt 11:30

729. Isa 63:5

730. Ps 6:3

731. Ps 88:50

732. Ps 43:4

733. Ps 43:5

734. Job 34:33

735. Mark 14:8

736. Heb 12:5-6

737. Heb 12:7

738. Heb 12:8

739. Matt 22:14

who appear to themselves as rich and powerful. Have I sinned against you in being good to you? You murmur because I do not invigorate you. Unless I had invigorated you, you would have already collapsed. You are groaning under my yoke. You are being exhausted under my burden. Charity creates my yoke's charm and my burden's lightness. If you had charity, you would experience that charm. Your flesh would not toil if it loved you. And if it did toil, charity would alleviate it. You will not be able to carry my burden and my yoke alone. If you have charity as a partner in this carrying, you will immediately be surprised at their gentleness.

13.3 *I Respond*: Lord, this is what I've said. *What I have been capable of, this I have done.*[740] What I seem to have received in my ability, my miserable body and weak limbs, these I have given over into your service. If it had been in my power to have charity, I would already have been perfect long ago. If you do not give it, I do not have it. If I do not have it, I cannot continue. You know, you see how little I can do. Take as much as you wish from this little itself; relinquish to me that fundamental and perfect charity.

13.4 *The Lord*: Am I to make good what you are less able to accomplish, and then add on what you are requesting? But, my son, *take hold of discipline.*[741] The journey is going nowhere unless through the way. You are looking for charity. You have entered on the way that leads to life. If you do not abandon the way, you will arrive where you are going. *I go before you.*[742] Follow just as you see how I have gone before. *I have toiled and endured.*[743] You too need to toil. I have suffered many things. You need to suffer some things. Obedience is the way to charity. Cling fast to it, and you will arrive. Yes, you may be sure, charity is a great thing, and worthy to be purchased at a price, a great one at that. *For God is charity.*[744] When you have arrived at this, then you will no longer toil.

13.5 *I respond*: Lord, *there is nothing hidden from you, neither my bones that you have made nor my substance in the depths of the*

---

740. Mark 14:8

741. Ps 2:12

742. Exod 13:21

743. Isa 1:14

744. 1 John 4:10

earth. Your eyes see my imperfection.[745] I do not dare, nor do I wish to seek that I should not labor, but in the meantime, while I do not have charity, who will endure the labor with me?

13.6 *The Lord: I have made you, and I will carry you.*[746] But if you are ungrateful for the gifts you have received, you will be judged unworthy to receive greater ones. You have already received charity to a degree, but either you do not know it, or you are ungrateful for it. Charity is proper to wisdom, and *the beginning of wisdom is the fear of the Lord.*[747] Already the fear of God has led you to this point. At another time, it established you in this place. If the end finds you there, you will come out safely. It has led you to this point, it has established you here, and it holds you here. Have you made so little progress? Is this something insignificant that you have received?

13.7 *I respond*: Yes, truly, *Lord, you are made our refuge.*[748] I have fled to you for help. *Teach me,* and make me *to do your will.*[749] You are compassionate and merciful to the people following you in the desert. And you have given them food so they will not faint on the way.[750] I have begun to follow you, the leader, into the desert. *I have vowed and determined to keep the judgments of your justice.*[751] With your gift, I will not abandon you. I will not pull myself away from you until either you lead me to the place you have begun for me or I faint in following you, if I should be able to faint in following you. For I know that even if the body is weak, and if sometimes the spirit grows weary, even if I have not deserted you, I will not faint, but I will make progress despite my infirmities,[752] if only you do not desert me by taking patience from me.

13.8 *Lord, have mercy upon me. Look at my humility* and poverty. *Help me*[753] and carry me, weak and helpless in both mind and body. Inspire your sons and servants, who love you, to help me and carry me and, because of my misery, acquire the reward for their patience and sympathy. *I am yours. Save me.*[754]

---

745. Ps 138:15-16

746. Isa 46:4; Med 1:2

747. Prov 1:7

748. Ps 81:9

749. Ps 142:10

750. Matt 15:32

751. Ps 118:106

752. 2 Cor 12:9

753. Pss 118:94; 30:6; Luke 23:46

754. Ps 118:94

I commend my spirit into your hands.[755] Teach and guide it. Encourage, console, and illumine it. *Grant me wisdom, the consort at your throne, that she may be with me and work with me,*[756] that I may know what is pleasing in your sight at all times. *Do not cast me out from your children, as I am your servant,*[757] and the servant of all your servants.

Lord, I do not know what to ask of you for my body, yet you know what is useful for me concerning it. If it so pleases you, let it be vigorous and healthy. If you so please, may it languish and be infirm. And when it has seemed good to you that it die, may it die. Only may its spirit be saved in your day! Concerning my body, I ask one thing of your mercy—that while I live, you teach me how to guide and guard it so I do not acquiesce in any of its pleasure, nor take away anything from its need.

13.9 *The purpose of a precept is charity,*[758] and the purpose of my prayer. Grant me charity, you who have willed to be called charity, that I may love you more than myself, not caring in the least what I do with myself, as long as *what* I do *is acceptable in your presence.*[759] Father, grant that I may always be your faithful little servant and *a sheep of your pasture,*[760] though I dare not say a son. Lord, speak sometimes to the heart of your servant. *May your consolations delight my soul.*[761] Yes, teach me to speak to you more frequently, and to bring back to you, My Lord God and my Father, all my poverty and need. *My Strength,*[762] have mercy on my weakness. Yes, may it be your great glory that my helplessness perseveres in your service. Amen.

755. Ps 30:6; Luke 23:46 758. 1 Tim 1:5 761. Ps 93:19
756. Wis 9:4; 9:10 759. Wis 9:10 762. Ps 117:14
757. Wis 9:4-5 760. Ps 78:13; Ruth 2:13

The Beginning of William's Contemplative Ascent into Intimacy with the Triune Divinity as Presented in His *Meditations*

A Monastic Commentary

Two Protagonists: *Meditation 1.1–6*

The entrance into William's contemplative ascent[1] into an intimacy through participation in and relationship with the triune God takes place through the blending of two verses from Saint Paul's Letter to the Romans (Med 1.1). It begins with Romans 11:33:

> *O the Depth of the riches of the Wisdom and Knowledge of God! How unfathomable are his judgments, and how incomprehensible are his ways!*

And it continues,

> *For who has known the thought of the Lord, or who has been his counselor? For you show compassion, Lord, to whom you show compassion. Lord, you offer mercy on whom you will have had compassion. In fact, it is not because of the one who wills, nor of the one who runs, but of you, Our God, having compassion.* (Rom 9:15-16)

These two verses serve as the foundation for William's work, presenting contemplative depths in the drama of life's intimate bonding between the two protagonists, the leading figures in this contemplative ascent: God and the human person, here embodied in William. These verses thus lay a grid for the *Meditations*.

William's development of these verses reveals wisdom and knowledge, compassion and mercy, as elements defining God's

---

1. William of Saint-Thierry, *On Contemplating God* 1 (hereafter Contemp) (CCCM 88:153; CF 3:36). *On Contemplating God* opens with words expressing the theme of ascent. Scholars accept this work and *The Nature and Dignity of Love* as William's first treatises.

foreknowledge and predestination. He presents personal choices as composing the truth about oneself. He establishes the incarnation as spanning the chasm between the two protagonists, between earth and heaven, between time and eternity, placing the incarnate Christ as principal, crucial in this ascent. Dense and challenging, these initial paragraphs elucidate the intimacy between Creator and the created, leading at once into William's use of the familiar metaphor of a potter forming a pot, from Jeremiah 18:1-10 and Isaiah 45:9, to give insight into the verses from Romans (Med 1.2).[2]

These foundational verses also establish the secret depths of conscience and consciousness. Sin and its effects initially launch persons as vessels of reproach, William says, but love, *your love*, changes them into vessels of honor, often with an alternating growth process, leading to a complete turnaround as one clings to the divine fingers of faith, hope, and charity (Med 1.3–4). This complete turnaround (Song 7:10 Vulg)[3] reforms people, their lives, and the likeness and image—which sin has distorted—into the image of God, and it empowers them to progress according to their likeness to God.

The two verses from Romans also reveal principles essential for opening the depths of the drama between the two protagonists. The nature of divinity means that in divine foreknowledge God knows all things that have happened from the first moments of creation and that will happen in the future until the very end of time. God knows every detail pertaining to every person who has ever lived or will live. There can be no surprises in divinity. Further, divine predestination gives every individual a worthy place in life, earthly and heavenly, through divine foreknowledge. Truth and mercy are gifts offered to everyone. Their use rests on human freedom.

---

2. William uses two words: (1) *figulus,* "a potter," which calls attention to the fact that the pot is in the potter's hands, and if it falls, it is reduced to nothing; (2) *plastes,* the way the potter gives a particular shape or form to the pot in the process of molding the clay.

3. "Our turning": *conuersio nostra* (Augustine, Conf 1.1.1).

The inscrutable depth of divine wisdom, which arranges all creation, and of divine knowledge, which comprehends all things, establish the bonding between eternity and time, a bonding essential to William's teaching about the human contemplative ascent with its fulfillment in the incarnate Word. Humans, because of their free choice, either ascend into intimate bonding with God or circle around the truth of their lives while evading their own truth because of some form of pride. Pride, which William defines as avoiding the truth about oneself, is that which most damages the chance of an intimate relationship with God incarnate. Humility is the direct path of ascent into truth. These are the themes opening the *Meditations.*

William's discussion of these two passages, Romans 11.33-34 and 9.15-16, in his commentary on *The Epistle to the Romans* provides insight into his reason for using them to introduce the *Meditations.*[4] Indispensable to William's thought in both works is his discernment that knowledge and understanding do not by themselves introduce people into the incomprehensible depths of God. Rather, he opens the *Meditations* with a personal experience of truth and mercy as conveying an inkling of the divine depths. Such an experience of truth and mercy, he says, conducts people into these divine depths according to the quality of their willingness to participate in the mystery of divinity. For William, this is the underlying grid of foreknowledge and predestination.

Implicit in William's approach is the idea that people cannot restore themselves. Created by God, they are endowed with the Holy Spirit of God and God's selfless mercy in the person of Christ. They are to render with their lives the praise and glory due to God and not remain entrenched in murmuring and complaining about their lives. These opening verses from Romans establish perspectives for people's proper attitude and behavior in relationship with divinity.

4. Exp Rm 6.10 (CCCM 86:159–64; CF 27:220–26); Exp Rm 5.8 (CCCM 86:137; CF 27:187).

William here poses some of the questions arising in the human heart, such as "Why are some persons saved and others not?" "Why is divine mercy bestowed on the persons on whom God has compassion and seemingly not on others?" Furthermore, he presents divine foreknowledge as comprehending how each person will use personal freedom in deciding how to live, arranging their own circumstances accordingly, either advancing toward participation or not. Such is the unfathomable depth of divinity. A possible source for William's teaching here is Origen's work on *The Epistle to the Romans,* which would have been available to William through various Latin authors,[5] perhaps even Rufinus's Latin translation of Origen's work itself, *Commentary on the Epistle to the Romans.*[6] Origen's concept of *knowing* is more than having information: it embraces concepts of devotion to another person and affectionate love in relationship with someone, for through love people get to know one another. God invites people into an intimate relationship of *affectus,* "ardent devotedness."[7] The quality of their response provides the answer to William's questions.

Foreknowledge and Predestination: *Meditation 1.2–6*

William introduces foreknowledge and predestination by speaking of the creator-potter as *carrying* the vessels that he has created, so placing the emphasis on the delicate care and intimate

5. E. Rozanne Elder, "William of St. Thierry and the Greek Fathers: Evidence from Christology," in *One Yet Two: Monastic Tradition East and West,* ed. Basil Pennington, CS 29 (Kalamazoo, MI: Cistercian Publications, 1976), 265.

6. The English translation of Rufinus's translation of Origen's commentary, 8.13 (Origen, *Commentary on the Epistle to the Romans,* trans. Thomas P. Scheck, The Fathers of the Church, vol. 104 [Washington, DC: The Catholic University of America Press, 2002], 185–90).

7. The Latin word *affectus* is difficult, if not impossible, to render in English that captures the nuances in William's use of it. I have translated it as "ardent devotedness" in the *Meditations.*

devotedness, affectionate love, that the creator has for each individual vessel he has created. These vessels, he says, "acknowledge you as their creator and potter" (*figulus*). Indeed they are the clay molded in God's hand with its divine fingers, and woe to them if they fall from this hand. "They will be broken, crushed and reduced to nothing!" (Med 1.3). With this idea of carrying William refashions the usual definitions of foreknowledge and predestination, inserting predestination into the divine foreknowledge that desires that all persons be transformed by faith, hope, and love. Augustine Klaas, writing of William's approach here, notes that "the first meditation, on divine foreknowledge and predestination, accentuates the characteristics of "theologians of foreknowledge," such as Irenaeus, Origen, and the Greek Fathers, rather than those of Augustine, the 'theologian of predestination.'"[8]

William offers another insight into an integral aspect of God's foreknowledge when he writes, "Lord! Hold us lest we fall from your hand. Fire *our inner depths and our heart* by the fire of your Holy Spirit, and *strengthen the work you have accomplished in us*" (Med 1.4). The double scriptural quotation emphasizes the presence of fire in one's inner depths, that is, the Holy Spirit creating the work that God has accomplished for a person. William ends his *Meditations* with the theme of this sacred fire of the Holy Spirit at work in a person (Med 12.30), the foundation for his distinctive use and teaching on *your love*. He clarifies this teaching about the Holy Spirit throughout the *Meditations* as fundamental to the contemplative ascent that the work describes. Here William prays, "Bring us to completion, you who have made us! Bring to completion the all-embracing form of your image and likeness according to which[9] you formed us!" (Med 1.5).

8. Augustine Klaas, Review of Guillaume de Saint-Thierry's *Méditations et Prières,* and *La Miroir de la Foi, Theological Studies* 9, no. 1 (March 1948): 132.

9. "According to which": *ad quam*, conveying the nuance of being intentionally shaped by the potter into his image and likeness. This prepares for the concept in Med 1.8 of life being in the Word.

Divine Foreknowledge as Eternal Wisdom:
Meditation 1.7–10

William explains divine foreknowledge as threefold, simultaneously divine wisdom, divine truth, and divine goodness. No creature can comprehend divine foreknowledge. In William's discussion this first aspect of divinity's unfathomable depth shows the great distance between God and all creatures, a distance that creatures can never grasp. Yet a bonding between creator and creature comes about in the consubstantial incarnate Word of God, in whom are created all things. For this reason, Christ's incarnation, human nature, and divine nature, hypostatically united, hold a distinctive role in the *Meditations*, incarnating the mystery of *your love*. Understanding this union is integral to William's grasp of predestination, of contemplative ascent, and of the bond between the eternal and temporal now, themes unfolding throughout the *Meditations*. The Second Person of the Trinity became incarnate, William says, to span the vast distance between creator and creature. Accordingly, then, all life past, present, and future rests in the Word. In the Word is life (Med 1.8).

Divine wisdom embraces all created things, for all things have been created by it. William articulates what is essentially impossible to fathom. Divinity's knowledge embraces and arranges all things. There can be no alteration or modification in divinity's wisely ordering all things. But creatures can change, for they are created changeable by the gift of free will, a changeableness that divinity knows.

Divine truth is for William twofold. As an integrated part of divine foreknowledge, divine truth embraces what God has foreseen for each person. Concurrently, divine truth contains human truth, that is, the life people shape for themselves because of their choices with their consequences. Persons are endowed with the ability to make their own decisions. William uses the term *liberum arbitrium*, "free will." God also knows this latter truth and executes judgment upon it, with appropriate punishment if need be, based on a person's accepting or refusing divine mercy. People are able to know and embrace their truth through the humility of self-knowledge.

God's foreknowledge is likewise God's goodness, the Holy Spirit. From eternity this goodness has been prepared for all creation, although it has not been accepted by all, since people are free in their choices. Consequently William describes virtue as the spontaneous assent of a will to good (Med 1.6) so as to participate in divine goodness, the Holy Spirit.

Divine mercy is both goodness and graciousness, constantly being offered to all people, who are free to accept or reject the goodness and graciousness that God imparts. If they accept mercy, they live a life in the consubstantial incarnate Word that only the Holy Spirit, divine goodness, can offer.

God's ways of acting, William explains, are always ways of truth and mercy. Truth and mercy meet and integrate, creating a joyful life. They do not impede one another. All things are created in this wisdom, and nothing, not even a sinner or sin, can defile or tarnish divine wisdom, because it is unable to be defiled or tarnished.[10] It gives free will to each person. Divine foreknowledge is never wrong and does not force free will. *O the Depth of the riches of the wisdom and knowledge of God,* William exclaims (Med 1.1). Accordingly, he deems all life, temporal and eternal, as present in the triune divinity, as he clarifies in his teaching on *your love.* He assigns a distinctive emphasis to life penetrated by eternal happiness, as it is established in the prologue to the Gospel of John. For William, a vision of heaven is vital to the life of humans while they are on earth, shaping the bonding with the divine that they need.

Bonding between Eternity and Time: *Meditation 1.8*

Dom Jean Leclercq's remarkable book *The Love of Learning and the Desire for God* has a chapter entitled Devotion to Heaven.[11] This

---

10. Wis 7:24-25.

11. Jean Leclercq, *The Love of Learning and the Desire for God,* trans. Catharine Misrahi (New York: Fordham University Press, 1961), 65–86.

chapter demonstrates the importance that heaven and eternity, the heavenly or the new Jerusalem, had for early monastics, Cistercians included. As examples, he points out Bernard of Clairvaux, Aelred of Rievaulx, and Helinand of Froidmont, who communicated distinctive characteristics of this theme in their treatises.[12]

William offers a comprehensive and practical approach to this theme in the *Meditations*, based on his own experiences and insights. He creates his own exegesis of Saint Paul's phrase *our way of life [conuersatio] is in heaven* (Phil 3:20) by making an intimate connection between our way of life and heaven. Two words—*aeternaliter* and *temporaliter* ("eternally" and "temporally")—introduce this intimacy, which William characterizes as a profound bond between what is happening in time and being present in the *now* of eternity, and the importance of a way of life leading to eternal joy proper to that *now* (Med 1.8). This bond, essential to both of William's ideas, of foreknowledge-predestination and of contemplative ascent, becomes clearer in later parts of the *Meditations*. It is especially present in William's understanding of prayer before the crucified Christ.

Divine foreknowledge does not force or determine what takes place in time. Nor does what happens in time determine divine foreknowledge. The human mind simply stands in awe of this enigmatic union between time and eternity. As William says, "if the thing were to end up not being this way in time, it appears that it could not exist eternally in the Word of God."[13] And again: "Yes, for you nothing is past, nothing is future, but you are always

12. Timothy M. Baker, " 'Be you as Living Stones Built Up, A Spiritual House, A Holy Priesthood': Cistercian Exegesis, Reform, and the Construction of Holy Architectures," PhD dissertation, Harvard University, 2015 (Baker-dissertation-2015 .pdf). Baker shows that early Cistercians created an architecture centered around this orientation to heaven.

13. *Nam si sic non esset futurum temporaliter, uidetur in Verbo Dei non posse esse aeternaliter.*

what you are. But in whatever way a thing may exist, either past, present or future, it is life in your Word!" (Med 1.8).[14]

Ascending vs Circling: *Meditation 1.9*

William states that God's foreknowledge is the same as God's goodness.[15] The consequence is that God eternally bestows this goodness on all persons, although not all are ready to accept it. Here William employs the metaphor of a circle to illustrate the reality of those who do not accept God's goodness. At the center of the circle is divine goodness. Those who refuse to face the radical truth about themselves also refuse to enter into a meaningful relationship with their Creator. They simply walk around in a circle of error,[16] on the perimeter, strictly avoiding this center of truth and never ascending.

William goes on to explain that the divine goodness in the center of the circle is the Holy Spirit. Picking up a theme from the Book of Genesis about creation, he continues, saying that the Holy Spirit hovers over all persons in self-manifestation, offering the grace that God's foreknowledge has prepared for everyone.

In his commentary on *The Song of Songs,* William introduces his understanding of predestination, addressing the soul, the bride of Christ:

14. "It is life in your Word": *In uerbo tuo uita est.* The implication is that of being alive in the Word of God, bringing one's image and likeness to God to its full realization.

15. In Med 3.2, William presents the countenance, *uultus,* of God as divine goodness, which attracts us. This divine goodness, he says, is the Holy Spirit resting upon all persons.

16. Augustine uses the phrase "circle of error" twice in *Confessions,* XIII.1 and 2, but appears not to use it elsewhere. William appears to use it only in the *Meditations. Center of truth* appears again only in Med 11, where William uses it six more times, in paragraphs 25–28 and 31. As far as I know, these are the only places in all of his works that he uses the phrase. Aelred of Rievaulx develops a similar theology of walking around in a circle in his Sermon 136.

The strength of your significance in life is recognizing grace, provided you are not ungrateful that you were known beforehand, predestined, chosen beforehand, and thus recognized [by God]. For God's foreknowledge about you is his goodness with regards to you. Predestination is his goodness already working [in you]. Choice is the hallmark of grace. About this, the Apostle says, "God's foundation stands, having this hallmark: The Lord has acknowledged who were his!" If you recognize, be sure of this, that you are foreknown! If you choose, be sure of this, that you are chosen. If you believe, you are created for belief. If you love, you are formed in love.[17]

Divine Predestination/Intimate Relationship:
Meditation 1.11

This teaching about truth and mercy is fundamental to William's understanding of predestination and the gift of free will with its freedom of choice. William's understanding of predestination is that God has called and preordained every person for heavenly happiness, the place of supreme good, even before anyone was created. Predestination is the grace given for this purpose.[18] The responsibility of accepting this grace, a good, rests on individuals' using their free will to do so. William shows that the Holy Spirit assists people on their ascent into the Trinity, leading all to the place for which they were created according to their image and likeness to God.

The heart of William's teaching on predestination is that God predetermines all people to heavenly happiness and offers them

17. William, Cant 62 (CCCM 87:51–52; CF 6:53–54, my translation).

18. This teaching on predestination appears Augustinian, as these two formulas are taken almost verbatim from Saint Augustine: "The predestination of God in regard to the good is the predestination of grace; grace itself is an effect of predestination" (Augustine, Praed sanct X.19; Adnot in Job 26.2).

the grace to attain it.[19] That is, even when individuals did not exist, God predestined them to glory. This concept of predestination contains the further element that God has created for each person an individual place in time and eternity. God rejoices as people move forward, ascending, attaining their place. The quality of free will's love and its proper choices bring them into this place,[20] also known as their perfection. Their place is unchangeable in God, but changeable in themselves, according to the quality of their choices, whether good or evil. God knows human choices in advance, but, William declares, "Nevertheless, because he foreknew the vessel would be this way, God predetermined it to destruction" (Med 1.9).[21]

Through predestination God has planned for human nature to ascend into the splendor of the triune divinity, but that can happen only if one enters the incarnation of Christ. The *Meditations* reveal the manner in which God accomplishes his purpose in a person's life with the proper use of imagination as an integral part of the approach to ascent. As sin turns a person away from God, so God invites that person to himself on a daily basis. Sin cannot do what only God's grace can do: justify a person. Sin makes one

19. This teaching on the Holy Spirit is penetrated with the doctrine of Augustine. In particular see C Max Arian; In Ev Ioann, 98.3; C S Arr 32, and "No one comes unless he is drawn. Whom he draws and whom he does not draw, why he draws one and does not draw another—do not wish to judge if you do not wish to err" (Augustine, In Ev Ioann 26.2).

20. *Place* is a significant word in William's thought. He uses it some 244 times in his treatises, 14 times in the *Meditations* alone. *Place* normally refers to the abode that God has foreknown and destined for a person, unless that person freely chooses another, namely, a place of destruction. When used in reference to divinity, it is where God is. In an earlier treatise, *The Nature of Dignity and Love* (Nat am 1 [CCCM 88:177; CF 30:47–48]), William provides some detail in developing the way authentic love leads each person to his or her place. The quality of one's love directs one to either a terminus of destruction or one of eternal joy in God.

21. The Latin (CCCM 89:5) reads, *Quod tamen quia* sic *futurum praesciuit, in interitum praedestinauit.* This is a classic example of William's use of *sic.*

earthly minded; God's grace glorifies. These are the riches of the wisdom and knowledge that God reveals and bestows in Christ's incarnation.

Pride: *Meditation 1.12–13*

Now William returns to the metaphor with which he began the work, of God as the potter creating vessels for various uses. He now expands it, moving onward from the intimacy of the relationship between potter and vessel, turning to the magnificent graciousness of God's mercy in destining all vessels for glory. God's mercy, he explains, is the basis of every relationship between the potter and vessel, between the Creator and the created. God's delicate care and infinite devotedness to each individual vessel enhances this graciousness, as God carries each vessel and holds it as precious, in his own presence.

The arduous challenge is for each vessel to move away from self, to move away from that spur-of-the-moment tendency always to question God by saying, "Why have you made me this way?" (Med 1.12). The question here reflects William's experience of his own truth, an experience that will appear more fully later in the *Meditations* as his center of truth. A vessel achieves the move from a focus on self by cultivating a vibrant awareness of the potter's tenderness and an accompanying acknowledgment and understanding that one is simultaneously clay and a vessel in the hands of God.

This awareness and acknowledgment are the fruits of God's creating grace that gives a personal shape or fashion to each vessel. The Holy Spirit offers each vessel a glaze consisting of faith, hope, and charity. Faith demands a radical trust in God so as to remove every trace of self. Hope positions a person on a dead center toward God. Charity gradually transforms a person into unconditional self-giving, participating in God's lavish gift of self in Christ's incarnation and the conferral of the gift of *your love*, the Holy Spirit. For God is good and has done all things well. When all is said and done, there is basically no difference among all the vessels. All are fundamentally identical because of free will, with its responsibility for shaping each individual life. William thus defines virtue precisely as the spontaneous assent of the will to good (Med 1.6), an unconditional "yes" to good.

But pride, inappropriate esteem for oneself, questions God, the potter, *why have you made me this way? Why have you predestined me for destruction?* (Med 1.12). The authentic and appropriate question should be, "why am I scorning humility?" This false sense of power and influence endeavor to make God responsible for an individual's bad choices and deeds: "Why have you made me this way? It is your fault!" These are the elements at the root of a person's bad zeal.[22] God, who has destined all individuals for a place in eternal glory, is not responsible for their unscrupulous choices and devious deeds. William concludes, "Therefore, pride is both what is deserved and a sign[23] of rejection, just as humility is both what is deserved and a sign of election" (Med 1.12). The paradox is that one is both free to be a humble or proud person and at the same time predestined for what one deserves in one's relationship with God.

---

22. See RB 72 for Benedict's explanation of good and bad zeal.

23. "What is deserved and a sign" = *et meritum est et signum*. The Latin phrase, used for both pride and humility, indicates simultaneously what one deserves and a sign of what is to come; it conveys the paradox of being at once free and predestined.

Go to Him and be Enlightened: *Meditation 2.1–3*

An initial element of the ascent, William shows, is arriving at an intimate relationship with God by an openness to God's will, the ability to say "yes" to this divine will. A person demonstrates this openness by making appropriate life choices. William recognizes that each person's rightful place is in God[1] and that ascent into God is empowered by an authentic good will, with its appropriate zeal. It is thus natural for a person to want to know more about God. This foundation flowers into an ardent and intense desire to be enlightened by a vision of God in order to make the ascent. But that very ardent and intense desire to know God more intimately, so as to be with God through divine enlightenment coming from a personal vision, surprisingly brings forth in William an adverse effect (Med 2.1).

William begins this series of ideas by declaring his utter dependence on God, recalling the intimate perspective initiated in the metaphor of the potter and his pots. To convey that, he returns to the earlier intimate perspective:

> without you I cannot possibly exist. I could not remain alive, remaining alive anywhere in any way, either in body or in soul, save by your ever-present power. I could not desire you or seek you save by your ever-present grace. I could never find you were not your mercy and your truth running to meet me. (Med 2.2)

Later he expresses an almost physical experience of God's presence, describing himself as conscious of the divine Spirit as a whistling

---

1. William, Nat am 44 (CCCM 88:211; CF 30:107).

gentle air flowing over him, and as like a falcon spreading its wings to the sun (Med 2.7). He is encouraged to continue approaching or ascending into God. He speaks of God's "Ever-present power . . . ever-present grace" (Med 2.2), which enable him to remain alive. Ever-present grace, power, and being alive—the three form a delicate connection among themselves that will begin to resolve the previously articulated painful paradox. They constitute essential and initial elements of the divine vision.

But, paradoxically, the very awareness of his relationship to God leads to a crisis that William conveys with powerful metaphors and images, elucidating the full dimension of his capacity for God. They are his technique for approaching authentic self-knowledge, a redefining of the truth about himself. The sense of being alone and ashamed, along with an ardent desire to be with God, simultaneously indicates God's enlightening companionship: "But if I am myself absent from you in thought and ardent devotedness when you are present to me bestowing your favors,[2] then in this situation these benefits of your grace shown me appear as a devoted and meticulous burial rite shown to a dead body" (Med 2.3). The combination of his desire for God and his sense of his own confusion leads him into the terrifying experience, or inner sense, that because of his own sinful life, he is not with God. Awareness of his inappropriate choices has resulted in a devastating sense of loneliness. These choices, rooted in a love that is inappropriate or sinful, cannot bring the inner openness or expansiveness that comes from a proper love, a love that is of God and that leads into God as William's proper place. William's desire for intimacy in his relationship with God unveils the complexity of this terrifying experience. He is grateful for God's presence, which gives him life, yet his experience of being in the divine presence burdens him with

---

2. Being absent from God in thought and ardent devotedness when God is present bestowing his favors are generic themes found in Augustine and Gregory the Great (Mor 18.LIV.89 [CCSL 143A:953; CS 259:136]).

the fear of being left alone, a vessel fit for destruction because of his inner confusion.

William uses verse six of Psalm 33—*Go to him and be enlightened, and your faces shall not be ashamed*—to articulate the human experience that while ascending into God, one becomes sensitive to a deep inner confusion, along with the need for personal change—a paradox surfacing from the intimacy of God's presence. But shame, as the psalm suggests, is removed by divine enlightenment. William says that he is ashamed because of hideous and horrible confusion within himself. Accordingly, he unleashes a barrage of metaphors and scriptural images to articulate and describe his anguish.[3] He portrays his inner life as a dead body receiving a meticulous burial rite, like the Canaanite woman of the gospels, like a dirty dog, like a deaf and blind person, like one dead at heart, like one sound asleep in the full sun, like soil without water, like an oil lamp with no light. His soul, he says, is a sleepy drunk person.

William consequently experiences the door of divine vision as shut before him—quite different from the previous metaphor of a potter and his clay, which he has used as a powerful symbol of intimacy with the divine. This painful paradox exposes his intense desire to be enlightened by God, and an awareness of perplexity stemming from the inner confusion that separates him from God, confusion that can only be resolved by God's enlightenment. Nevertheless, he recognizes that this paradox bears the blessing of being alive, and he sees as inseparable the twin fundamentals that are vital to an ascent to God: correct thinking concerning oneself and ardent devotedness to God. These bring to birth and configure one's responsibility in God's intimate presence.[4] God's grace is working in one's inner life, in conscience and consciousness.

3. In this passage William explains his shame as due to his past sins. In Med 12.9, however, he admits another type of shame: the fact that he has not loved *your love* sufficiently.

4. This process is the reasoning in Saint Benedict's first step of humility (RB 7).

William experiences this paradox as a beginning of a change—or, better, purification—in his conscience and consciousness and therefore in his choices. What is the far-reaching significance of God's companionship in one's life? To be alive! William understands truth to be an accurate evaluation of one's life and of one's person. This accuracy of evaluation results from being in the presence of God, so attaining a truthful judgment of who one is and what one has done. Living in the presence of God in this life brings no surprises when the time arrives for entering into eternal happiness. Truth and mercy are the ever-present grace and ever-present divine power that make a person truly alive. The correct human response embraces an awareness of God's ardent devotedness, enabling one to use free choice properly. Otherwise, the benefits of divine grace in one's life are nothing but a devoted and meticulous burial rite performed by God over a dead body. William's is a remarkable illustration of an unhappy personal experience in a relationship with God, yet one that conveys the positive elements of truth and mercy so vital in one's relationship with God.

A Remarkable Scriptural Image and Metaphor:
Meditation 2.2–8

William insists throughout the *Meditations* that one should never give up on pursuing God, regardless of one's inner confusion, because God is always present. To illustrate the need for persistent determination in seeking God, William uses a remarkable scriptural image and metaphor. The first is a brief reference to the scriptural passage of the Canaanite woman's persistence, found in the gospels of both Matthew and Mark. Furthermore, to etch even more intensely his shameful conscience, with its deep inner confusion, William introduces as his second metaphor the image of a dog. To show persistence, he calls up a dog's devotion to the master, always returning to receive daily sustenance regardless of how often it is beaten and driven away. Since a dog is a fine example of thriving on intimate human companionships, William professes that he cannot live his life without an intimate relationship with God, regardless of his inner confusion, conveying an easily recognized human experience. *Intimate relationship* here translates a Latin term William uses to express this idea of intimacy with the Lord: *contubernium,* a military term for a tent dwelling where eight soldiers live intimately together while on a military campaign (Med 2.4). By using *contubernium* for tent only in reference to dwelling intimately with the Lord, he thus refers implicitly to contemplative intimacy.

Divine and Human Darkness: *Meditation 2.5–8*

William continues to develop his inner darkness, explaining it as composed of dullness and perverse habits, sedating conscience and consciousness. It is everything, he says, that makes him dead in soul and spirit,[5] making him insensitive to God's enlightening ways hidden in the gospels, the liturgy, and the lives of holy persons. Above all, he experiences God as seeming far away in a divine darkness. Experiencing this combination of divine darkness and human darkness, he feels himself to be dead at heart. Yes, he may have some light, yet God still appears unutterably distant. William thus makes an anguished plea, again using the metaphor of a dog searching through the city looking for food. His dilemma is an experience of the self as having to seek through the city of God, a city encompassing both earth and heaven, in search of God. He is searching for someone to receive him, even some saintly soul from the heavenly tabernacle-tents (Med 2.6).[6] He begs for assis-

---

5. This continues the idea introduced above, of a devoted and meticulous burial rite conducted for a dead body.

6. Here William uses the word *tabernacula* for the saintly communal heavenly dwelling with God as distinct from *contubernium,* the tent of intimacy with the Lord in daily life. The Latin word is *tabernacula,* which I have translated as "tabernacle-tents" to distinguish it from the word used for dwelling with divin-

tance from anyone either on earth or in heaven. Yet no one offers support in his darkness, or so it seems.

Regardless of the manner in which a person encounters these two forms of darkness, the encounter itself is a grace; it is the Holy Spirit tenderly speaking to the human spirit, saying, *Go to him and be enlightened*. When experiencing such darkness, William is astounded[7] to find himself drawing in the Holy Spirit,[8] ever so gently. As he begins to realize this fact, he changes his way of thinking by discerning his inner thoughts. He opens the depths of his sleepy, sluggish[9] inner self, his *nocturnal conscience*[10] as he calls it, to this divine presence. With the metaphor of a falcon spreading its wings to the warming sunlight, William, accepting his inner darkness and incomprehension, begins to unfurl himself to the divine light by the hand of exercise,[11] probably referring to a practice of one or another virtue (Med 2.7).

---

ity in the intimacy of daily life. (Another use for this word appears in Exodus, when the *tabernacula* or tabernacle-tent of divinity during the exodus from Egypt was God's special dwelling place.)

7. *Astounded = destupesco.* This is the only time William uses this verb in his writings. He may have created this verb by adding the prefix *de* to *stupesco,* "becoming astounded."

8. The text has "I draw in this Spirit," translating *Attraho spiritum.* William uses these Latin words another two times in his works. In Contemp 20 (CCCM 88:167; CF 3:61) he uses it for drawing in the Spirit; in Nat corp 42 (CCCM 88:117; CF 24:120), about the nature of the body, it refers to the natural breathing process. In the passage above William uses *Spirit,* as his theme is the Spirit's voice awakening William. It fits nicely with the passage in Contemp 20, where the metaphor is that of the soul as a wild ass sniffing the scent of the beloved.

9. *Sluggish = depigrescant.* To my knowledge, the Latin word is not found in any Latin vocabulary, and this is the only time William uses it. It is possibly his own coinage.

10. The meaning of the "nocturnal conscience" is William's opening up his deep inner self to the Divine Light. He powerfully expresses the result of this process at the end of Med 10.12, where he states that Christ dwells in one's conscience.

11. *Exercitii manu.* This is the only time William uses this Latin expression in all his treatises.

In his treatise dealing with the human soul, William envisages the experience of darkness, human and divine, as indicating human incomprehension bonding with divine incomprehensibility.[12] Human incomprehensibility parallels and mirrors divine incomprehensibility. Furthermore, incomprehensibility is a subtle enlightenment offering an insight into the divine vision that William is so ardently pursuing. The mutuality of such incomprehensibility incarnates the necessity for persistently seeking God despite any darkness, with the effort climaxing toward the end of the *Meditations* in Christ's dwelling in one's conscience (Med 12.10). At the moment, however, the requirement as William explains it is to begin to enter into virtuous ways of life that cleanse and bring to birth an ever-more-ardent devotedness to God. Yet a virtuous way of life is not to be considered to be an end in itself.

Imagination in Respect to a Vision of God that Enlightens:
Meditation 2.9–12

William's theory of understanding God—that is, seeing or having a vison of God—is drawn from Augustine, who presents three methods of vision or of seeing. The first is vision with one's bodily eyes, seeing physical objects. Augustine uses the Latin term *corporalia* for these objects seen by one's eyes. His second category is *spiritualia,* those concepts and thoughts that are seen only in the mind, such as abstract ideas coming from imagination, dreams, and the like, having no physical existence. Finally, he names as *intellectualia* understandings or insights that come from neither physical nor mental sense. William accepts these three categories but divides the category of *intellectualia* into two, one coming from reason (rational), and the other coming from above. He then

12. William, Phys an 72–73 (CCCM 88:128–29; CF 24:133).

develops these Augustinian categories as three ways of seeing or understanding God, three ways to think about God.[13]

As a virtuous way of life gradually accomplishes its cleansing by leading a person away from a life captivated by the physical senses,[14] a glimmer of intellectual life comes to birth, beginning gradually in the imagination. William views the operation of the imagination as a kind of intermediary step between a mind totally dedicated to an exterior and superficial way of life, one immersed in the five physical senses, and a mind having a more intellectual dimension, with its consequent insight. Imagination can draw the mind away from total entanglement with the physical senses and their objects, orienting it to the early stages of conceptual thinking, not purely based on the physical senses. However, if one does not know how to think or understand except by using images of sensory things and physical objects, then that can cause a difficulty in one's prayer life. William intimates that this problem is the muddling of imagination, which does not know how to think or understand anything except through images of sensory things. To illustrate his point, he offers the example of prayer.

Persons tend to pray the way they think, William says, because thinking of God leads to thinking of the Trinity, and when the imagination enters, it can bring about serious consequences. Divine revelation in the catholic faith and in sacred Scripture gives some grasp of the Trinity, of one God and three Persons:

13. Augustine, Gen ad litt 12.27.55. In the introduction to his translation of "The Prayer of Dom William" (Orat), David N. Bell gives a clear explanation of William's theory of seeing as coming from Augustine's threefold distinction (Bell, "The Prayer of Dom William," 21–26, esp. 25–26).

14. William, Ep frat 60 (CCCM 88:241; CF 12:32) develops this teaching. This treatise also develops the distinction between a person who is *animalis* and one who is *rationalis*. *Animalis* is usually translated as "animal," which does not quite convey in English the concept of a person whose life is totally nourished by the senses, either in terms of a sensual life or in terms of a good life, even a holy life, that is based only on external actions, things, external devotion. This is the dynamic of consumerism, creating needs for external objects.

God the Father, Son, and Holy Spirit. But when the imagination enters in an attempt to understand the Trinity, it is inclined to picture the Trinity as numerical, each person having its place. William reflects on his prayer as veering towards individualizing the Father, Son, and Holy Spirit, passing from one to another as if they were three differentiated bodies. With that kind of understanding, the Trinity can function in one's prayer life in sense forms, with all that that implies. For example, the Father can appear inappropriately as an old man, the Son as a young man, and the Holy Spirit as a dove. This manner of praying rests on the level of one's physical, bodily senses and so retains the person who prays at that level.

When the mind is in its mode limited to imagination, only faith, with reason and authority, prevents it from dividing up the substance of Father, Son, and Holy Spirit into matters of time, place, number, or confusion of Persons. In theological understanding, as taught by faith, reason, and authority, divine unity does not imply solitariness, and the threefold unity does not admit plurality of number. It is essential to think and speak correctly about the Trinity with an understanding formed by revelation and faith and supported by reason. When one is mentally and correctly attempting to grasp the concept of the Trinity, or invoking the Triune God in prayer, reason can guide the mind away from the approach provided by imagination, leading to the threshold of faith. Faith's teachings give authentic explanations of revelation, including about the Trinity. But faith reduced to doctrinal belief can leave a person without ardent devotedness, which is the heart of prayer. William sees this deficiency as a form of darkness, a theme to which he returns throughout the *Meditations*.

William ends this section on the experience of imagination in prayer by implying that in the context of this divine trinitarian darkness there is a small glimmering of enlightenment, offering an insight into a divine vision of God: "Truly, your grace, Lord, coming to us in advance of any merit, any carefulness of expertise and virtue, gives us however small a degree of knowledge we have of ourselves and of you" (Med 2.12).[15]

Two Categories of Understanding: *Meditation 2.13–15*

In order to comprehend the insights that convey understanding grouped by Augustine in one category, *intellectualia,* William divides that one into two, one derived from reason, with its thought processes, and another that he calls *enlightened* or *illumined* and that he explains as coming from above, from "the abode of your greatness" (Med 2.13). This category is pure grace, granting an understanding that comes from God, not from any human effort. William establishes this distinction as a preparation for his discussion of seeing the face of God, which he develops over the course of the *Meditations.*

The gift of grace brings a humility necessary for accepting the authority of revelation and the catholic faith that shapes understanding of this type. This acceptance in turn helps to prepare one to receive the understanding that comes from above. For reason does not teach faith in order to bring faith to understanding. Rather, faith prepares reason to accept the enlightened understanding that comes from the Father of lights. The grace of ascent as William develops it is a movement from the understanding that comes from reason to the enlightened understanding that comes from above.

Enlightened Understanding Coming from Above:
Meditation 2.14

Enlightened or illumined understanding or insight is the reward of faith; it is formed by divine wisdom, and it does not rest on reason or images. This understanding is like the fountain from which

15. This paragraph shows possible influence from Odilo of Cluny, Sermon 12.

it flows: it enters the mind of the believer, takes reason to itself, and conforms reason to itself. Accordingly, it is not reasonable in terms that reasoning can elucidate. All the while, it is vivifying and illuminating one's faith. It does not supersede faith. Understanding from above does, however, communicate a certain integrity, with intense devotedness, to the aspect of faith it presents to one's mind. It is ineffable: essentially impossible to convey in words, for it is in its essence distinct from verbal categories. It must be experienced. In such an experience, consciousness is transformed and devotedness is enriched. Individuals come to prayer before God and stand, holding themselves in their hands and offering themselves in reverential awe to God.

In his short *Prayer* (*Oratio*), William reveals a loathing for what he calls "idols," images of God that come from his imagination, the phantasms of his heart. While imagination can lead a person away from concern with physical objects into a thinking based on concepts or reason, he says, it cannot lead into comprehending divinity.[16] William sees his faith as accurately describing divinity, yet his mind in its human understanding is inadequate to see God. The *Prayer* reveals his passionate desire to see God, but he is greatly troubled, hardly able even to believe in God, because even as he yearns for the illuminating light from above, he does not experience it. He no longer wishes to remain at the level of human understanding; he goes so far as to hate himself, wondering whether he has any love for God, as he sees himself enmeshed in understanding limited to reason. His is a vehement plea for the light—that is, the understanding that comes from above—to illumine his darkness. He desires the understanding that only God can give, that will vivify and illuminate his faith, opening him for an experience of intimacy with God, of looking intently on the divine face.

16. David N. Bell discusses the role of what William calls idols and other aspects of his thought in *Oratio* in "The Prayer of Dom William."

The graces of humility and faith have already prepared William to be receptive to enlightened understanding coming from the Father of lights. Enlightened or illumined understanding will also come as a grace, formed by divine wisdom, which does not rest on images or reason. Ultimately, as God wills, William will receive this understanding. As he comes to grasp the disparity between these two types of understanding as though standing as a wall between them, he fervently prays, "*How long, O Lord,* how long! If you do not *light my oil lamp,* if you do not *light my darkness, I shall not be rescued from this trial.* Nor, *unless in you, my God, shall I pass through this wall*" (Med 2.15).

Face and Countenance: *Meditation 3.1–5*

William's fervent prayer to pass through the wall that separates him from God leads him into prayerful *lectio divina* on two passages from the Book of Exodus, chapters 3 and 33. These scriptural verses present two divine revelations allowing Moses to encounter God (Exod 3:6; 33:11). In the first revelation, Moses comes to know God as *I am who am* (Exod 3:14). In the second one, after having repeatedly met with God face to face, Moses is told that he may not look intently upon the face of God: *you cannot see my face, for no one may see me and live* (Exod 33:20; Med 3.1). God's words here are particularly distressing to William, because although looking intently[1] upon God's face is central to his understanding of the ascent into the Triune God, he is told that he must not look upon it. At the same time, William is not entirely ignorant of what he is seeking, nor does he fail to understand that some form of dying is necessary if one is to see God. These two concepts—the necessity for both some degree of knowing and some type of dying—lead to William's desire to go beyond understandings of the Trinity proposed by imagination and reason.

The result of insightful *lectio* on the passages from Exodus is that William now differentiates between the face of God (*facies*), and the countenance of God (*vultus*). He explains the divine face as what God is, and the divine countenance (an expression of the face), as divine goodness attracting the seeker into the divine face.

William draws three important clarifications from these two chapters of Exodus. First is education about the names of God: Who God is, *I am who am.* Second is revelation of the face of

1. "Look intently" = *intendere.* This verb is distinct from *respicere,* "to look back or to gaze upon."

God, which Moses cannot see and which William understands as the divine nature or essence, what God is. Finally comes invitation through the countenance of God, which attracts one to God. William sees in his *lectio* that while Moses was denied the sight of the divine face, he was given a vision of divine goodness in seeing the back of God (Exod 33:23), which William explains as God's countenance.

Meaning of the Face

As the *Meditations* unfold, William expands these three clarifications by defining them. In terms of divinity, the Face is what God is: the intimate nature, or the very depths of God. Eventually William explains this depth of divinity as manifested in the person of Jesus Christ, the incarnation, who contains the depth of God's selfless love. It is selfless love, *your love,*[2] that empowers a person to become by grace what God is by nature. This understanding explains William's placing such prominence on the hypostatic union of Christ's two natures. The transforming power of selfless love in humanity would be impossible without this union, the bonding of divinity and humanity in Christ's incarnation.

Meaning of the Countenance

Countenance is the expression that a human face always bears. *Countenance* understood as the expression on the Face of God is the splendor of the divinity, or the highest good, attracting, helping, and shining on a person for the purpose of conveying him or her into the intimacy of the Divine Face. As a grace from God, Goodness leads a person into selfless love, that is, into what God

2. William introduces *your love* in Med 3.6.

is, for fidelity to goodness eventually removes all focus on and trace of one's self.

A Succinct Unfolding of the *Meditations*

As the *Meditations* unfold, they present the Divine Face and the Divine Countenance as coalescing into Christ Crucified, the magnificent revelation of God. With the grace of understanding coming from above, William comes to comprehend his own life as *concrucifixus*, crucified with Christ. *Your love*, which he defines as the heart of the life of the Trinity, is the participating grace given by the Spirit. Meditation Thirteen, which in this volume follows the *Meditations*, shows the difficulty of accepting and living life as *concrucifixus*, and the full implications of divine predestination for William.

The Paradigm of Your Countenance

In the third chapter of Exodus, Moses hides his face when God speaks with him. William's own desire to behold the Face of God is so intense, though, that he claims that he would be willing to die to see God, or that seeing God, he would be willing to die. At the same time, he says that, like Moses, he covers his countenance, not daring to look directly upon the Lord face to face (Med 3.1). William thus experiences the paradox of desiring to cover his own countenance while at the same time yearning to look intently upon the Lord's countenance.[3]

---

3. The Vulgate version of Exod 3:6, which William probably used, says that Moses hid his face, not that he covered his face (*Abscondit Moses faciem suam non enim audebat aspicere contra Deum*). Scripture says that the Prophet Elias covered his countenance with his mantle (1 Kgs 19:13: *Helias operuit vultum suum pallio*). William's Latin here uses words from both Exod 3:6 and 1 Kgs 19:13, perhaps switching intentionally, or perhaps quoting from memory and confusing the passages.

In covering his countenance, William appears to imply that the countenance of God, divine goodness, shapes the way a person is to live, opening oneself to the goodness of God, to be shaped by it rather than living in imitation of it. The implication is subtle, but basic and important: persons are not to live according to their own understanding of holiness, their own countenance, but to be transformed by the enlightened or illumined faith that comes from above, God's countenance: "They live according to what they read and comprehend within the paradigm[4] of your countenance" (Med 3.3).

William thus presents God's countenance, with its power to reshape human lives, as a foundation for any contemplative union with the Triune God. To walk in the light of God's countenance means that God's countenance—divine goodness—structures one's every choice. It is no wonder that with that insight William is ashamed of his sins and their inner turmoil, and of his own way of life, seeing that his sinful life makes him unable to live by divine goodness, even while he desperately desires to see God.[5]

William knows that God is present to him, and that he himself truly lives and moves in the divine presence. Furthermore, he knows that Christ has taken away his sins and so removed the barrier between them, and that this is ultimate goodness. Christ has given him this gift in a profound act of *caritas*: Christ's selfless love in his passion and death. Yet William's own cry of anguish goes on as he sees that despite all this, he is not with God.[6] Like a blind beggar,[7] he pleads to see and understand God's presence in his own way so as to be with God (Med 3.3). In other words,

---

4. "Paradigm" = *exemplar.* This word denotes more than a pattern or imitation. It is a comprehensive inner re-formation, a true reconfiguring—the apogee of participation in this present life.

5. To live according to one's own idea of holiness could be seen as a modern form of Pelagianism.

6. Augustine, Conf 10.27.38; Bernard of Clairvaux, Ep 85.1. These two sources express similar thoughts.

7. Gregory, Mor 18.LIV.89 (CCSL 43A:952; CS 259:136).

William, like every person, requires to know the divine selfless love within his own life as it is restructured by the paradigm of the divine countenance. The implication here is that each one lives this selfless love according to one's own life's circumstances and to who one is. By God's gift, and according to William's own being, he will be able to see and, through experience, to some degree to understand *caritas:* what God is. With profound significance, William explains self-knowledge as knowledge of God, in the familiar phrase that to know oneself is to know God.

William thus shows that the mystery of selfless love, *your love,* is itself understanding.[8] Charity is simultaneously the place to live generously and to die generously in order to see God. This gift of selfless love persistently urges William forward into the divine vision and the eternal festivity of the divine face.

Your Love: Meditation 3.6–7

Now William subtly introduces a feature vital for understanding the phrase "with face unveiled, looking intently into the glory of the Lord" (Med 3.6), contrasting Moses and Saint Paul. Moses covered his face, he says, for he represented a people fleeing from the face of God: "Lord, that Moses of old may have covered his countenance and veiled his face before you, bearing the form of your people whom he was leading, who were always fleeing from the face of the Lord" (Med 3.6; Exod 34.35).[9] On the other hand, William considers Paul as one who in his desire to see God kept his face unveiled; as he wrote to the Corinthians, "*All of us, gazing with unveiled face on the glory of the Lord, are being transformed into the same image from glory to glory, as from the Lord who is the Spirit*" (2 Cor 3:18). So Moses, with veiled face, and the Israelites

---

8. *Amor ipse intellectus est* (Ep frat 43.173 [CCCM 88:264; CF 12:68]).

9. Here William writes of Moses' covering both his countenance and face, whereas in Med 3.1 he says merely that Moses covered his countenance.

flee the Lord, while Paul and his followers, with faces unveiled, behold the Lord. They flee not from but into God's Face. Consequently, the clarion call of Paul, the trumpet of the New Testament, is to live with face unveiled, in longing and in *your love*, looking intently into the glory of the Lord as he is manifested in his passion, death, and resurrection, and thereby being transformed into the same image, from brightness to brightness. William equates *your love* with Trinitarian glory, that is, the life of God as revealed in the life of Christ. The life of Christ is the face of God, revealing who God is.

William embeds the most important feature of the ability to look unveiled and intently toward God in his words *your love*: *amor tuus*.[10] He has already explained this term in what was probably his first treatise, *On Contemplating God*, written around 1119–1120. Here he declares that *your love* is the Holy Spirit, who is the love of the Father for the Son and the love of the Son for the Father, and that this divine love, the Holy Spirit, is exquisitely bestowed in the depths of one's heart. Once present in persons, this divine love transforms and sanctifies their affections.[11]

In his *Exposition on the Song of Songs*, written between 1136 and 1139, William delineates a more comprehensive understanding of *your love*, adding that not only is the Holy Spirit God loving himself, but that God accomplishes this self-love through or in human love. *Your love* occurs a number of times in this treatise,

---

10. William uses *your love* some sixty-nine times in the course of his treatises. In the *Meditations* alone he uses it twenty-seven times, nineteen in Med 12.

11. *Cum que amor tuus, amor Patris ad Filium, amor Filii ad Patrem, Spiritus sanctus habitans in nobis ad te est quod est, id est amor, omnem captiuitatem Sion, id est animae nostrae omnes affectiones in se conuertens et sanctificans, amamus te uel amas tu te in nobis, nos affectu, tu effectu* (Contemp 17; CCCM 88:165). (And when your love, that is, the love of the Father for the Son, and the love of the Son for the Father, and the Holy Spirit living in us, is to you what he is, that is, love, turning toward himself and hallowing all the captivity of Sion, that is, all the affections of our souls—then we love you, or you love yourself in us, us affectively and you effectively.)

but William, addressing God, articulates its richest meaning in this passage:

> May your spouse, our soul loving in you, fathom in your very love what she is to accomplish in herself. Furthermore, you dwelling in her, God, who are yourself your love in her, accomplish in her that she love you through yourself, O her love! May you yourself in her love yourself through her. May you accomplish this in her and through her, and arrange everything according to yourself.[12]

These passages, two of many, demonstrate William's teaching in his treatises on the contemplative ascent into a participating intimacy with the triune divinity by means of God's love, the Holy Spirit. The presence of the Holy Spirit, the love-bonding between Father and Son, means that the life of the Trinity is alive within one's life or soul, transforming and sanctifying one's own love. This act of transforming and sanctifying renders possible one's unity with the Spirit's bonding,[13] wherein the Father loves the Son and

---

12. *Sponsa tua anima nostra amans in te, in ipso amore tuo intelligat quid faciendum sibi sit de se. Quin potius tu habitans in ea, Deus qui es ipse in ea amor tuus, fac in ea ut amet te de te, o amor eius; et tu ipse in ipsa, de ipsa ames te; et de ipsa in ipsa facias et ordines omnia secundum te* (Cant 12 [CCCM 87:90; CF 6:104]).

13. Unity of Spirit, *Unitas Spiritus*, is another characteristic of William's teaching complementing *your love*, a profound union of the divine will and a person's will, and their love binding them together. William gives one explanation of this unity in a rather complicated sentence in *On Contemplating God*: *O felicem et felicissimam animam, quae Deo sic a Deo meretur affici, ut per unitatem spiritus, in Deo solum amet Deum, non suum aliquid priuatum, nec nisi in Deo amet seipsum, et Deus in ipso amet uel approbet quod amare uel approbare debet Deus, id est, seipsum; immo quod solum debet amari, et a Creatore Deo, et a creatura Dei* (CCCM 88:159). (O happy and most happy soul who merits from God to be so affected by God that through unity of spirit she loves in God only God, not something belonging to God, and loves herself only in God. God loves and approves in himself what God must love and approve, that is, his very self, that is, only what ought to be loved, both by God the Creator and by the creature of

the Son loves the Father in one's own love, so that, lifted up by this bonding, one ascends into the trinitarian mystery. Over the course of the *Meditations* William continues to develop various aspects and dimensions of *your love* dwelling in a person. This trinitarian life within a person coalesces into a vision of God that is a vision of love, and William shows that his own sanctification has been brought about by his participation in divinity.

Divine Revelation: *Meditation 3.7–8*

Paul's desire, uttered in longing and in *your love*, to look intently with face unveiled into the glory of the Lord, and to be transformed into the same image from brightness to brightness, focuses on seeing God as God is. William perceives the fire burning intensely in his heart, though, as a desire to seek something more. Indeed, he longs to seek the face of God. He wishes to see God as God is: *as you are*, but in the dimension of Trinitarian relationships. Accordingly, he questions, what does *as you are* mean?

> And what does it mean: "as you are"? Does it mean quality, or quantity?[14] In fact, you are neither quality nor quantity. Neither quality nor quantity is in you, because you are what you are. What, therefore, is "as you are"? To see this is beyond us, because to see what you are—this is to be what you are. (Med 3.7)[15]

God.) For a comprehensive and masterful study of the changing ways the phrase *unitas spiritus* was used over the centuries, and the uniqueness of William's use, see F. Tyler Sergent, "*Unitas Spiritus* and the Originality of William of Saint-Thierry," in Sergent, Rydstrøm-Poulsen, and Dutton, *Unity of Spirit*, 144–70.

14. "Form" = *qualis*; "quantity" = *quantus*. *Qualis* and *quantus* are terms probably coming from Ps-Dionysius, *Mystical Theology*, 4.

15. *Hoc uidere supra nos est; quia uidere quod tu es, hoc est esse quod es.* The final sentence of this passage prepares for and leads to William's explanations when he writes of seeing God.

In this prayerful quest, William has arrived at the threshold of the enigma of the Trinity. Not content with theological descriptions, he now opens himself to the revelation found in the Gospel: *"For no one sees the Father except the Son, and the Son the Father"* (Matt 11:27). To be the Father is to behold the Son, and to be the Son is to behold the Father. Now William continues in Jesus' words: *"and to whomsoever the Son wishes to reveal him"* (Matt 11:27). This revelation to a person in prayer is not new, for divine revelation is complete and definitive. Rather, deeply personal experiences of insight are granted to individuals so that they may grasp a facet of divine revelation that allows them to commit themselves to the mysteries of the life of Christ.[16] Such experiences form a matrix for the two types of understanding mentioned above, experiences that transform a person's ability to fathom divine insights. William deems it possible for a person to behold God, to some degree, as the Father beholds the Son and as the Son beholds the Father because of their mutual love. William concludes his explanation of this concept somewhat hesitantly: "absolutely, yet not exactly in the same way" (Med 3.8).[17] So he says that as any person begins to experience a life penetrated to this degree by *your love,* the divine selfless generous love, he has a transforming inkling of the trinitarian bonding between Father and Son. This type of revelation, with insights from above, is bestowed through the Holy Spirit and tailored to the individual. Such a revelation is an essential aspect of the contemplative ascent, William declares, with the understanding that the Trinity-God is revealed to any friend of God whom God wills to grace. This view is the foundation for his teaching on unity of spirit.

---

16. *Catechism of the Catholic Church* (Mahwah, NJ: Paulist Press, 1994), 23. If an understanding that seems to be from above surpasses or corrects divine revelation in Christ, it is inauthentic, not coming from the Father of Lights.

17. *Sic omnino, sed non per omnem modum.*

Understanding from Reason: *Meditation 3.9–11*

William's exegesis of Saint Paul's sentence—"*Looking intently at the glory of God we are changed*" (Med 3.8)—embraces both longing and *your love*. The longing rises out of the transformation of one's ordinary understanding[18] by selfless love. William explains the process of transformation by analogy with the medieval scientific understanding of the way the physical senses allow perception, so that the degree to which one perceives an object depends on the way the perceiving sense is transformed in the process. For any of the five physical senses to function properly, according to the theory, they must be stimulated by an object, and that stimulation in some way creates a mental image of the object in the perceiving sense so that, as William says in his work on the Song of Songs, "he who perceives is transformed into the thing perceived." So when the eyes perceive a physical object, a visible element of that object is formed in the mind. Thus an object experienced by a physical sense can be said to change a person, opening the way to one type of knowing and understanding.[19]

William applies this understanding to the concept of an ardent willing, so desiring love. Love, an intent looking or awareness, develops one's perception of willing. In reaching out to what is loved in ardent devotedness, one's life is transformed by what is loved and so partakes of it to some extent. This understanding, grounded in medieval scientific theory, underlies William's deep concern about his love of God and its authenticity, and his metaphorical description of himself as a blind person seeking to see God. Yet William does not appropriate to himself the nature of

18. *Physicus intellectus.*

19. William, Cant 8.90 (CCCM 87:69; CF 6:76–77). William also refers to this theory of sensation in his *Mirror of Faith* (Spec fid 97 [CCCM 89A:118–19; CF 15:70–71]). See also Bell, "The Prayer of Dom William," 32, n. 53.

the object loved. As he frequently says, we become what God is by grace, not by nature.

As William muses on this understanding, he goes directly to his concern with *your love*: "Yet does a person ever see God as the Father sees the Son, or as the Son sees the Father? For them, as was said, to see one another is not to be two different things but to be one God" (Med 3.8). That is, the three divine persons beholding one another are but one God, not three gods. William fearlessly continues to declare that a person can see the Father, Son, and Holy Spirit as they see themselves: "Absolutely, yet not exactly in the same way" (Med 3.8).[20]

This dynamic of the matter is this: The Father and the Son mutually behold one another in a union who is the Holy Spirit. One can enter into this vision, this unity, to the degree that one strives as far as possible to have one will with the Will of God, unity of spirit, *Unitas Spiritus*. This unity takes place through selfless love, *your love*. The grace of striving to have one will with God assumes that one can be graced to some extent to see and comprehend the mystery of the Trinitarian relationships as this mystery unfolds in the incarnation. Yet one can never totally comprehend this mystery of God, although the consequence of participating in it is a contemplative intimacy.

Ardent willing is nothing other than love, and love carries people to their ultimate place.[21] This being the case, love is the essential dynamic in human life,[22] and as a person begins to love God, God's attractiveness and selfless love gradually transform that person into selfless love by the working of divine grace. The experience of God, the awareness of God's selfless love, has a renovating effect on William. It makes him like God, although it gives no indication of what eternal life will be like or of what he shall be in eternal splendor. This is a key concern for William, as the

20. *Sic omnino, sed non per omnem modum.*
21. William, Nat am 3 (CCCM 88:179; CF 30:53).
22. Saint Augustine holds that sense knowledge, or the experience of which the body is the cause, is transmitted to the soul (Augustine, Gen ad litt imp 5.24).

Meditations gradually reveal, a concern that underlines his extravagant exclamation:

> O Charity, Charity, you have brought us to this point, that by loving God and the Son of God, *we are called and we are gods and the children of God. And if it does not yet appear what we shall be, when he will have appeared we shall be like him because we shall see him as he is. Lord, it is good for us to be here.* It is delightful to stay here! O, would that it be permitted to die here! (Med 3.11)

Even ordinary understanding transformed by selfless love, that is, by divine charity, prepares one to receive the understanding from above when the Holy Spirit chooses to bestow it.

Understanding God: *Meditation 3.12–13*

William, driven by love of *your love*, offers a further clarification. He now explains that understanding that arises from reason, grounded in revelation and perfected by charity, requires a balanced, concise, and orderly presentation of the incarnate Jesus as the revelation of the Trinity and of God's selfless love. William longs to experience Jesus as God's incarnate selfless love when he thinks, speaks, and meditates about Jesus in the sacred Scriptures. He is not a scrutinizer of God's grandeur and majesty, seeking to acquire powerful intellectual insight, but a poor person, seeking God's fragrant grace to assist him to penetrate into the divine presence, the very life of God.

But understanding from above is not totally sufficient. It gives insight into one or another mystery of divinity, but the mystery of divinity as mystery nevertheless remains. However, the understanding from above does give birth to an intense desire, a love penetrating into a face-to-face vision. William realizes the importance of that understanding from above as allowing him to touch and attain something of God or of divinity itself in this life, bringing fragrance to his experience. He declares that understanding to be unequaled by anything in human experience:

> What use are physical senses here? What use is imagination? What can reason accomplish? What can rational understanding do? For although reason sends us to you, God, by itself it cannot attain you. Nor by the same token can understanding, which consists of reason's inferior insights, pass beyond the limits of reason. Nor does it have the capacity of reaching all the way to you. But *what is truly from above* has the fragrance that is from on high. Nothing human is present; all is divine. (Med 3.13)

So William explains that in this understanding from above, the Holy Spirit gently touches a person's consciousness with divine fragrance, urging him or her to move beyond all that God is not and to enter into prayer, resting on an experience of love. God is not contained in images, thoughts, reasons, or other such ways of understanding him—ways that in his *Prayer*, William calls idols. The experience of divine love brings a vision of who God is, though the one receiving the vision may not yet see God face to face, as God is.

The understanding that comes from above is undeniably clothed in mystery. William expresses his intense desire for the vision in the life to come in eternal life, the vision that will be face to face. Nonetheless, he recognizes the importance of the understanding from above as allowing one to touch and know something of God himself, even now.

Understanding the Trinity: *Meditation 3.14*

In this life, the understanding from above provides a proper knowing, an intimate loving relationship, with the Trinity. This understanding, this intuitive apprehending, has its own manner of transporting a person into some aspect of the divine mystery of the Incarnate Word. Such intuition functions independently from rational understanding, which does not of itself enable the ascent into God. Such intuition, resting in faithful consciousness,[23] carries something of the divine fragrance, since it is all divine, and there is nothing human in the relationship. One experiences the Trinity as Three yet One, without attempting to reason how that can be:

> [It] divides nothing, blends nothing together in the Holy Trinity. For the Holy Spirit gently touches a faithful consciousness when and as and in what manner he wills, so that persons praying to you or contemplating all that you are not have sometimes gone beyond. Through this very contemplation of all that you are not, they may see to some extent who you are, although they may not see you as you are. Nevertheless, this intermediate insight may soothe something in the devoted mind. For it is evident that it is not from those things that you are not, and even if it is not entirely all that you are, it is nevertheless not foreign to what you are. (Med 3.14)

Whereas a rational understanding may be tempted either to divide or to blend the Persons in the Trinity, the understanding that is from above does neither. Indeed, the understanding from above rests on an authentic teaching[24] describing the triune relationship among the persons of the Godhead, explaining them as co-indwelling, co-inhering, and mutually interpenetrating. It

---

23. "Faithful consciousness" = *sensum fidelem. Haec in Trinitate Sancta nihil diuidit, nihil compingit, sed sensum fidelem sic quando et quantum et quomodo uult Spiritus sanctus perstringit, ut orantes te et contemplantes omne quod tu non es supergressi nonnumquam, per hoc ipsum quod tu non es, uideant aliquantenus te qui es, quamuis te non uideant secuti es; sed tamen medium quid deuotae mentis demulceat intuitum, quod constet nec de eis esse, quae tu non es, nec, etsi non sit omnino totum quod es, alienum tamen esse, ab eo quod es* (CCCM 89:19).

24. This is the doctrine of *perichoresis*, explaining the relationship among the divine persons in the Trinity. It is integral to William's understanding of Unity of Spirit, *Unitas Spiritus.*

allows the individuality of the Persons to be maintained while insisting that each one shares in the life of the other two.

John's gospel provides an application of this understanding when Jesus prays, *Father, the hour has come; glorify your Son that the Son may glorify you* (John 17.1). Here the Son brings glory to the Father, the Father brings glory to the Son, and the Spirit is the glory bonding the Father and the Son. This understanding of glory reveals the selfless love expressed within the Godhead by Father, Son, and Spirit as they give glory to each other.

Embracing the Trinity: *Meditation 3.15–16*

William now explains something of the transformation that takes place in such a moment of understanding: "For in this way, the Spirit of the Lord suddenly clothes the serene and humble person upon whom he rests" (Med 3.15).[25] He has previously indicated that allowing the imagination to work in thinking about the Trinity can muddle a person's prayer (Med 2.11), but at the same time the very incomprehensibility of the three divine persons and their unity can mystify people in prayer. But the incomprehensibility that troubles rational understanding, William says, "does not darken the charity of the person rejoicing in the delightful love between the Father and Son" (Med 3.15),[26] for charity is the Holy Spirit, the Unity of the

---

25. The idea is not that one is changed into an entirely different person, but that participating in the presence of the Holy Spirit makes a major difference in one's life. The Holy Spirit resting on a humble person is a favorite theme with early Cistercians. See Bernard of Clairvaux, *Homilies on the Annunciation* 1.3; *Sermon on the Nativity of the Blessed Virgin Mary* 4.9; 6.10; *Sermon for Pentecost* 3.1; and Aelred of Rievaulx, *Sermons on the Prophetic Burdens of Isaiah*, Sermon 14.

26. The Latin is *non contristet substantiae unitas caritatem Patris et Filii dilectione gaudentis.* This statement could be anticipating William's teaching on Unity of Spirit in *A Letter to the Brethren of Mont Dieu,* Ep frat 263, where he explains that the Holy Spirit, charity, so transforms a person's spirit that it finds itself in the midst of the embrace and kiss of the Father and Son.

Trinity. William reflects on the change in himself that takes place as a result of the enlightened understanding of the Trinity that he obtains through charity, *your love,* working in his life. Through it he obtains a devoted and realistic understanding that simply "by not comprehending" helps him to "comprehend the majesty of divine incomprehensibility" (Med 3.15).[27]

So one is enabled to delight in the joy of the Holy Spirit, who confers both insights from above and confidence of obtaining eternal life:

> Suddenly, from the fullness of the highest good, this person is so delighted with the joy of the Holy Spirit that if it is brought to perfection in him, he will be confident of having obtained eternal life. As it is said, *this is eternal life, that they know you as the only true God, and Jesus Christ whom you have sent. Therefore, go to Christ and be enlightened, and your faces will not be ashamed, for you will have received understanding from above.* (Med 3.16)

27. Pseudo-Dionysius, *Mystical Theology* 1.

Personal Change via the Lord's Prayer: *Meditation 4.1–5*

William's experience of his transforming change conveys an understanding of God's devotedness, mercy, and compassion. He perceives that his own will must have these selfless inner dispositions if, under the influence of grace, his will is to receive the Holy Spirit. Here he expands on the earlier theme of a clay vessel's being open and willing to say yes to the Creator God. God is the judge who challenges him to be truthful in discernment of himself and merciful to others. God forgives, because God has made persons forgivable and capable of the divine characteristics of devotedness, mercy, and compassion. William's words—"finding what you are doing so that you may be gracious to us" (Med 4.4)—suggest that God finds reasons to be reconciled to humans, because God has given copious grace for reconciling. To realize and accept this fact is central to a person's accepting forgiveness. Furthermore, the Holy Spirit exhorts one to pray, and the Lord himself has taught how to pray.

The prayer the Lord composed, The Lord's Prayer, reveals God, judge and advocate, as not failing William in his need. This way of praying, acknowledging God's goodness, also obliges William not to fail others in their need for mercy. The Lord's Prayer brings in abundance to William divine characteristics proper to the Holy Spirit, such as devotedness, compassion, and mercy. By offering this prayer, he is praying for these gifts.

William also emphasizes that an additional condition for contemplative ascent is awareness that rather than fleeing a person, the Holy Spirit manifests himself with all fragrance—he "*who helps our weakness and interposes[1] for us with inexpressible sighs* (Med

1. The Vulgate here uses the Latin *postulare* (to demand, request, etc.).

4.3). The Father is constantly working in persons to be gracious to them at all times. To realize and accept that God multiplies loving kindness, and that mercies abound over all God's creation, including the human person, is a fundamental aspect of this teaching. Nothing is beyond the Father's gracious forgiveness.

William's personal change emerges from this dimension of the Lord's Prayer. The graciousness of God reaches far into the depths of William's conscience and consciousness as he solicits total openness in listening to God's voice. The Holy Spirit produces in him a spirit that rejoices in divine consolation, a spirit that comes to life when any humble person perceives the touch of divine presence, which produces a faith that leaps for joy, a confidence that delights, a heart that is set on fire, and tears that fan the newly lit fire. Speaking from the perspective of his own experience, William explains these tears as flowing from a loving devotedness to the divine sweetness working in him in the midst of his poverty, troubles, and disordered life, restoring him as a lost sheep to the pasture of the Creator.

Nine Factors Bringing Personal Change:
Meditation 4.6–19

William now articulates in some detail the ways in which the Holy Spirit is at work within him. In this section he reveals ten prevenient graces that effect this change. They may be succinctly summarized as graces for opening up personal depths, accepting the consequences of solitude, operating out of a good conscience, establishing a proper *ratio* or orientation for choices, meeting one's personal God, desiring to see and taste or delight in God, pursuing the place of God, removing all the types of idols that one is accustomed to use for comprehending God, cultivating an accurate comprehension in one's religious life, and, finally, living while authentically listening to the voice of God.

1. Opening Inner Depths: *Meditation 4:6*

To arrive at the truth about himself, William knows that he must open the dark inner depths of his conscience and consciousness, seeing himself as he truly is. He must thoroughly open this dimension of himself, with its dark obscurity and inner confusion, and expose it to God so that the enlightening divine presence can illuminate and transform his life. He knows that he has been predestined for eternal happiness, but his choices have not always led him in that direction.

In discussing the need to expose one's inner self to God William uses the scriptural image of eating of the tree of the knowledge of good and evil, with the help and consent of his flesh. In so doing, he sees his own shame, not God's graciousness, a vision that reveals to him his infamy, his nakedness, and a kind of liberty that needs control and restraint. In God's presence, William finds himself naked, lacking those attributes that other persons thought they perceived in him. In God's eyes, he experiences himself as shameful, having no place of refuge, no escape, from himself or from God. His poverty overwhelms him. At the same time, his perception of the truth about himself, overpowering as it is, prevents him from circling around and around the periphery of his center of truth (Med 1.9).

William explains that solitude has played an important role in his contemplative ascent, bringing him face to face with the truth of his inner self and inner life, where he must cope with the thorns and thistles of conscience, a verbal reminder of the exile from Eden (Gen 3:18). He recognizes himself as now dwelling in this place of truth, as a solitary wild ass (Hos 8:9). Conscience, and its opening forth into consciousness, is where God speaks truth to a person, raising such questions as Who am I? From where have I come? Where am I going? Such questions cause William to assess his former life, to flee to the Lord, and to enter deeply into the place where the Lord is speaking.

In the same sentence with which he laments his suffering in his solitary exile from Paradise, William recognizes the enduring presence of God's fragrant love, lyrically calling up another biblical echo: "*I have put my mouth in the dust, if perhaps there may be hope, like a solitary wild ass breathing in the scent of his Beloved"* (Med 4.7). In this experience he does not hear God demanding an account of his conscience, nor does he question and discern, as is proper in examining one's conscience. Instead, he sits humbly in silence in his center of truth with his *thorns and thistles*, "hearing *neither the voice of one demanding,* nor the noise of a hostile encounter" (Med 4.7).

The dynamic of this portion of the work is a movement from self-consciousness giving birth to an appropriate self-knowledge, and consequently the birth of a wholesome relationship to God, established on humility. William now begins to acquire a deeper realization of God working in his life. He cannot as yet touch God with a good conscience, but he is beginning to realize that God is working in him, graciously, devotedly, and mercifully. Self-knowledge is thus beginning in him to become the foundation for knowledge of God—but as he makes clear, self-knowledge can be unpleasant: "I have been expelled from the paradise of a good conscience. I am made an exile in a foreign land, in a region of unlikeness."[2]

William can no longer camouflage his deep inner self, but must face it, however unpleasant he finds it. But in his awareness of God's loving divine presence he allows the birth of a profound humility. Now at last he is able to recognize the reality of his life, the center of his truth.

2. Good Conscience: *Meditation 4.10*

Over the course of the *Meditations* William increasingly sees awareness of one's place—the Paradise of a humble conscience with its consciousness—as the way into the presence of God. So he proposes that displaying a good conscience before God allows personal restoration. One emerges, he says, from the land of unlikeness to God, where one walks in a circle, circumventing the center of truth. William acknowledges to God, "you did not create me for Paradise,

---

2. Augustine, Conf 7.10.16; Augustine, En in Ps 99.5.

but Paradise for me when you made me a human upon the earth" (Med 4.10). Through a good conscience before God, he recognizes that the land of unlikeness, of thorns and thistles, is transformed into the land of likeness: so the rational life[3] is coming to birth.[4]

3. Reason in Its Proper Responsibility: *Meditation 4.11*

William teaches that the dignity of the human person rises from an inner harmony resulting from the proper use of reason, but he understands reason[5] not simply as a matter of being logical, as in deductive reasoning, but as being ordered to an end, to the place foreknown and predestined for a person by God. The faculty of reason uses the movements of life's affections and intelligence so that they may be no longer instruments of weakness but instruments of happiness. Such a harmony is the result of reason used properly, for the body to adjust to spirit and spirit to God, for all aspects of the body and intellectual life need adjustment to reason. Here is the new heaven and new earth of personal restoration.

4. Knowledge of One's Personal God as the Fruit of Solitude: *Meditation 4.12*

The next transforming factor is an awareness of God as a personal God, the fruit of the traveler's experience of wilderness and solitude.[6] At this point, William shows, awareness begins to co-

3. Soul-*animus* / reason-*ratio*.

4. Our Image, the *animus* or intellectual soul, consists in rationality, along with the concupiscible appetite and irascible appetite. Virtues of faith, hope, and charity foster the proper use of these three respectively. The land of unlikeness is a common Cistercian theme. See William, Cant 65; Augustine, Conf 7.10.16; Augustine En in Ps 99.5.

5. Reason, here *ratio*, is to be identified with the *animus* or the rational person.

6. The idea of a personal God in the *meditations* is not intended to convey the idea of God known personally or individually, but rather to convey the idea of a

alesce into intimacy with God. His ordering to God is not simply a direction proper to reason, but a relationship. Grace orchestrates this new way of experiencing God. The context for this section is the second chapter of the prophet Hosea, which speaks of harmony between the physical and moral world.[7] William applies Hosea's theme to the human composite of body and soul. Solitude, he says, begins this integration of body and soul, placed in the presence of God.[8] Such solitude means, then, not that one is utterly alone, but that God is present and will be able to pick up the one who falls:

> Give me, Lord, the consolation of my solitude, a solitary heart and frequent conversation with you. For I will not be alone as long as you are with me, my God. But if you leave me, *woe to the person who is alone.* For if I fall asleep, there will be no one to keep me warm while I am sleeping. If *I fall, there will be no one to pick me up.* (Med 4.14)

William's implicit reminder here, though, is that where God is absent, only suffering remains: *Woe to one who is alone.*[9]

5. A Desire to Taste, See, and Delight in This Personal God: *Meditation 4.13–14*

Closely associated with the experience of a personal God and the recognition that one is not totally alone is the intense desire for a greater intimacy with God. In this portion of the meditation

---

personal relationship not shared with anyone else, on the model of a spousal relationship.

7. J.-M. Déchanet, *Méditations et Prières,* Éditions Universitaires (Brussels: Les Presses de Belgique, 1945), 186.

8. William here first touches on *eucrasis,* the quality of one's inner life as manifested through the physical body.

9. Some medieval Cistercians take this idea in the literal sense and apply it to the need or reason for a communal living and way of living.

William recognizes the demand that this threefold desire to taste, see, and delight in God makes on him.

The ascent has so far progressed from identification with the lower impulses of his narcissistic self—a selfish love, i.e., pride, vanity, passions, and other egocentric desires—into an identification formed by appropriate relationships with things, other persons, and God. By gradual purification of these relationships through sincere love as taught in the gospels, William has discovered a still greater, more magnanimous self. An authentic love experience has challenged him to give all and hold nothing back. But the ascent to God now incorporates an identity shift for him, with identity no longer to be formed by appropriate relationships, but identity rising out of an intimate union with God. The description William gives to this identity shift is *being led into the desert* (Med 4.15).

6. Pursuing the Place Where God Is: *Meditation 4.15*

William asks to ascend by being led into the place where God is, into God's desert, into that selfless love, *your love*, that cleanses him of every encumbrance, leaving only clean and pure affections: "where the holy soul that has won admittance into this place is all aflame" (Med 4.15). This sentence contains two significant terms: *where* and *into this place*, both important for understanding the burning-bush experience.

William understands that for him as for Moses, this experience is not a question of seeing One who cannot be seen, or of covering his face, but of having his ears uncovered to listen to the One who is saying, *I am who am!* One must be thoroughly humble, not desiring to see face to face, but desiring to listen and learn obedience as the way to advance and ascend into God. William's insight here is essential, causing a major shift in one's relationship with God. Here, in this place, in *humility of obedience*, one listens with close attention so as to hear the Lord speak: "With the humility of obedience one's listening is focused with attention so as *to hear what the Lord his God is saying within him*" (Med 4.15). This is the only time William uses the phrase *humility of obedience*[10] in all his writings. It may have been inspired by the opening words of chapter 5 of the Rule of Saint Benedict: "The first degree of humility is obedience without delay." The focus situates one's attention on hearing what the Lord, one's personal God, is saying within oneself as indispensable for ascending into the secret place of God. This secret place implies a relationship so intimate that one experiences oneself as the burning bush where God appears and speaks within.

7. Removing All Types of Idols Formerly Used to Comprehend God: *Meditation 4.16*

In this secret place is an authentic ministry or service in God's service, where there are no idols and no forms whatever, even spiritual ones that any other ministry or service might contain.[11] Now William's thrust is dedicated to listening to God's voice. This authentic ministry in God's service is a living expression of the sixth and seventh degrees of humility as spelled out in chapter 7 of the Rule of Benedict. It is a place of total acceptance and surrender to God, allowing one to listen in obedience. Christ's humility in his death on the cross is the service he offers to the Father and to

10. *Sed in humilitate obedientiae exerendus auditus ut quid in eo loquatur Dominus Deus suus,* a quotation from the Vulgate Gallican Psalter. In using it, William has made meaningful alterations. In the Vulgate the sentence reads, *audiam quid loquatur in me Dominus Deus.* William changes the first person active *audiam* "I will hear" into the noun *auditus* "[sense of] hearing." The addition of *suus* underscores that the God who speaks is one's own personal God. On the phrase "humility of obedience," see Gregory the Great, *Homilies on the Gospel* 34.10; Isidore of Seville, *Etymologiae* 7.5.24.

11. For a comprehensive presentation of William's understanding of idolatry and its effect on a contemplative union with God, see Bell, "The Prayer of Dom William," 21–26.

humanity. Entering into an intimate relationship with God in the secret place where God is, with the cross as the desert of God, demands a total self-stripping, removal of all hindrances and affections that are not of God, idols of any type or kind that one uses to approach God in prayer. When this stripping takes place, William senses that he will encounter God, not seeing God, but hearing God say, *I am who am.* William hears but does not see *I am who am.*

This life-long process of stripping oneself in humility has a profound effect on one's conscience and consciousness or awareness, bringing one into conformity with God's way of thinking. This process creates a positive acceptance and surrender to the aspects of one's vocation in life. Such a surrender is by no means easy, though one would wish it to be. It complements the opening theme of the *Meditations* of the potter tenderly creating vessels for various uses. Meditation 13 contains William's final struggle in his desire to be under God's law, to acknowledge God's yoke and the light burden that supports and does not crush him.[12]

8. Becoming Intelligent and Devoutly Knowledgeable:
Meditation 4.17

While being recreated by God, William shows, one progresses in understanding and insight about self and God, and along with that comes a vision of a new earth and new heaven. Authentic listening to God blossoms in a desire to know the good, the acceptable and perfect Will of God so as to be intelligent and devoutly knowledgeable, realizing even the divine nods that God might give to a person, a charming metaphor that William employs to illustrate one's willingness to listen and obey. He perceives that seizing

12. See Augustine, Sol I.1.5.

and being seized by God is the realization of faith's enhancing and fulfilling his inner life as rational and intellectual.[13]

At this juncture, a further stunning shift surfaces in William's quest for God. Delicately, he moves from a focus on his inner life, which is rational and intellectual, to a preparatory stance for his spirit to enter into what he will develop as the concept of unity of spirit. Here his spirit becomes intimately united with God's Holy Spirit, who is the bond between Father and Son. This shift towards unity of spirit inaugurates an additional re-creating of a phase of his life that he will express in a new way of life. His steady ascent will evolve through his authentic listening to Christ as the Word of God, that is, his divine nature, and as his prayer, especially the prayer on the Cross in his human nature. Christ on the cross invokes William's being crucified with Christ. Here William enters a bodily dimension in terms of his way of life, supporting his inner life in his quest for the Triune God.

9. Authentic Listening to God: *Meditation 4.18–19*

The outcome of these steps in renewal is a person who listens authentically to God—equivalent to praying without ceasing. Such a listener is devout, pure, and full of joy. Although this prayer does not forget one's sinfulness or the experience of finding oneself in dire straits as a result of sin, it is nevertheless truth. For the grace of authentic listening receives only what comes from above, from God. Authentic listening understands the language God speaks in numerous ways (Heb 1:1), predominantly in the passion, death, and resurrection of Christ. Authentic listening has the ability to contemplate, to comprehend, and to understand so as to receive the understanding from above. Such listening is the joyful work and gift of the Holy Spirit.

---

13. This is the fulfillment of one's *ratio fidei*, which William describes as faith giving focus to reason in his ascent.

Faithful to his monastic call by praying by listening, William knows the challenge of the gospels and the Rule of Benedict. At the Transfiguration the voice of the Father thunders, *Behold my Beloved Son, in whom I am well pleased! Listen to him!* (Matt 17:1; Mark 9:1; Luke 9:28; 2 Pet 1:17). In this vein, as if to lead his disciples into the Transfiguration experience, Saint Benedict opens his Rule with the word *Listen.*

The Prayer of Jesus: *Meditation 5.1–3*

Fidelity to a total openness in listening to God's will leads William now to focus on Christ crucified and, accordingly, to desire to be instructed in this school by none other than the Lord Jesus himself, the Wisdom of God the Father. William finds this instruction in the Lord's Prayer and, strikingly, interprets his transforming change in having found his place, *locus*, in the prayer of Jesus.[1] The *Meditations* unveils this school of the Lord's Prayer by presenting the pattern that Jesus gave for an all-embracing prayer. William reflects on this pattern and the ways Jesus prayed: sometimes alone, sometimes in the midst of a crowd, sometimes in exultation of spirit, once in a bloody sweat, and once exalted on the cross.

As William continues to reflect on the way his own prayer needs to be empowered by the prayer of Christ, he realizes that such empowerment is a distinctive grace. When praying alone, he perceives that he lacks a sufficiently pure conscience and the abundance of grace requisite for prayer of exaltation in Holy Spirit. Praying alone is not being in a physical, solitary place, but praying from a solitary heart. This place is an uncontaminated conscience: a solitary heart is one that is not caught up in idolatry of any sort. William emphasizes a personal encounter with God rising out of an ardent devotedness of love rather than resting on any image, mental or physical, of the divine. Inner awareness or consciousness requires a sharp focus on God, one that integrates all that a person encounters in life so as to be able to respond yes to God. Prayer of this nature leads to a martyrdom of conscience, that is, a faithful yes to God's will in all circumstances of one's life.

1. A prayer for every situation, *perfecta oratio*, literally "perfect prayer."

Self-knowledge as knowledge of God is a well-known axiom. Sincere interior knowledge of oneself, self-knowledge as truth, is transmuted by grace into a knowing of God.[2] A little later William uses the imagery of Christ crucified as a means of contemplating the divinity of Christ and gazing upon its brightness.[3] Fascinatingly, William, previously having rejected all images as idolatry, proceeds to use imagination, with its images, but not as ends in themselves—as a means, a kind of metaphor, to open out onto an experience of divine selfless love or charity and goodness. Opening out or leading beyond is indispensable to prayer with images lest they somehow assume the form of an idol.

Prayer as Being Crucified, *Concrucifixus,* with the Lord Jesus: *Meditation 5.4*

William pleads for the Lord to come to him in advance with divine grace so that he will be able to pray with a pure conscience. William also wrote in his other works of this prevenient grace, Christ himself coming in advance. Meditating on how one can identify with Jesus' ways of praying leads William to a critical decision that he requires a prayer "to sweat out and the cross to crucify" what is in him. So he acknowledges his martyrdom of conscience:

> For when I am conscious of what there is in me that prayer needs to sweat out and the cross crucify, indeed I do not have a bloody sweat, although my heart sweats bloody tears before your eyes. Nor does my body find a cross on which to be crucified, although my unhappy soul is crucified[4] in itself beyond every sorrow of a cross. (Med 5.4)

2. Bell, "The Prayer of Dom William," 31, n. 41.

3. Bell, "The Prayer of Dom William," 27.

4. William uses the Latin word *excruciare* three times in the *Meditations,* always in Med 5, §§4, 8, and 14. The usual translation of the word is "to torture or to torment either physically or mentally," but here he uses it meaning "to crucify," in terms of his soul. *Torture* and *torment* convey the wrong idea.

William here enters explicitly into an experiential, contemplative participation in Christ's passion and death.

Traditional monastic teaching recognizes that monastics are crucified with the Lord Jesus on the cross by their profession, vowing fidelity in their monastic vocation throughout their life. Meditation on Jesus' crucifixion reveals that no death, no life, no sacrifice can make an adequate response to his loving selflessness. This manner of *meditatio* assists the monastic to realize that the world, having been redeemed by the cross, not only pays no attention to the cross, but despises the cross. Commitment to meditation emphasizes the significance of upholding this union with Christ as both personal and living in the one who meditates. For William, this manner of *meditatio* is the heart of what it means to pray.

Concrucifixus and Its Consequences: *Meditation 5.5*

William shows that Christ's crucifixion stands at the center of history and that monastics keep it vibrant and alive in their daily life. He emphasizes that meditation allows the mystery of the cross to transform who he is when he distinguishes between the pain of his cross and the pain of his heart, a transformation that maintains this divine work vibrant and alive throughout the remaining years of his life.[5] This style of meditation is not simply

---

5. In Med 5:5 William speaks of the pain of his cross as distinct from the pain of his heart. He appears to say that his monastic life as a Benedictine before entering the Cistercian abbey of Signy was a form of embracing the cross. After his entrance into Signy, the pain of his cross, now the Cistercian way of life, was initially excruciating, but he was now able to carry it by the grace of Christ crucified. This is perhaps an allusion to the trial that he experienced after his entrance into Signy, experiencing severe discouragement and despair until a vision comforted him. God's grace and this vision were so fruitful in his life that afterwards he was able to bear with ease the heavy yoke of Cistercian discipline (see Jean Marie Déchanet, *William of St Thierry: The Man and His Work*, trans. Richard Strachan, CS 10 [Kalamazoo, MI: Cistercian Publications, 1972], 44).

a mental devotional exercise grounded solely in the imagination's reflecting on the Crucified Christ. William's phrase, using a Latin passive form of the verb "to vivify," illustrates a highly delicate nuance.[6] This form of *meditatio* has the transforming effect of *concrucifixus* as one is crucified with Christ, opening loving pain in the heart of one ardently devoted to Christ. William avows, "I am crucified[7] with you, Lord Jesus . . . . on the cross of profession that daily and continually I offer you" (Med 5.5).

This use of Jesus' crucifixion reveals that there is no adequate response of ardent devotedness to the mystery of the Incarnate Word. For William, such appropriation reveals that his life is crucified by monastic profession, by the inward agony caused by the just and unjust things of life. This is the gist of Benedict's teaching contained in his fourth step of humility, in chapter 7 of his Rule. Although monastics' bodies are not physically crucified, by the grace of Jesus each monastic is able daily to offer Jesus this crucifixion of humble charity, the service of selfless love that participates in the trinitarian *your love*. William articulates these consequences of his prayer:

> May your cross crucify whatever has been collected through *concupiscence of the flesh, concupiscence of the eyes, and pride of life* in the vast expanse of my negligence. May whatever *has been singed and undermined by the flesh's will* and the mind's consent be destroyed at the rebuke of your countenance. (Med 5.14)

6. *opus tuum in medio annorum uiuificatum,* from Hab 3:2. In the Vulgate the sentence reads *vivifica*. With the past participle *uiuificatum* William indicates that Christ's redemption stands at the center of history, that his redemption has been kept alive throughout the centuries, and that frequent, if not daily, meditation keeps the mystery of Redemption vibrant and alive, not merely a theological axiom.

7. *Concrucifixus.*

A Treacherous Problem: *Meditation 5.6*

Having completed his portrait of himself, his self-understanding as one crucified with Christ, William now points to the treacherous problem present in this meditation: the danger of being dulled by habitual meditation on Christ's passion and crucifixion and so failing to maintain it as living and alive. He explains this danger by noting that habit can desensitize a person: "Because of habit itself,[8] we are desensitized when seeing you crucified, thinking of you as dead and buried." Rather, William urges, "What should pierce through further into the heart" of worshipers is this: that "struck on the face with blows, scourged, mocked, spat upon, pierced by nails and the lance, crowned with thorns, given gall and vinegar to drink," Jesus on his cross thirsted "for nothing but our salvation." He continues:

> *The earth trembled* when you were crucified; we laugh. Heaven with its lights was obscured; we burn to shine in the world. *Rocks were rent*; we harden our hearts. *Graves broken open* gave up their dead; we, luxuriously resting upon beds of lewd playfulness, are the dead burying our dead. (Med 5.6)

Christ's Prayer on the Cross: *Meditation 5.7–10*

Seeing the crucified Christ upon the cross in his meditating prompts William to recall again the three prayers Jesus offered to the Father from the cross, embracing everything that would be accomplished by his blood in his passion. He prayed for himself, for his friends, and for his enemies. When he prayed for himself, though, William says, he did not labor, "for as the Apostle says, he was heard by reason of his reverence" (Med 5.7). He prayed

8. *Vsu enim ipso iam pro nihilo habemus.*

also for his friends who had persevered with him in time of trial, and for his enemies who were crucifying him, not knowing what they might be doing.

But now a new question arises: where is the prayer for those persons who sin knowingly? He concludes that such persons are beyond the open arms stretched out, beyond the embrace of Jesus, because they have deliberately placed themselves there by an absence of the repentance that would identify and unite them with Christ crucified, identity and union involving sorrow, blood, suffering, and crucifixion. This thought confirms William's sense of his need for repentance in order to find his place and insert his monastic call into Christ's passion.

The implication of this concern is of course that people must be especially concerned about the quality of their prayer when they have knowingly sinned. They cannot be excused for conscious behavior, because they have sinned knowingly and willingly:

> Therefore, the Apostle says, *no sacrifice for sins is left for us who sin willingly.* Unless repentance removes these sins, unless a bloody sweat expels them and the cross crucifies them,[9] I do not find persons sinning willingly and knowingly to have a share in the prayer of the one sweating blood or hanging in sacrifice on the cross. (Med 5.8)

Despite judging himself for his life's sin, though, William asserts a little later that he has not trampled the Son of God underfoot because he has never denied him as Peter did: "But have I trampled you underfoot, Son of God? I have trampled you underfoot if I have denied you, although I do not allege Peter to have trampled you underfoot, he who, as it happened,[10] denied you. He loved you

9. *Nisi sanguineus sudor exsudet et crux excruciet.*

10. William presents his own sin as a parallel to Peter's threefold denial, insisting that both men always ardently loved Christ, despite Peter's denial, but William argues that love excludes contempt and appears to be taking the edge off of Peter's responsibility: "who, as it happened, denied you" = *quem contigit negasse.*

most ardently even as he was denying you once, twice, and a third time" (Med 5.10). The guiding principle for William is that authentic self-knowledge, an accurate evaluation of one's self, ought to give an understanding that shapes one's way of life.

To continue participating vibrantly in the prayer of Christ while persevering on his monastic cross, William perceives his need to pray that Jesus will whisper to him that his sins are forgiven, and to tell him what is indispensable if he is to atone for his sins. The word *whisper* has overtones not only of intimacy, but also of being positively ingratiating, of being capable of gaining or giving a favor, or to be intimately pleasing to someone. For Christ to whisper to a person is a powerful encouragement of conversion, elaborating on the idea of God with us.[11] Since William has always loved the Lord, he does not hesitate courageously and affectionately to ask the crucified Christ to whisper affectionately and intimately to him.

Love and Truth: *Meditation 5:10–12*

Despite his passionate rejection of the idea that he has ever denied Christ, and his earnest request that Christ whisper encouragement to him, William soon remembers who he is and has been. So once again he descends into anguish, now about the sin that he has committed despite his awareness of God's goodness to him:

> Truly, Lord, I have sinned *willingly and greatly after having received the knowledge of truth,*[12] *and I have abused the Spirit of grace,* from whom I have freely received the washing away

11. "Whisper" = *insinua.*

12. Knowledge of truth = *notitia ueritatis.* Augustine uses this phrase about three times, but it appears five times in William's works: Nat am 11; Exp Rom 1; Med 5.10, 12; Med 7.8. He first uses it in Nat am 11, stating that sinning after receiving knowledge of truth is to crucify again the Son of God. His use of the term here implies experiential insight that brings with it a knowing of God that shapes one's conscience. In developing two kinds of understanding (Med 2.9) William elaborates on his experience of the knowledge of truth.

> of sins in baptism. And, after receiving the knowledge of
> truth, I have returned to sin *as a dog* to its *vomit*. (Med 5.10)

William is now approaching the theme of love's intensity, distinguishing between truth and love. He realizes that his love has not always been as devoted toward God's love, *your love, amor tuus*, as it should have been, and he understands himself as having sinned,[13] but he declares that he has not denied Jesus. His sins are not sins of contempt, for he has always loved, and his faith in Christ has always been present despite temptations to abandon it. But he is nonetheless concerned about the quality of his love:

> I have always believed in you. I have never denied you. I have
> always loved you, even when I have sinned against you. I am
> sorry for my sin until my death, but I am not sorry for your
> love [*amor tuus*]. I am only sorry that even then I did not
> love you to the extent that I should have. For if I had loved
> you to that extent, I would not have sinned. (Med 5.11–12)

This kind of sin does not imply contempt of the Lord. But it does imply that when one must choose, love of one's self tends to take precedence over the selfless love, *your love, caritas*, even though the Holy Spirit, *your love*, is persistently present within the depth of one's heart.

William is beginning to understand the significance and consequence of *your love, amor tuus*, the bonding between Father and Son, as operative in the depths of his life in conquering his love of self. But scrutinizing his willingness to sin is pivotal in this process, leading him into the depths of his love and truth.[14] Again

13. Saint Bernard makes the same statement in Letter 27: "I ask that you pray for me without ceasing, for I have never ceased to sin."

14. In his treatise *The Nature and Dignity of Love* (Nat am 14 [CCCM 88:188–89; CF 30:70–71]), William speaks of the apostle Peter and King David as never having lost charity even when they sinned greatly, the former by denying Christ and the latter in his behavior. They were readily able to confess their sin because

he declares his faithful love to Christ: "Virtue is the willing assent of the mind to good. You know, my Lord, how I have always kept my willing assent in fidelity to you. Keep it in me until the end!" (Med 5.11).[15]

William goes on to probe his experience in light of his love of God. Recognizing the ultimate importance of recognizing the truth about oneself, he now asks a different question about sin and its impact on his final end. And again he considers his sin in light of the persistence of God's love:

> Yet alas, how I fear lest the fact that I have loved you may bring me forth into Judgment, because if it is so serious to sin *after having received the knowledge of truth*, how much more serious is it after the most sweet tasting of your good, after having received the sweetness of your delightful love? (Med 5.12)[16]

William's Bonding to the Human and Divine Natures of Christ: *Meditation 5.14–15*

William's reflection on his love's intensity leads him to the scriptural woman (Luke 7:36-38, 47–50) whom Jesus forgives because she has loved much. This scriptural pericope exemplifies William's use of imagery to ascend into the brightness of Christ's divinity. When William comes into the holy place, the *locus*, as he calls his judgment before Christ, he wants his love to be of such intensity

---

they still possessed charity, the love of God. That is, they both had a basic love for God, a certain selflessness or humility, that enabled them to repent; this might be called a grace of conversion.

15. This definition of virtue is a classical Augustinian definition: *Virtus est uoluntarius assensus animi in bonum* ("Virtue is the willing assent of the mind to good"). This is the only time that I have translated *animus* as "mind" in the *Meditations*.

16. This statement is an extension of William's teaching about Peter's denial and King David's sin.

and greatness that all his sins will be forgiven. Prostrate at the feet of Christ, as a sinner but also as a person who has great love for Christ, he washes these feet with the abundant tears of confession, and he anoints them with the ointment of love's ardent devotedness: "This is my whole substance, however small it is, either in body or in soul, as the price of an ointment pleasing to you, which I will pour out upon your head—*whose head is God*, [1 Cor 11:3]—and over your feet, the lowest part of our humble nature" (Med 5.15).[17]

William here acknowledges both the divinity of Christ, as his sins are against God, and the humanity of Christ, as he brings the ardent devotedness of his love to the incarnate Christ. William has now entered into the depths of the mystery of the incarnation and requests that Christ's perfect love, which is the attractiveness of divinity, may overpower the will of his flesh and his mind's consent to his will.

Mutual Anointing and the *Amplexus*: *Meditation 5.15–19*

The example from Scripture that William now uses points to a mutual anointing between Christ and William, with William giving ardent devotedness to Christ in his humanity, and Christ bestowing the compassionate prevenient grace of merciful love, breaking down the long-standing wickedness and hardness of William's nature. So William will be ready for Judgment, according to the quality of his love. This love, however, is nothing other than his sharing in the cross of Christ, that is, a life lived as crucified with Christ, *concrucifixus*. This is their mutual embrace in Christ's crucifixion, as William desires to share in everything the cross

17. William does not use 1 Cor 11:3 exactly with regard to God as the head of Christ. Rather, he here understands Christ as combining his divinity in his head (that most elevated part of a person) and his human nature in his feet, the lowest part of a person (see Bernard, P Epi 2.1).

brings, crying out to Christ, "Lord, do not exclude me from the embrace of your redemption. For in everything I desire to share in your cross" (Med 5.17).

William thus conveys the fullness of being *concrucifixus* with the embrace of Christ. As Christ's body is crucified on the cross, William's body is crucified by fidelity to the cross of monastic profession,[18] that is, his loyalty to the daily monastic routine with its implications for his conscience and his conscious life. The two bodies are joined and sealed by a mutual and ardent love. So William asks to be judged on the evidence of his love for Christ's love. This constitutes one of William's fundamental themes: as love is the foundation of one's life, it is essential to be judged on this basis. As he writes elsewhere, "Love is a power of the soul, leading her by a kind of natural gravity to her place."[19] And "our heart has been prepared by the gift of loving, pulling us to our place!"[20]

The essence of this crucified love is a heart prepared, so that neither William's heart nor his body may withdraw from doing the divine will. So William prays for the grace of fidelity to his monastic life:

> Command whatever you wish, but grant me to understand and to be able to do what you command, you who have given me a *heart prepared* for this so that neither my heart nor my body may withdraw in anything from doing your will. *You have known my sitting and my rising, and all my most recent and former thoughts.* Unform me from a world to which I have conformed myself and conform me to [Christ], the form of your grace, from whom I have fled. And give to my heart a form of penitence pleasing to you. Furthermore,

18. Med 5:4–5 and 8:4–6 are also important passages for William's concept of *amplexus.*

19. Nat am 1 (CCCM 88:177; CF 30:47–48). The place, of course, is God; see Orat (CCCM 88:170; CS 268:34); see also Augustine, Civ Dei 11.28; Conf 13.9.10; Ep 157.2.9.

20. Contemp 1 (CCCM 88:153; CF 3:136).

grant to me, Lord, a faith unadulterated and devoted, conscientious, strong, and unshaken, so that, giving grace for grace, you can also say to me, *Go, for your faith has made you alive.* (Med 5.18–19)[21]

This, William understands, is the essence of a fidelity to monastic life, and the essence of anyone's fidelity to his or her vocation.

21. "Alive" = *saluus,* "safe, intact, well, whole, alive." I translate it as *alive,* since the word gives a powerful accent to faith as giving life, unlike the life of sin, which brings death. See also the ending of Med 1.8: "alive in Your Word."

Heaven's Open Door: *Meditation 6.1*

A life crucified with the crucified Christ is an authentic life to the degree that one is not conformed to the world. In the previous passage William has prayed to be unformed from the world, so initiating his movement into what is opposed to the worldly life, namely heavenly life—the day of eternal happiness, the objective of his contemplative ascent. He further develops this theme in the next section of the *Meditations,* in a natural sequel to meditating on Christ crucified and his saying to the repentant thief, *Today you will be with me in paradise* (Luke 23:43). Thus William continues reflecting on Paradise, or heaven. Using the book of Revelation to express his thoughts, he writes, "*I saw a door opened in heaven,* says John, *and the first voice, which I heard, was like a trumpet speaking to me, saying: Ascend to here*" (Rev 4:1).[1] As William describes it, ascending into heaven is what heaven is, with the ascent and heaven appearing to be identical. William's thoughts on heaven and participation flow naturally from an identity with Christ crucified, an identity that is correspondingly a participation with him.

Earthly Heaviness and Human Pride: *Meditation 6:2–5*

William presents earth as a place full of curses and heaviness because of human pride, because of sin—full of change, alternations, and misfortunes of all sorts, whereas he sees heaven as a place cleansed of pride, as pride has been cast out with the proud angels. Heaven is now the only proper place for the humble. According to

---

1. William uses the word *ascend* ten times in this section of the *Meditations,* so connecting it to Christ's ascension.

Benedict, humility is the heart of the monastic way of life. Humility ascends into that perfect love that casts out all fear, that is, the Holy Spirit (RB 7).

William goes on to say that saints rejoice in an inner tranquility that flows from authentic charity, so delightfully celebrating a day of the continuous vision of God's glory. Nothing could interrupt enjoyment of the festival of the divine countenance. He goes on to focus on heaven as joyful relationship. If on earth, he says, a gathering of two or three with God in their midst creates a life filled with the goodness, pleasantness, and fragrance of the anointing of the Holy Spirit, what must the joyful happiness be where the saints are gathered together with God?

He continues to develop the theme of this joyful intimacy. On earth, he explains, the commandment of love, the Lord's Testament to love one another, generates intimacy, a community of blessing, revealing that love is more important than sacrifice: "Then how much greater is it where you [Lord Christ] have gathered together your saints, who have preferred your testament over and above sacrifices and, having become heaven, now proclaim your justice?" (Med 6.5).[2]

By teaching that heaven is a loving intimacy, William reveals justice to be more fundamental than sacrifice. In this passage the saints and God relate to one another justly. William labels this interchange peace, understanding it as a profound dimension of intimacy with Christ. Justice of this nature initiates an intimacy found in a community of blessing on earth and reaches fulfillment in the everlasting intimacy between God and the saints.

William's concept of justice as more fundamental than sacrifice raises questions. What is God's justice? What is human justice? He suggests that God's justice is God's rightly having mercy on people. Human justice is people's confessing truthfully who they

---

2. *Quanto maxime ubi congregasti sanctos tuos qui ordinauerunt testamentum tuum super sacrifice, et facti caeli annuntiant iustitiam tuam?* (CCCM 89:34).

are, on the basis of their accurate self-knowledge: they are not circling around themselves in error. Accordingly, William says, people and God relate to one another justly, with humans confessing accurately and truthfully that they are sinners, and God rightly having mercy. Accordingly, mercy and justice meet in God (Med 8:2–3). God's justice is a human life saturated through and through by authentic divine merciful love. This mystery is brought to perfection in heaven—eternal happiness.[3]

Jesus, Incarnate Merciful Love, Is the Open Door into Heaven: *Meditation 6.6–7*

William goes on to say that the open door into heaven for human nature is Jesus: "You have said, *I am the door. If anyone enters through me, that person will be saved.* You are the door, then" (Med 6.6). Incarnate merciful Love! This open door is an invitation for all to enter so as to leave the earth, a place full of curse due to human pride, due to sin, full of all sorts of misfortunes. Interestingly, *amor* is the Latin word William uses for love describing Jesus as the open door, rather than *caritas*, selfless love. William elucidates, quoting the Apostle Paul:

> *The one who ascends, he it is who descends.* Who is this? Love. For the love in us ascends there, into you, Lord, because the love in you descends here to us. Truly, because you have loved us, you have descended here, to us. By loving you, we ascend there into you. (Med 6.7)[4]

---

3. This entire section of the *Meditations* reflects the teaching of William's Orat (Bell, "The Prayer of Dom William," 21–36).

4. *Quis ascendit, ipse est qui descendit. Quis est hic? Amor. Amor enim ad te, Domine, in nobis illuc ascendit, quia amor in te ad nos huc descendit. Quia enim amasti nos, huc descendisti ad nos. Amando te, illuc ascendemus ad te* (CCCM 89:34).

Why does William use *amor* for "love" here? As he explains in the opening paragraphs of his *The Nature and Dignity of Love,* it is *amor,* love rooted in human nature, that conveys human nature to its proper place, in this case into heaven, with human love having been touched by grace, empowering human nature to ascend and bestowing a sense of happiness or well-being.

The Proper Way to Think Regarding Heaven and Earth:
Meditation 6.8–9

As William explains, God incarnate, because of his divine and human natures, is entirely present on earth and in heaven. This proper manner of thinking about God incarnate is crucial. In the perspective of his incarnation, Jesus proclaims that he is the open door on earth leading into heaven. William's critically nuanced focus on heaven has a single-mindedness that prevents thinking about God in a purely human manner, with the emphasis on earth. As William says in addressing God, "You are entirely everywhere, if entirely is a word that can be established in you or about you, in whom there is no division" (Med 6.8). Yes, God is entirely present everywhere on earth and in heaven. The ascent of the Incarnate God maintains this focus of being always in heaven.

The Lord's Prayer also gives the proper approach for thinking about God, William shows. Those who accept this prayer affirm the belief[5] that God our Father is in heaven, for they understand and grasp the truth about God contained in this prayer: that God the Father dwells in heaven. These words assist one to form an outlook founded on truth about something incapable of being thoroughly understood by the human mind.

---

5. "Belief" = *sententia,* a technical term for a juridical pronouncement that can in turn be used in jurisprudence. William appears to use it here to describe those persons who understand or grasp something, so implying that they are grasping the truth about something.

Further Thoughts on Heaven: *Meditation 6.10–14*

The notion of place, *locus*, plays an important role in William's teachings, as is seen earlier in the *Meditations*. In one of his earliest works, *The Nature and Dignity of Love*,[6] William writes that love's place is in God. God has implanted love, *amor*, in the human heart so that love might carry one back into God. William further delineates aspects of place in these paragraphs of the *Meditations* to guide his readers to a clearer way of thinking about God. He quotes Christ's response to those asking about his place: "I plead, reply to persons reaching out for you, thirsting after you: *Master, where do you live? You respond immediately, saying, I am in the Father, and the Father is in me*" (Med 6.10).

This is a revelation of oneness, that Jesus is in the Father and the Father is in Jesus, with the bond between them the Holy Spirit. This is the place where Jesus dwells. They, the triune persons, are their own heaven. Heaven is not an otherworldly place: it is the Trinity.

William goes on to show that persons also participate in and in a sense become this place of oneness in the Trinity: "However, when you dwell in us, we are your heaven, indeed!" (Med 6.11). Yet the triune God is not here defined as having a dwelling place; rather, he makes a dwelling place for people. The triune God exists as the heaven into which they can ascend and dwell.[7] This is to say that their dwelling is in the triune God—or rather, the triune God dwelling in them is their heaven. Accordingly God's dwelling place is the bond between eternity and time, between heaven and earth. This is God's tremendous gift, bonding men and women to God as their mutual place.

William explains that the mutual bonding and indwelling of a person and the triune God have as their birthplace the gift of the Holy Spirit, the gift of selfless love, *your love*. The transforming

6. William, Nat am 2 (CCCM 88:136–37; CF 30:48–51).
7. Augustine, En in Ps 122.4.

objective of this indwelling is that people may live and manifest in their way of life the selfless love proper to the triune God. Once so vivified and transformed, they are indeed children of God. As William exclaims, quoting Scripture, "*Behold the manner of charity the Father has given us that we may be called and are children of God*" (Med 6.12).

William reflects further on this birthplace of the mutual bonding and indwelling. There are two births, he explains, one of divine nature, the Son begotten by the Father from all ages, and the other a birth that is an adoption by grace, for persons baptized into Christ. The birth of the Son is itself one of unity and bonding, the Holy Spirit. The birth by adoption into Christ is made possible through the gift of the Holy Spirit. It is a birth that people cannot bring about themselves, as William writes: "surely this birth is beyond the manner of human nature, yet it falls short of the essence of divinity" (Med 6.13). Those adopted in this way are born of God by grace. Furthermore, William explains (including himself among those of whom he writes), the vision of God confers

> the likeness of God, whereby we will see God, not what God is, but as he is! Yes, that likeness whereby we will be like God! For the Father to see the Son, this is to be what the Son is, and vice versa. However, for us to see God, this is to be like God. (Med 6.13)

At the same time, he encapsulates an essential distinction between who God is and what it is to be like God.

William's thought on the two kinds of birth is not a digression, but a perception into the concept of the mutual bonding and indwelling of the triune divinity and those who are baptized into Christ, the place effected by an anointment of the Holy Spirit. The concept of birth is but one feature of William's concept of heaven and of his contemplative ascent from a present life in the triune divinity to an eternal life in the Trinity. Birth is an understanding of the way likeness to God is brought about through unity of Spirit:

"But in you is the highest harmony, highest clarity, highest plenitude, and fullness of life" (Med 6.13).[8]

Heaven is Likeness to the Creating God: *Meditation 6.15*

Heaven, then, is a type of birth with mutual indwelling, with God dwelling in a person and the person in God, a likeness making possible the highest harmony, highest clarity, highest plenitude, and fullness of life. This concept of heaven evokes the perfection in divinity and divinity's having preordained all things for each person, a theme that William has enunciated at the beginning of the *Meditations*. For divine foreknowledge has predestined for each person his or her own place, as well as dwellings of virtues in this life and eternal happiness in the next: "no repulsiveness in your creature is repulsive to you, nor does malice harm, nor does error lead astray" (Med 6.15).[9] All are to arrive at the place preordained for them.

This is the divine splendor, the height, the depth, the wisdom, the power manifested in the highest harmony, highest clarity, highest plenitude, and fullness of life. This is the heaven to which Jesus, Son of the Father, in whom all things have been created, is the door. Here is the mystery hidden from all ages in God who created all things including all human life.

The Comprehensiveness of the Incarnation: *Meditation 6.16–19*

William continues with insight into the comprehensiveness of the incarnation of Christ,[10] the fullness of divine revelation, which he has perceived as the open door into the triune divinity.

---

8. Augustine, Sol 1.1.4.
9. John Scotus Eriugena, *De divisione naturae* III.20; Augustine, Sol 1.1.1.
10. This section is a summary of William's profound insight in Med 6:16–19.

He initiates this theme with the Old Testament image of the ark of the covenant, which was both the divine presence among the chosen people and a living reminder of the prodigies God had done for them during their exodus from Egypt toward the land God was giving them. William offers the ark, then, as metaphor for the mystery hidden in the Godhead from all ages and finally revealed in the incarnation of Christ. This is momentous metaphor. The contents of the Old and New Testaments identify this mystery, once hidden but now revealed and accessible to all people. This great wonder of God, the ark, says William, is the two natures of Jesus, human and divine, comprising the fullness of Christ's revelation, his mercy, and the dignity of his eternal priesthood.[11]

Exodus describes the ark as having two cherubim sitting in adoration on its top. For William these two cherubim, supported by the ark, represent every aspect of humanity and creation as supported and sanctified by the incomprehensible mystery of the incarnation, represented by the ark. The cherubim's location, hovering above and overshadowing the mercy seat, is not due to their preeminence, but to a need to be supported and carried by what is in the ark. This relationship shows, William says, that all humanity and creation are supported and sanctified by every charm of heaven that has been poured out upon the earth in the Person and incarnation of Jesus Christ.[12]

The Obedience of Charity and the Charity of Obedience:
Meditation 6.18

William now initiates a dual combination of obedience of charity and charity of obedience to elucidate the overwhelming depth of

11. Origen, In Num 10.3.

12. Many sources contribute to this paragraph, e.g., Origen, In Num 10.3; Augustine, En in Ps 79.3; Cassian, *Collationes* 14.10; Gregory I, *In euangelia* 14.10; Isidorus, *Etymologiae* 7.5.22; Gregory of Nyssa, *Vita Moysis*. In addition, William here quotes and refers to Heb 9:4.

the incarnation of the Son of God, "when he himself rendered to [the Father] a most pure obedience of charity for our salvation, and to us the charity of his obedience (Med 6.18). Charity, selfless love, is the Holy Spirit, the Spirit of Unity between the Father and Son. Their triune unity or one will is expressed in the second chapter of the Letter to the Philippians. The Second Person, the Son, did not cling to equality with his Father, but accepted human nature, and accepted it to an extreme extent, even to death on the cross. In his human nature, the Second Person was able to give perfect and supreme obedience through his selfless love to the Father. By means of this perfect and supreme obedience, God incarnate as selfless love, *your love,* is poured forth upon all persons who are willing to enter into the divine mystery. Human obedience can now assume its own divine dimension of selflessness in love, the charity of obedience.

This manner of obedience has a divinely sanctifying element. The combination of obedience and charity in Christ constitutes the contemplative ascent into heavenly participation for those who are living a life in Christ. This ascent is a road well worn[13] by the footprints of the apostles, martyrs, and all the saints, who by the example and grace of charity received from Christ have loved Christ to the extent of disregarding themselves, not fearing even to lay down their lives for Christ.[14]

Obedience of charity and charity of obedience, the embodiment of *your love* as lived in one's own life, has the divine power to penetrate and transform a life focused on images and imagination, removing the possibility that such images might become ends in themselves in personal devotions—idols, in William's terms. In opposition to such idols of the imagination, obedience of charity and charity of obedience are able to convey a person beyond them into the profundity of Trinitarian life! This development is

13. Gregory the Great described Saint Benedict's ascending into heaven by a magnificent road (*Dialogues* 2.37).

14. "Lives" = *animas,* the word with which William denotes a definite physical or bodily dimension in laying down one's life for Christ. See also Augustine, Civ Dei 14.28.

conceivably the nearest one can arrive at a contemplative grasp of Trinitarian divinity.

The Pierced Heart of Jesus: *Meditation 6.20–22*

William emphasizes that the dynamic interaction between obedience and charity as selfless love at the heart of the life of Christ climaxes in Christ's passion and death. The crucifixion so reveals the comprehensiveness of the incarnation that William pinpoints it in the piercing of Christ's side, the opening of his heart, the very depths of his soul as the seat of divine mercy, the fullness of God. The pierced side of Jesus, his open heart, is thus, he says, the ark, the open door into heaven.[15] It is significant here that the risen Lord Jesus invites the apostle Thomas to enter him by inserting his hand into the pierced sacred heart and his finger into the pierced hands, thus entering into his crucifixion mystically as a *concrucifixus*, the glorified open door to heaven. The profundity of this invitation to enter is that the crucified and risen Christ is the Way, the Truth, and the Life for all people. Such is the penetration of the Divine Person of Jesus, whose secrets are now accessible through the sacraments that flow from him.

Beholding the fullness of this revelation, William addresses Christ: "O Good Father, Delightful Brother, Charming Lord, you are whatever is good, delightful, and gentle, in whom so much goodness abounds" (Med 6.22).

A Yearning to Rejoice with the Saints:
 Meditation 6.23–27

William now passionately pleads that Christ will open for him an entrance into heavenly intimacy with Christ, although he declares that he does not deserve its full effects. Having received

15. Augustine, Adnot in Job 120.2.

some inkling, only glimpses, of this divine magnificence with its exaltation and praise, he desires it intensely. Despite having heard of it,[16] he is still sad that he is not permitted to enter permanently, and he prays that his rejoicing now may be similar to the rejoicing in heaven. He yearns for intimacy with the denizens of heaven so as to share in their life of rejoicing there: "May I become known to your citizens, not those rejoicing here, but like *all those rejoicing* and dwelling there" (Med 6.23).[17] For to share in the rejoicing that takes place there would indicate that he is in some degree already in heaven and beholding the face of God, the source of this divine exultation.

William now expresses a rather curious thought. Being denied entrance through this open door makes him sufficiently sad to feel so tired of life that he would find it pleasing to descend into hell—but still, to descend there alive, for to descend there dead would leave him unable to render praise to the triune God. When he finally observes what is happening in hell, though, he prays not after all to descend into hell.[18]

All these experiences, insights, and glimpses into the fullness of Christ have made William eager and impatient: "Lord, my heart is

16. *Subaudire:* understanding something from hearing a voice, but not necessarily hearing individual words.

17. *innotescam ciuibus tuis, illis non laetantibus sed sicut laetantibus omnibus habitantibus illic.* Although Bruno the Carthusian's commentary on Ps 86 uses identical language to say that persons who glory here below in a good conscience are like those who are glorying in heaven, his idea is the opposite of William's, as Bruno's word *like (sicut)* expresses similarity, not shared experience. A certain Oddo Astensis uses *sicut laetantium* to express that our rejoicing in this life is "like" that rejoicing in heaven, that is, similar to heavenly rejoicing (Oddonis Astensis, "Expositio in Psalmos: Expositio Psalmi LXXXVI," PL 165:1247). I am indebted to Sr. Grace Remington for this observation.

18. See William of St Thierry, *The Golden Epistle: A Letter to the Brethren at Mont Dieu*, trans. Theodore Berkeley, intro. J.-M. Déchanet, The Works of William of St. Thierry, CF 12 (Kalamazoo, MI: Cistercian Publications, 1971), 21, n. 74. Descending alive enables one to reflect on the pains of hell and be converted.

restless and impatient for you" (Med 6.25).[19] In this life he can go only so far in an ascent experiencing the joys of heaven. Set afire, he asks to be able to proceed further so that heaven's members will recognize him when he is permitted to enter permanently.

In all of this William echoes early Cistercian teachings, which centered the monastic way of life around the pursuit of ascent into God, seeking to live in this life as do the saints and members of the household of God already rejoicing in eternal life. William, however, is particularly mindful of the bond between eternity and time in the eternal now (Med 6.26).[20]

As a result, he takes an audacious stance and makes a mighty request to see God face to face. This stance and request merge into a profound prayer:

> O, if at any time or other I will have heard, *Enter into the joy of your Lord,* may I so enter as never to come out from there. *Lord, you are mighty and your truth surrounds you.* Bring to perfection what you have made! Give what you have promised! (Med 6.27)

19. See Augustine, Conf 1.1.1.

20. The language of twelfth-century Cistercian ascension theology drew from a number of scriptural motifs for its expression. So for example, Bernard of Clairvaux describes his monastery as the heavenly Jerusalem and his monks as Jerusalemites; Aelred of Rievaulx writes of living stones, building up the Temple of Jerusalem and rising up as sacred incense; and Helinand of Froidmont exhorts his monks to climb the mountain with Christ and to raise up within themselves a temple of living stones, becoming bearers of Christ like Mary, his holy mother. In the case of these and other Cistercian exegetes, the goal remained the same: by interpreting Christian Scripture and tradition, they sought to transform the monastery into a sacred space, bridging the gap between the human world and the realm of God, so that they and their brethren might ascend as living stones built up, a spiritual house, a holy priesthood (see Baker, "Be You as Living Stones").

Boldness in Seeking God's Face: *Meditation 7.1*

William is aware that his charity and humility are still insufficient to stand in the presence of God, face to face, yet he still desires to be united with God in the divine depths. Nonetheless, he is bold enough to declare his desire to see God face to face: "*My heart has spoken to you: My face has sought you. Lord, I will search for your face. Do not turn away your face from me. Do not avoid your servant in anger*" (Med 7.1). His words here demonstrate *parrhesia*, "personal assurance or boldness," as found in the New Testament and in Greek mystical doctrine.[1] Although he is aware that because of his own injustice he ought to flee from the justice of God, he will not turn his face from God's face, because God knows that William wants to love God and to love nothing other than God.

William is coming to realize the importance of two elements in his life that support his boldness in wanting to see God face to face: humility and ardent charity, selfless love. In this passage he shows his growing humility and selfless love coalescing into a profound reverence before the risen and glorified Lord Jesus, following the example of the apostle Peter, who declared to Jesus, *You know that I love you* (John 21:15). William too declares, though with more humility, "You know that I want to love you" (Med 7.2).

Two Aspects of Humility: *Meditation 7.2–4*

William's previous monastic training has enabled him to embrace and cultivate the humility that is contempt for one's own

---

1. *Parrhesia* "to speak openly, truthfully, candidly," and especially "boldly or with boldness." Some form of this word is used about forty times in the New Testament, and it was carried over into early Christian writings.

excellence. He sees that as long as he acclaims his own excellence, in however small a matter, he is not really humble. He is familiar with Benedict's definition of pride at the beginning of the Rule, that any form of self-exaltation is pride.

William also strives to embrace and cultivate another feature of humility, that is, an authentic way of assessing self-knowledge. If he is to be judged according to what he knows about himself, he says, "then it is all over with me," as "I have put out my foot into the justice of your judgment" (Med 7.4). On the other hand, if God judges this boldness to be virtue and if William's sins are always present to God, William considers himself to be not after all lacking in humility. Meanwhile, when he focuses on better things, the filthy face of his sins so thrusts itself before the eyes of his mind that he loathes himself on account of them. This ignominious face, the filthy face of his sins, he says, is the face of his conscience.

This face does not, however, lead William into despair, as it is necessary for participation in God and for its own transformation. It leads him to despise everything, including his unwitting pursuit of trivial honors[2] and indeed his very life, while he all the more ardently desires to see the face of God. This fusion of the humility that is the opposite of self-exaltation and the humility of authentic self-knowledge is ready to receive the "illumination of your [God's] countenance" (Med 7.5). So William now seeks to be receptive or enlightened by the goodness of the divine countenance, which draws his conscience.

William makes it clear that God's gift to a humble person is ardent charity, selfless love. As the Rule of Benedict says in chapter 7, the relationship between charity and humility results in an ardent charity that casts out fear.[3] Such charity is a manifestation of divine essence, *your love*, and is a gift from God. William declares his great desire to love God in this authentic manner, not caring what

---

2. Bernard says some of the same things; see Ep 42.19; Hum 1.2.
3. RB 7: "Ad charitatem Dei perveniat illam."

kind of vision he has of himself so long as he can see God. Consequently, he does not flee from the face of God. As his humility fosters confidence, he professes himself to be a friend of God. He reflects that while Moses, the apostle Paul, and the beloved disciple, all friends of God, were not allowed to see God face to face, King David writes so frequently and familiarly of God's countenance and face that he must on occasion have experienced it.

David, William notes, affirmed that his decisions came from the experience of the divine face and that he was filled with joy in anticipation of beholding it, even declaring that his people walked in the light of the divine countenance. The fact that the psalms of David convey this grace of walking in the light of the divine countenance gives William hope. So, considering Moses, Paul, and David, he develops a concept of the face of God that guides him in his contemplative ascent, so that his decisions, joy, and walking may also come from the divine face.

Signs of the Divine Face: *Meditation 7.6–8*

Up to this point in the *Meditations* William has been presenting a highly nuanced understanding of truth. He has explained knowledge of God's truth as seeing both the divine countenance, that is, God's goodness, and the divine face, what God is—*caritas, your love*—as encompassed in divine foreknowledge and divine predestination. Human truth, then, he says, is found in embracing and acknowledging every aspect of one's self in the presence of God's truth. It thus behooves William to display his own good will in his own countenance and face, so to embrace God's truth, for good will is opposed to self-will.

William now further considers David's words about God's countenance and face,[4] recalling for instance that in the Psalms David

4. The Latin Vulgate's psalms uses *facies,* "face," some sixty-six times, and *vultus,* "countenance," some twenty-five times in reference to the divine face.

beseeches God *"that every one of his decisions may come forth from it*, and he anticipates being *filled with joy from your face."* William recalls that David pronounced "a blessing on the *blessed people who know rejoicing,"* and that he declared, *"Lord, they will walk in the light of your countenance"* (Med 7.7). William thus pleads that David's vision of God's face and countenance may be the source of his own decisions and happiness.

To Know by Not Knowing: *Meditation 7.9–11*

In these paragraphs William has been applying Augustine's ways of seeing God, that is, of understanding and thinking about divinity. They suggest a vision, either *corporalia* or *spiritualia*, rising from mental images or from some type of thought that shapes a person's decisions and contours a way of living. In the following paragraphs, however, William attempts to articulate the inexpressibility of such a vision in words and images. Remembering that the face of God—what God is—is the divine essence, and that the countenance of God is God's goodness, he perceives the importance of the means of attracting a person to God.

William explains that one kind of knowing God is a highly intimate experience that comes from above, a pure gift from God, a kind of knowing that Augustine calls *intellectualia*. This kind of knowing is pure grace: no person can bring it about. It is a way of seeing God that enables one to comprehend something about God, to experience insight into divinity. But this insight is incapable of being expressed in words, thoughts, or images, for God gives it to each person as an individual gift, not to be shared. It is a transforming moment in one's life, a participation in one or another aspect of revelation given through Jesus Christ. It overcomes the general incomprehensibility of God, as William had declared it in the first words of the *Meditations:* *"O the Depth of the Wisdom and Knowledge of God! How unfathomable are God's judgments, and how incomprehensible are God's ways! For who has known the mind of the Lord, or who has been the Lord's counselor?"* (Med 1.1).

After long urgent efforts to reach through that divine incomprehensibility, William now returns to Moses, whom he now understands as exemplifying the knowing of God by not knowing:

> there is another face and another countenance of your knowledge. Moses was told concerning this, *You will not be able to see my face, for no person will see me and live.* In this life, sight or knowledge of your divine majesty is better known by not knowing, and to know something by knowing the ways in which one does not know it, this is the highest summit of knowledge in this life. (Med 7.9)

Remarkably, then, the very impermeability of human ignorance and human blindness—human inability to comprehend God—gives those who are truly seeking God some inkling of the mystery of the Godhead. Furthermore, William declares, addressing God, that God's hiding place in human nature, a form of God's divine presence in persons, is found precisely in the human inability to comprehend God: "O Lord, . . . *you made the darkness* of our ignorance and human blindness *the hiding place* of this face" (Med 7.10).

William earlier presented incomprehensibility as one of the seven ways in which people are like God,[5] kinds of likeness between God and his human creatures that give some possibility of participating in God. For while God's ways are incomprehensible to the human mind, those who examine that incomprehensibility can come to a glimpse of the divine nature that created them to its image and likeness and thereby both appreciate and enter into some degree of participation in the divine nature (Med 3.12).

Another way of expressing this participation is that since the human person is the image of the incomprehensible God, it stands

5. David N. Bell, *Image and Likeness: The Augustinian Spirituality of William of Saint Thierry*, CS 78 (Kalamazoo, MI: Cistercian Publications, 1984), 119. The seven ways are unity, ubiquity, royalty, dignity, stability, liberty, and incomprehensibility.

to reason that people are incomprehensible to themselves.[6] It is a way of seeing God as God is. As individuals experience their own incomprehensibility, they are able to come to some understanding of divinity. For while divinity is certainly not incomprehensible to itself, human incomprehensibility can recognize the incomprehensibility of divinity, so becoming able to taste and experience the sweet gentleness of the divine majesty (Med 3.12). Even here and now people are able to know in what way they do not know. This knowing by not knowing—as seen in Moses—is an approach that fosters a contemplative and quiet peacefulness in the divine presence.

These paragraphs, which fall at the center of the meditations, are an exquisite and highly nuanced presentation of mystic darkness and of knowing by not knowing. Stepping backward so as to reconsider and build on where he has already been, William uses this reconsideration of the role of the divine incomprehensibility in human knowing to present yet another characteristic of the bonding between eternity and time, considering human relationship with the saints and their continued responsibility for human life with the image of the tabernacle-tent (*tabernaculum*). While the highest knowledge of God is in the depths of divine darkness, and shared with persons through their own incomprehensibility, the tabernacle-tent, as William presents it, is composed of the saints' surrounding divinity in brilliant light, because they have been enlightened by Christ. They have blazed and shone forth in Gospel splendor, and their example is thus able to enlighten and set ablaze persons still living on earth:

> O Lord, although *you made the darkness* of our ignorance and human blindness *the hiding place* of this face, still *your tabernacle-tent* [*tabernaculum*] *surrounds* you—those resplendent saints of yours who once lived. Sharing the intimate companionship [*contubernium*] of your own light and fire, they blazed and shone, *enlightening and setting others*

---

6. William expands this idea in Nat corp 72–73 (CCCM 88:128–29; CF 24:133).

ablaze by their word and example. And they declared to us
the festal joy of this knowledge of you, coming unexpectedly
in the life to come where we will see you as you are, or face
to face. (Med 7.10)

This vision of God, the festal joy of knowing and participating in
God, is made possible by the intimacy the saints shared with Christ
while still living on this earth. William introduces a paradoxical
nuance into the discussion by using the word *contubernium*[7] to
portray the intimacy saints had with God in their human life.
Sharing such intimacy with God's own light and fire, the saints
blaze and glow, setting an example and encouraging those still on
earth to understand that enlightenment by God is possible through
participation in God.

The saints' participation in the flashing splendor of divine truth,
William declares, has illumined the earth's orb. People of good will
and good zeal who are receptive to this manifestation of divinity
in the lives of the saints may profit from and rejoice with them,
enabled to see and accept God's working in any aspect of their
lives. But those who do not make this step forward, who love
another category of darkness more than the light, are shaken up
and thrown into confusion as they walk, circling the center of their
own truth without ever entering into it, always remaining on the
perimeter of their own truth (Med 1.9; 11.25). As Origen explained
it, "Those who see . . . see more clearly, but for the blind, they
remain in their darkness."[8]

The Implication of Being Illumined: *Meditation 7.11*

In his passionate desire to progress and to rejoice by being
wisely illumined, William concludes this meditation with a prayer

---

7. *Contubernium* (Med 2.6) is the term for military tents on a campaign where
six to eight soldiers live in close relationship to one another.
8. Origen, Com in Cant 2.20.

celebrating God's gift of vision to those living in darkness, in the words of John the evangelist:

> O Wisdom of God and Light of Truth, when you came into the world, you through whom the world was made, *you enlightened every good person coming into this world, yet the darkness has not embraced you. On the other hand, to as many who have received you* and the light of your truth, *you gave the power to become the children of God.* (Med 7.11)

Good Will, Good Zeal: *Meditation 8.1–2*

As William begins the next meditation, he continues to pray intimately, now moving from the general celebration of God's gift to all those who seek him to a declaration of his own longing to see God's face, implicitly identifying himself with the bride of the Song of Songs:

> *O Sun of Justice*, illuminating all *with the light of your countenance* and the splendor of your truth, you invite your spouse, whoever she may be, saying, *Show me your face, my sister, my spouse.* And immediately, a person of good will, to whom is announced the peace from heaven—who is the brother of Christ, whose soul is designated his sister—desires just as she is to *appear this way before you in your holy place, and to see light in your light.* (Med 8.1)

Invoking God in one of his favorite expressions, *O Sun of Justice*, William requests to be illumined in seeing the face of God, that is, to be allowed to show God his own face. He perceives God as addressing him as sister, spouse, and brother of Christ: a person of good will who desires nothing other than to be in the presence of God, ready to respond to the gracious divine invitation to contemplative union. To be illumined with splendor from Divine Light, William says, in the rays of the Sun of Justice, entails giving God one's good will and good zeal. These comprise one's face. Good and zealous persons long to show their faces to God in all humility and boldness: to appear before God.

Every such person who stands before the Sun of Justice has a face searching for the face of divine mercy, William suggests. Sinners who desire goodness will run to meet the Sun of Justice, with their own faces of justice revealed through facing the truth about themselves. As William earlier explained it, one's own truth is an accurate self-knowledge, allowing oneself to avoid circling around the truth of oneself (Med 1.9). Entering into one's center is a matter of accurate self-knowledge. There the divine face encounters one's own, because the just Lord loves justice and truth. However, the unblushing sinner flees the truth, and therefore rushes headlong into God's most furious justice.

The human soul has as many faces as it has affections, all of which stand in the presence of this Sun of Justice. Divine truth entertains all of them, adapting itself to all of them while itself remaining unchanged. The face of a humble person presents the truth about itself, as does the face of a sinner presenting his truth. Truth and mercy become operative when the truth of divine justice and the truth of human justice meet in the affirmation of a just soul receiving mercy. Justice involves relating to another person equitably: punishing, acquitting, and giving others their rights and proper due. Thus a person and God relate to one another in justice, as the person confesses truthfully, and God rightly has mercy. Mercy and justice meet in the divine presence.

The Kiss of Truth and Mercy: *Meditation 8.3*

William explains a further feature of this development: the seeker's encountering of God's truth and mercy. As he presents it, the countenance of a devout soul offers the kiss of an authentic, truthful confession, and the Sun of Justice receives it with the kiss of peace. Truth and mercy thus become operative, with the truth of divine justice and the truth of human justice meeting in the affirmation of a just soul receiving mercy. William calls this meeting the kiss of peace between humanity and divinity. He understands it as initiating a new dimension of intimacy with Christ.

The Passion of Christ as a Contemplative Spousal Kiss:
Meditation 8.4–5

William now adds a distinctive dimension to his discussion of the passion of Christ, introduced by the metaphor of a kiss. With this sign of an appropriate physical and spiritual union between people,[1] he establishes the concept of an intimate and contemplative union with Christ. Although he articulates this union in terms of images, both corporeal and mental, he also transcends them, revealing a profound union of spousal intimacy in the embrace of a person crucified with Christ, a *concrucifixus.*

William here inserts Christ's passion into the language of spousal intimacy, showing the passion itself to be the kiss of bridegroom and bride. The intimacy implied with this language flows from the Christ's union of divinity and humanity in his incarnation. This mystical intimacy ushers the reader into the suffering and abuse that the divine face sustained in his passion. William's foundation for this perception is chapter seven of the Rule of Benedict, which teaches that radical humility is a way to suffer and die with Christ and so to share in his resurrection (Col 3; Phil 2:6-8). In this passage of the *Meditations,* where William explains the divine face as what God is, he identifies the divine face as God incarnate, he who did not hesitate to set aside divinity in order to bond intimately with humanity, so suffering even the death on the cross, the great Paschal mystery, to achieve that bond.

In this context of the mystical marriage, William shows the effect of the passion on humankind, explaining that Jesus' face underwent the passion so that the human face could appear lovely and beautiful in his sight. The logic of William's explanation is

---

1. William explains the meaning of a kiss in Cant 30 (CCCM 87:33; CF 6:25–26), identifying the Bridegroom as the Incarnate Word. Bernard of Clairvaux also discusses this passage in Sermon 2 of his sermons on the Song of Songs (CF 4:9–15).

that the human face would be unable to appear before the face
of divine justice had Jesus not suffered in innocence for humans.
Thus William declares the marriage of the divine face with the
human face to be Jesus' innocence and his sufferings in buying
human salvation:

> This is a kiss of a bridegroom and bride. That her face may
> be found worthy of your kiss, O Lord, your face was spat
> upon. That hers may appear lovely and beautiful, your face
> is made black and blue by being slapped with human hands
> and blows from rods. That hers may appear exquisite and
> beautiful before your eyes, your face was *drenched with dis-*
> *grace* before human eyes. Why not? For over and above all
> this, you have prepared for her a bath in your most precious
> blood, wherein she may be cleansed. (Med 8.4)

William cultivates this spousal intimacy with Christ as an all-
embracing embrace, with a bodily feature. He presents the passion of Christ in its power to transform the human body—in this
case William's—so that he may live appropriately as the spouse
of the Crucified. By the power that comes from Christ's suffering
in each part of the human body, the face, hands, feet, eyes, ears,
heart, and even death receive the grace of being used in following
Christ. William sums it up: "This is the kiss of your sweetness to
your spouse. This is the embrace of delight for your friend" (Med
8.5). This embrace has the power to transform not only individuals but whole groups of those whom Christ loved: "Publicans
and sinners, whose fellow dinner guest and friend you became,
were drawn tightly together in this embrace. Present there are the
converted harlot *Rahab, Babylon that knows you, strangers, Tyre,*
and the black Ethiopians" (Med 8.5).[2]

Implicit in this discussion of the passion is William's understanding that divine truth and the divine face are present in the

2. Augustine, En in Ps 86:6.

incarnation of Christ and his life as revealed in Scripture and tradition, especially in his passion, death, and resurrection as both the quintessence of *your love* and the bonding between human truth and divine truth. All who contemplate and enjoy divine truth itself expressed in the life of Christ, revealed in Scripture and tradition, will walk in its light, arranging their steps and all their dealings according to the declarations of this divine light, and be caught in Christ's embrace. Knowledge of God's truth—both perceiving the truth and living the truth—is God's face illuminating a human face. For the entire life of Christ as revealed in Scripture and experienced in tradition and the liturgy can open and prepare a person for the experience of truth, with its understanding from above that is beyond images and thoughts. This experience of truth becomes the defining moment for the meeting of the faces of human and God, shaping the lives of those who truly seek God's face and countenance.

The Sacred Heart as Hiding Place: *Meditation 8.6*

Continuing, still contemplating Christ's passion, William demonstrates his devotion to the wounded side and pierced heart of Jesus, the place where Jesus draws one into intimacy. Now he asks, "Lord, where do you draw those whom you embrace[3] and clasp close to you if not to your heart?" Here in this place, one rests protected for the time between this first and last coming; his Sacred Heart is the hiding place, the most secret place of spousal intimacy with the Sun of Justice. And William goes on to celebrate all those who have found rest here, returning again to the darkness and incomprehensibility of God: "Blessed are they *whom you have hidden in the hiding place* of that hidden place, *in the depths of your heart, that they may be covered over with your embrace from*

---

3. "Your embrace" = *scapulis tuis,* your shoulder-blades or shoulders.

human turmoil."[4] With *they,* William repeats and expands the communal reference in the previous paragraph to make it clear even while celebrating the individual's intimacy with Christ that a community of Christians may also receive the divine kiss, the intimate gift of the incarnation.

Those whom Christ has embraced by his passion, who are not grumbling in discontent about their life's circumstances, are joyfully safe in Christ's heart: "*hidden in the secret place* of your heart, charmingly sleeping and rejoicing in affectionate anticipation *in the midst of the chosen lots,*[5] the merits of a holy conscience and anticipation of your promised reward, neither lacking because of faint heartedness nor grumbling because of impatience." In the Rule, Benedict presents grumbling as a serious vice; William here inverts Benedict's warning to define a person who is free from grumbling as one who is embraced by Christ, sleeping in his heart, in spousal union.

Ruminating on the Passion: *Meditation 8.7*

Grumbling, on the other hand, would prevent or destroy such an affectionate union. The remedy, William shows, is to meditate on Christ's passion. And at this point he initiates another prayerful practice, of continual rumination on the passion. Such ruminating,

---

4. William's Latin is rich with word play: *In abscondito absconditi illius abscondisti.*

5. "in the midst of chosen lots" = *inter medio cleros.* This may refer to what follows, William's celebration of the merits of a holy conscience and anticipation of the promised reward. Just a little later, in Med 8.13, William uses the phrase somewhat more clearly, referring to the outcomes that he knows await: "the destiny of death and life, of damnation and redemption, of anger and grace." Bernard sees the lots here as referring to the two comings of Christ (S 4 for Advent 1 and 4). In his Sentences, lots are a community bonding (Sent ser 3.108), or the Old and New Testaments (Sent ser 3.109). In SC 51.10 they refer to love and peace as the presence of Christ.

he says, brings about a deep cleansing of one's spirit and an intense affectionate devotedness to Christ, an idea he shows as inspired by Leviticus 11:3, which lists ruminating animals as clean animals, worthy of sacrifice.[6] William infers from that passage that one must be pure to enter into the passion and, further, that ruminating on the passion cleanses one's depths and so one's outward behavior:

> Like your clean animals, we bring it [the passion] up again from the depths of memory into our mouths, so to speak. Always ruminating with a new intensity of ardent devotedness in a new and unending service of our own salvation, we sweetly store up again in this same memory what you did for us, what you suffered. (Med 8.7)

William's reflection is a superb analysis of Cistercian *memoria Dei*, memory of God, as a transforming force of the spirit through commingling with the spirit of Christ. *Memoria Dei* is understood as the place where God dwells innately in a person. Remembering the passion of Christ—in fact, remembering the entire life of Christ as presented in the Scriptures—develops one's *memoria* in two ways, reshaping one's way of thinking so that one's life may be reshaped in Christ,[7] and drawing or carrying one into one's rightful place in eternal happiness.

William continues to elaborate on the metaphor of spousal embrace with its kiss, noting that those who embrace and kiss are affectionately filled with each other's fragrance. So he earnestly prays that the depths of his spirit may be completely changed into the charm and sweetness of Christ's spirit: "those who more affectionately kiss one another more affectionately mingle their spirits with one another. They are filled affectionately with each other's fragrance" (Med 8.7).

6. Animals worthy of sacrifice ruminate and have a divided hoof.
7. *In Christ* is a common expression throughout all Paul's epistles.

He speaks more explicitly about this commingling of spirits in his treatise on *The Song of Songs*:

> A kiss . . . is expressed not only by a union of bodies using the mouth, but even by a union of spirits from a mutual touching. . . . Furthermore, he extends to his Bride, the faithful soul, and impresses on her this same kiss when entrusting to her from the remembrance of common benefits her personal and unique joy, pouring into her the grace of his own love while drawing her spirit to himself and pouring his into her so that they may mutually be one spirit.[8]

In the *Meditations*, however, William goes beyond the commingling of spirits in the kiss of the bridegroom and bride, identifying it with the Paschal mystery, the Eucharist itself:

> Yes, pour into me your entire spirit, which is entirely fragrant, so that because of your charm and your sweetness, my spirit may no longer be foul smelling. O Most Affectionate Lord, may it always penetrate more deeply into me. This is what happens when we do what you commanded us to do *in remembrance of* you. There is nothing more affectionate for the salvation of your sons and daughters. Nothing more powerful can be provided than when we eat and drink the incorruptible banquet of your Body and Blood. (Med 8.7)

William has earlier said that people have many faces, according to their many affections or loves. The union that the Paschal Mystery of Christ effects is a purifying, coalescing, and arranging of these many human faces into one face that is able to enter into mystic union with the face of Jesus, the incarnate God. The eucharistic sacrament is the place and means for this union to unfold in a person's life.

As William continues to discuss the kiss that unites God and those who love him, he also expands on the idea of a transformed

---

8. Cant 30 (CCCM 87:33; CF 6:25).

way of life; as a person's many loves are purified, the person's spirit is refined, sharpening its focus toward Christ. William explores this idea by subtly explaining the bodily transformation that results from a transformation of one's spirit through the paschal mystery. Elsewhere[9] he has addressed the way the body reflects the quality of one's rational life or life in the Spirit—a life lived in accord with one's vocational orientation—endorsing good balance between body and rational life. A well-integrated rational life directly affects the body, becoming evident in a person's behavior and health, through the integration that comes from a deep faith, with love of God and a solid commitment to live this faith and love.

The spousal embrace with its kiss, commingling of spirits, and, especially, *memoria Dei,* are natural movements flowing from *meditatio* on the passion to its presence in the Eucharist. Nothing can be more intimate than the commingling of spirits that takes place in the sacrament of the Eucharist. Like the *Meditations,* William's work *On the Sacrament of the Altar* reveals his profound appreciation for this sacrament, which he envisages as a purification of the human spirit. Nothing more affectionate or powerful can exist than eating and drinking worthily of the banquet of the Lord's Body and Blood.

"When we do what you commanded us to do in remembrance of you" (Med 8.7), writes William, the eucharistic mystery penetrates one's *memoria Dei* and in turn unites one with Christ, so that one becomes bone of his bone and flesh of his flesh (Med 8.8). This union empowers people to manifest Christ's glory in their bodies by their way of life. As Christ prayed to the Father when he was about to enter into his passion that all would be one with him in his unity with the Father, William understands the eucharistic sacrament as the face of the passion, the death and resurrection of Christ, with the unity of wills between the Father and Son. The

9. William, Spec fid 52–54 (CCCM 89A:101–3; CF 15:41–44); Phys an 4 (CCCM 88:126–28; CF 24:131–32).

Eucharist is thus central in the incarnational bonding between earth and heaven.

Delightful Love: *Meditation 8.8–9*

William discerns the prodigious opportunity to be present in both tasting and seeing the charm of Christ in this sacrament. Here the face of Christ is turned to the face of the one who longs for him; this is the kiss of his mouth upon the mouth of the one who loves him. This sacrament is the embrace of his delightful love, reaching to his spouse who yearns for him, saying, "*My beloved is mine and I am his. He shall dwell between my breasts*" (Med 8.9). Now William responds with his own yearning, calling out in the words of the psalmist, "*my heart said to you: My face has searched for you. For if our soul's face does not look for your face, its face is not natural. Rather, it has put on some mask, that of a beast*" (Med 8.9).[10] With the word *natural* William here insists that the soul, created in the image and likeness of God, naturally—innately—seeks the face of God, its Creator, so once again recalling the beginning of the *Meditations*.

The Effects of Christ's Face upon a Human Face: *Meditation 8.10*

The effects of God's presence depend upon the truth, that is, the quality of a person's face coming face to face with Christ. In the presence of the divine face, he says, an enemy finds a furnace, a sinner finds traps, a proud person finds the power with which God resists the proud, and a hypocrite finds the light of truth that he hates. The face of wrath is tailored to sinners. All of these have consciences branded with a face of their own evil.

10. See Boethius, *Consolation of Philosophy* 4.3; John of Salisbury, *Letter* 155.

Christ's face, the integral knowledge of the triune God, imparts the truth that brings forth unrepentant faces, that is, different affections or desires needing purification. William perceives that what is natural to his face is to seek the face of God. He is ready to die—to sin and to self—for such a vision of God, and calling on God, he quotes Job as acknowledging that God had preserved him: "Have mercy, Lord. I would already have died—by what manner of death I do not know—had not *your visitation guarded my spirit*" (Med 8.10).[11] Christ's face seen in his passion and his death on the cross gives the truth that brings forth one's unrepentant faces—its loves and affections needing purification.

Torment of Hell: *Meditation 8.11–14*

The result of not knowing God can be degenerate thought and behavior. Those who are ignorant of God, William asserts, are doomed to eternal disaster, eternal separation from the face of God:

> They forge for themselves from a multitude of sins that strong, that tearful, long chain whose iron links make a charmingly clanking sound for the time being.[12] Painfully pulled tight, they drag their makers down into hell, where no one will ever more *praise you*, O God, where there is no hope, from where there is no exit. (Med 8.11)

The torment of hell, William here declares, is the realization that the enjoyment of God has been lost forever. There is in hell a no greater torment than to be without the vision of God, for hell consists in having been judged guilty of Christ's death, now seeing the face of

---

11. Bernard speaks of the divine visitations of the Word that bring life, not death (SC 57.2; 74.6; 85).

12. Augustine, Conf 8.5.10.

divine wrath: "they will be judged culpable of your blood, which they have trampled underfoot by sinning and not repenting. This is the *face of your fury*" (Med 8.12).

William naturally at this point desires to know where and how he stands before God. What will be his judgment on that last day? "*Where will I be found?*" he asks. In death or life, anger or grace? He calls out, "to be sure, O Truth, I know that I am seeking you, but whether I am truly seeking you, I do not know" (Med 8.13). Finally, then, he prays that he may see how his face looks to Christ's and Christ's to his. He prays for conversion, that the truth of the divine face will bring truth to his human face so that he may know his true self.

William repeatedly in these paragraphs speaks of truth, and of his desire never to lose sight of the center of truth, understood as his own face, and of his wish to know where he really stands in God's presence, so that the truth of the divine face will bring a personal truth to his human face. He knows his need for inner purification. Accordingly, he turns back to the depths of the house of his conscience to re-evaluate his inner self, to touch his misery and his desire to see the glory of God, the face of God—God's merciful look upon him.

William Descends into His Inner Self: *Meditation 9.1–2*

When William descends into this inner self, the house of his conscience as he styles it, he is confronted with such a density and immensity of misery that he appears unable to cope. He strives to advance in seeking God, but he consistently falls back into himself, into this inner darkness. He views his thoughts, desires, and affections as so many faces of who he is, a perception he had expressed earlier in the *Meditations*. In other words, he equates the many aspects of this inner human stream of consciousness with the many faces a person can have. This inner steady movement deep within him has added to his sense of personal instability.

Although William acknowledges that the face of God's goodness is always present looking toward him, he is nonetheless wrapped up in inner turmoil. By means of the Word of God as a light to dispel the fog of his inner blindness, though, he is able to acquire stability and to enter into his gloomy inner house, to discern the source of the darkness that separates him from the light of his heart. He is well aware that he needs to make peace with himself before ascending to the altar of God, the place of God.

Rowdy Thoughts Hinder Inner Peace: *Meditation 9.3–7*

When William enters into himself, what does he find with the assistance of this divine light? A crowd of thoughts—so insolent, so uncontrolled, so wide-ranging, so confused that the human heart that gave birth to them is not adequate to discern them. Straightaway he is overwhelmed by this crowd of wild and rowdy thoughts, thoughts like a plague of flies, he writes. He strives to analyze them, organize them, assign each one its own proper place, but they are flighty, scattering here and there. Control of one's thoughts is a mammoth task, impossible, he discovers. He strives to organize his thoughts to judge them, but they won't permit it. Angry with himself, he takes refuge in his good thoughts, those that are at base mindfulness of God: the *memoria Dei*.

So William shows that the initial step for controlling and organizing one's thoughts is to dissociate oneself from them. Put simply, persons are not their thoughts. Thoughts may take on an identity all their own, an objectivity distinct from the mind they inhabit, and William here appears to characterize them in their objectivity, as actors in his spiritual drama.

One's worst thoughts, William suggests, are unworthy of consideration; they are condemned straightaway by the judgment of conscience, and they receive their sentence without murmuring. The same applies for idle and hateful thoughts, which, as they observe one's sorting out in progress and fearing to interrupt it, disperse or become weaker. As regards thoughts about business and responsibilities, William deals with them reasonably, listening and processing them, then assigning them their proper time and place. They thus recognize themselves as being somewhat ignored, of little value since their purpose has come to an end. Embarrassed to be numbered easily among the idle thoughts, they withdraw.

The process William describes here clarifies the different kinds of thoughts that confront a person and considers how to distribute them. His method is to throw out the unclean ones immediately, and then to do the same with idle and troublesome ones. As for work-related thoughts and those requiring responsible consideration, once he has given them due consideration, they will dissipate and cease to trouble him.

Having accomplished this categorization and dismissal of his thoughts, William is able to go to their source, his affections and desires, and to recognize the need to place a guard over them. The grace of his vocation, with its love and ardent devotedness to Christ crucified, keeps all thought properly in bondage, oriented to its proper place, and at peace. William continually requests from the Lord a fidelity to this grace, praying to regulate his thoughts.

Total Openness in God's Presence: *Meditation 9.8–9*

This inner quiet that William has now reached by achieving the upper hand over his thoughts helps him to enter more deeply into intimacy with the divine presence, to place himself in the hiding place, the truth of the divine face. At this stage of intimacy with God, William has a new ability to lay open to God all the deep places of his conscience, casting off any masking of his inner disgrace and shame. He shows himself to God as naked as he was at creation, exposing all to God, both good and evil. He has at last entered into the center of his personal truth, a vision of his life from his creation onward, as emerges in a magnificent prayer of transparency before God:

> *You have created me in your image.* You have placed me in your Paradise. You gave me by name a place in the midst of the community of your children.[1] From the very time of my impure childhood, *you have imprinted, like a seal upon me, the light of your countenance.* I fled from your Paradise, and instead of the place you had given me, I found a sewer and concealed myself in it. Always I held on to the seal of your countenance in faith and intention,[2] but I rejected it in my behavior. For by following my concupiscence and my heart's vanities, I squandered my adolescence and almost engaged in the way of the flesh. (Med 9.9)

In this review of his life, William recounts the good things that from the beginning God did for him. But despite God's consistent goodness, William characterizes his life as spent hiding from God in a sewer rather than remaining at peace in the place God had predestined for him. He declares that although the seal of the

1. The *midst of the community of your children* may refer to William's baptism and baptismal name.
2. "Intention" = *uoluntate* (CCCM 89:54). *Intention* here fits the context better than the more literal alternative, *will.*

divine face remained in his spirit, his flesh, his actions and behavior, rejected God's enduring goodness towards him.

In this way William presents the struggle between flesh and spirit, understanding spirit as a basic orientation of love for God. This opposition reveals his view that flesh, which is to say the world's abyss, is not the place that reveals God's glory. At the same time, the struggle that he reports indicates that God does not abandon the sinner so long as the human spirit longs for the divine spirit.

Experiences of Alternations: *Meditation 9.10–11*

William now admits that he experiences alternation in his house of conscience, alternation between the times when he forgets God's presence and those when he recognizes what he has done. He declares that these moments leave him utterly exhausted, both physically and mentally.[3] He cries out to God, who immediately rescues him from the lake of this misery[4] and reinstates him in his former state, restoring to him the joy of God's salvation.[5] These experiences reveal not only human frailty but also a sensitivity to God's presence, both of which William views as ways of being transparent in God's presence, demonstrating accurate self-knowledge, which only the divine presence can call forth. While he admits the role of the evil one in causing him to consent to sin, he professes this transparency as his face before God, a face with no hidden corners or recesses. All is manifest. Because God has rescued him, William

3. "utterly exhausted both physically and mentally" = *Cum ad ultimum et corpore deficerem et mente.*

4. A brief anonymous meditation composed around 1135, "In Lacu," includes the phrase *lake of misery.* William's use of the phrase here points to his having arrived at a fairly comprehensive self-knowledge. See Stanislaus Ceglar, "William of Saint Thierry: The Chronology of His Life with a Study of His Treatise *On the Nature of Love*, His Authorship of the *Brevis Commentatio*, the *In Lacu*, and the *Reply to Cardinal Matthew*," PhD dissertation, Washington, DC: The Catholic University of America, 1971, 380–99.

5. Abelard, *Epistle to the Romans* II.4.5; *Explanation of the Apostles Creed.*

is able to declare himself with a certain boldness, *parrhesia*, with its complementary sense of security in being at home in the divine presence. Simultaneously, he shows that he has maintained the basic orientation that has led him into the divine presence. Love, despite its alternations, its ups and downs in his conversion and daily living, does control and finally orient his thoughts towards God. His sins will be forgiven, he understands, if he learns to love much.

Truth, Accurate Self-knowledge, Comes from God's Presence: *Meditation 9.12–13*

William, standing face to face with the Lord, now beholds both his own face of supreme misery and the Lord's face of supreme mercy. Nothing is now hidden from the Lord: this is William's truth. His greatest fear, however, is that he might want to deceive himself. He knows that that desire poses a real possibility, for he knows that he has harmed himself more than the enemy could have harmed him. He must take responsibility for his own life. His face-to-face presentation of himself to God is one aspect of the first step of Benedict's degrees of humility (RB 7). Additionally, its outcome will be unlimited faith and trust in God.

The Fullness of Love Depends on the Fullness of Faith: *Meditation 9.14–17*

With nothing more holding William back from trust and belief in the Lord, he ponders all the possible dimensions of his faith and concludes that he simply believes Christ. He believes because of who Christ is, and he believes in handing himself over to Christ. Nevertheless, he requests that the Lord continue to fill and expand his trust and faith, which he knows to be still inadequate, making this request emphatic by three times repeating a variation of *"I believe in you!*"[6] echoing Peter's threefold profession to the Risen Lord: "You know that I love you." William's equivalent is, "I still believe in you, I hope in you, and I love you, O Life Eternal" (Med 9.15). So he declares that hope flows from faith, and love from hope, testifying that love's quality is integrated with faith's intensity.

William is still endeavoring to follow a loving and undeviating course to God through faith. He claims little knowledge of the good things that exist, though he acknowledges himself to be well versed in the knowledge and the experience of bad things. So he asks to know how much time he has left in his life to gain the knowledge of the good he still lacks, by seeing God face to face: "Have mercy, Lord. Look, *I have run and aimed straight towards you! Arise to meet me and see!* Lord, *make my end known to me, and what are the number of my days, so that I may know what it is that I lack*" (Med 9.16).

While declaring that he stands firm in his faith, then, he hopes to progress further, and he passionately requests the gift of *your love,* the presence of the Holy Spirit, the Spirit of mutual love between the Father and Son that is the trinitarian mystery. He has moved from desiring simply to be in the heavenly fatherland into a plea for some experience of intimate divine love, trinitarian life itself. So he calls out in passionate longing for the face of God and the operating energy of *your love* in his life:

> O Love, O Fire, O Charity, come to us! Be our Leader and Light, the Fire burning and consuming in the repentance of sinners. Be our Paraclete, Comforter, Advocate, and Helper in the petitions of our prayers. Show us what we believe! Whisper within us that for which we hope! Give us a face like the face of God! Let us bring them together so that we can say, *My heart has said to you, "My face has sought you!"* (Med 9.17)

---

6. *Credo te, credo tibi, credo in te.* The Latin verb *credere* can take both the accusative (*credo te*) and the dative (*credo tibi*), a dative of reference.

An Intuitive Vision of God: *Meditation 10.1–2*

The prayer of William that ends Meditation 9 communicates William's awareness that a face-to-face vision with God entails a certain intimate affinity between William's own face and the face of God. The motif that controls the next section of the *Meditations* is the incarnate face of God crucified, to which the operating energy of *your love* leads William. Now he perceives that his vision of *your love* embraces the face of God, that is, the cross of Jesus. This love is thus his own life's personification, his life as *concrucifixus* with Christ. He explains that he has been changed and imprinted with the cross:

> *May it be far from me to glory save in the cross of Our Lord Jesus Christ.* My entire way of life is toward my crucified one. His cross is my glory. My forehead is signed with it. My mind rejoices in it. My life is oriented by it. My death is lovingly blessed by it. (Med 10.1)

He continues with a highly nuanced teaching of this vision.

The prophet Isaiah's vision of God seated high up in the temple, elevated in dazzling light upon a splendid throne, with his train descending to earth and filling the temple, inspires William to report his own vision of God. As William describes it, though, it is not he but the angels who behold God, in a vision embracing both the lofty magnificence of divinity and the majesty of Christ's humanity, descending and embracing all creation. They in turn joyfully communicate this vision to humanity, sharing it by revealing the many manifestations of God's Wisdom contained in the incarnation or human dispensation of Christ.[1] They announce

---

1. The essential revelation of the angels to humankind is the annunciation Mary receives from the archangel Gabriel.

their vision so that those who share in this mystery of Christ, the church of Christ on earth, may spread the news of Christ's dispensation, his incarnation as manifested in his public life and in his passion, death, and resurrection, throughout the universe, to unite all creation in him. The twofold aspect of the divine face that they behold—Christ's lofty divinity and his lowly humanity incarnating divinity—is the manifold or comprehensive wisdom of God.

William at once introduces another slightly nuanced aspect of this vision of God's comprehensive wisdom. He says that the angels are pleased to share their beholding of this comprehensive wisdom of God with the church, but they are unable to share its fullness. It is the glory of the church as the Body of Christ to make known to the heavenly principalities and powers themselves certain aspects of this manifold wisdom of God related to the mystery of the incarnation, as Saint Paul wrote to the Ephesians: *The manifold wisdom of God is made known to the principalities and powers in the heavens through the church* (Eph 3:10).[2] But William adapts these words to his own purpose, by saying that the angels behold divinity in the comprehensive wisdom of God and the mysteries of the incarnation for human salvation:

> May they delightfully contemplate in your wisdom the majesty of your divinity, which beheld what was before and after our epoch and which inserts all this past and future into the now of your eternity. *This wisdom reaches from end to end mightily* and has strewn our epoch, a time of the human dispensation, with your selfless love *charmingly arranging all things* on behalf of the daughters of Jerusalem, souls devoted yet still weak. (Med 10.3)

2. Augustine uses this quotation only three times in all his treatises. The three times are in Gen ad litt, twice in 5.19 and once in 9.18. William uses Augustine's thoughts on Eph 3:10 indirectly, quoting it only once in all his treatises. Bernard seems never to have quoted the verse.

Human nature alone can accomplish the task of making known the diverse aspects of the wisdom of God, for only human nature can participate in the human life of Christ, especially his passion, death, and resurrection. The angels, who lack corporeal bodies, cannot so participate. William desires to see the vision that the angels behold but is unable to do so in this life. Nonetheless, he desires to share in the angels' joy in seeing it.

William recognizes, however, that his desire to ascend directly into the angelic contemplation of God's wisdom is inappropriate: as a human being he must be satisfied by contemplating God's humility as given in his human dispensation. He thus beseeches the forgiveness of the angelic spirits for his presumption: "Therefore, may they pardon us, Lord, even in this: if your love sometimes leads us to the point that we desire to see with them what we love with them. We rejoice with perfect charity with those seeing what we do not as yet merit to see" (Med 10.2).

Earlier in the *Meditations* William has explained that *your love* is the Holy Spirit, the love of the Father for the Son, and the love of the Son for the Father, and that this divine love is the gift God bestows in the depths of one's heart. This divine love, present in persons, can transform and sanctify all their affections. William now turns from his longing to share the vision of the angels to explain another feature of *your love*, the wisdom of God as Christ crucified.

The Bonding Role of This Wisdom: *Meditation 10.3*

Divine wisdom on earth, Christ crucified (1 Cor 1:23-24), is a participation of divine wisdom in heaven, the Father's sending his only-begotten Son. The entire mystery of Christ crucified and glorified is present now, in eternity and in time, because of Christ's selfless love in his divine and human natures, and because of one's participation by grace in this glory of the incarnate God. This ordering of divine wisdom correspondingly orders human life on earth, but in a way befitting weak human faculties. In this life, one cannot contemplate the heavenly glory as the angels can, but through the wisdom of the cross, all people love to be touched and transformed by the humility that Christ assumed in order to be with them, and all love to be freed from the vigorous energy of the flesh in controlling the spirit. William's preparation for the heavenly vision of God is to appropriate through Christ, the face of God, the vision of divine humility. This vision is the bonding between eternity and created time. Entrance into this contemplative bonding comes about through unity of spirit, the human spirit bonding with the Divine Spirit. Furthermore, this bonding is the fundamental meaning of adoring God *in spirit and in truth* (Med 10.3).

Prayer with Images: *Meditation 10.4–10*

William locates the role of images in his affective prayer in the context of spirit and flesh. He recognizes that his own spirit is not prepared to enter into the unity of spirit, so he proposes a manner of praying founded in imagination, a prayer resting on and rising from images of Christ crucified. But such prayer celebrated with ardent devotedness demands that a person pass through any image in order to enter into the truth that the image epitomizes. When one prays in this manner, the grace of the redeeming power of Christ operates in one's soul and life. This is a vital aspect of meditation in the context of a vision of divine wisdom.

This manner of praying also enables one to embrace the profound humility of divinity. It is more than merely thinking about God; it is the means to enter into the now of time and eternity. William's description of the role of imagination in prayer emphasizes the eternal now, using the infinitive form of verbs, so *amplecti,* the infinitive of "embrace," *deosculari,* the infinitive of "to be kissed," and *lambere,* the infinitive of "to lick."[3] These three verbs parallel

---

3. This is the only time William uses the word *lambere* in his treatises. Aelred of Rievaulx uses a form of the verb (*adlambere*) in a similar context, guiding medi-

three present participles: *nascentis* of being born, *pendentis* of hanging, and *resurgentis* of rising:

> For as I have not as yet gone beyond the basics of my sensual imagination, you allow and will be pleased that my soul continues to exercise its weak character with its mental imagination itself vis-à-vis your lowliness, that is, to embrace the manger of the one being born and to adore your holy infancy, to lick the feet of the one hanging on the cross, to hold on to and affectionately kiss the feet of the one rising, to insert a hand into the place of the nails and exclaim, *My Lord and My God*. (Med 10.4)

His repetition of these verbs coalesces into a kind of now that comprises all the events in the life of Christ, the Wisdom of God, with an understanding that rises into a crescendo declaring the passion itself as eternally present, and the eternal nature of Christ at the right hand of the Father.

The human mind inclines to be occupied with physical, corporal objects, the *corporalia,* in Augustine's terminology. Conversely, a meditative single-minded focus on the vision of divine wisdom in the humility of God's human dispensation can allow a human mind or intellect to act according to its more noble qualities through the use of mental images, the *spiritualia*. And with the grace of God, intellectual comprehensions coming from above, the *intellectualia,* provide meaning that is in the nature of an insight, one that defies being put into words. Thus meditative single-minded focus parallels the angelic vision of seeing all things as now in the eternal beatific life, without past or future, in heaven's divine wisdom. In

---

tation on Christ's sweat being like bloody drops during his vigil in Gethsemane: "*suauissimus illas guttas adlambe, et puluerem pedum illius linge*" ("lick up those drops, and lick the dust from his feet") (Inst incl 31; CCCM 1:669). In Cistercian devotional literature, *lambere* is extremely rare in this early period, though it becomes more common in the late Middle Ages (see Brian McGuire, *The Difficult Saint*, CS 126 [Kalamazoo, MI: Cistercian Publications, 1991], 227–49, esp. 247).

the now that bonds heaven and earth, *eternaliter-temporaliter,* one touches this angelic vision of God.

This manner of praying also elevates a person into the trinitarian relationships between the divine persons. As the apostle Paul writes to the Philippians, it was the Father's good will for the Son to become incarnate, suffering crucifixion and then being raised in glory (Phil 2:9-11). The love uniting Father and Son for this triumph is their Holy Spirit. Accordingly, a person praying with a single-minded focus on the incarnate God embraces this Trinitarian mystery. The unfolding dynamic of *your love* prepares one to ascend into unity of Spirit with God. For Divine Wisdom in the humility of his humanity enables one's basic life—soul or *anima*—to be transformed into a mature human life or *animus,* and lifts a mature person devotedly and consistently into seeking the things of God, *spiritus.*[4]

Unity of spirit is the fundamental goal in William's life in God. It is the culmination of the person's contemplative intimacy with the triune divinity. Put succinctly, it is a person's ability to will what God wills, to be one spirit with God and so unable to will anything else.[5] This one spirit is none other than the Holy Spirit, *your love,* who brings about this union. As a person becomes intimately identified with Christ in the humility of his incarnation (Phil 2:5-9), especially in his crucifixion, the Holy Spirit brings about a taste for *your love* that is itself divine. The significance of the Holy Spirit's working is that by grace the person so inspired becomes what the Holy Spirit is by nature, the bond between the Father and Son, their love, unity, sweetness, kiss, embrace, and all that they have in common.[6] This arrangement coming from divine wisdom makes

---

4. Three dimensions of a person, *anima, animus, spiritus,* are systematically developed in William's Ep frat (CCCM 88; CF 12).

5. *Cum fit homo cum Deo unus spiritus, non tantum unitati idem uolendi, sed expressiore quadam ueritate uirtutis sicut iam dictum est, aliud uelle non ualendi* (Ep frat 262; CCCM 88:282; CF 19:95).

6. William, Ep frat 263 (CCCM 88:282; CF 12:95–96).

it possible for one to touch by contemplation the mystery hidden in eternal Triune God but revealed in human time.

William goes on to say that when a person is unable to worship God in spirit according to God's own eternal life, entrance into this mystery of divinity may come in a form not unfamiliar, in a face that one can perceive without any scandal of faith during prayer, even though in this life people are not yet capable of gazing into that brightness of the divine majesty (Med 10.5). William similarly writes in his *Exposition on the Song of Songs*, "Surely it is a matter of devotion to approach God even in this fashion . . . that is, thinking about one's likeness to God, one does not sin."[7] This earthly contemplation prepares one for the contemplation that is to come in heaven.

Significantly, William sees these two contemplations as occurring successively, in tandem. He clarifies that he no longer knows Christ according to the flesh on earth, but according to the glorified flesh at the right hand of the Father (Med 10.6).[8] Accordingly, this type of prayer, carried out in unity of spirit, allows him to ascend into the trinitarian relationship between the divine persons and so to touch divine Truth. In the now that bonds heaven and earth, *eternaliter-temporaliter,* one touches and is transformed by the angelic vision of God, embracing lofty divinity insofar as a creature is capable of doing so, and embracing the majesty of Christ's humility.

This teaching culminates with the twofold aspect of divine wisdom, grounded in Isaiah's vision in the temple, with another forceful image taken from chapter 10 of the Acts of the Apostles, to clarify the effect of Christ's passion in William's life. Recalling the passage in which the linen sheet containing both clean and unclean animals is let down from heaven and shown to Peter, William

---

7. William, Cant 15 (CCCM 87:26; CF 6:14).

8. William's teaching here may reflect Bernard's admonition against knowing only Christ-Flesh and not Christ-Spirit, something he argues in his *Sermons on the Song of Songs,* SC 48:7–8.

offers thanks for this vision: "We give thanks as it lifts us up into heaven, where we who are unclean are likewise cleansed" (Med 10.8). This linen sheet, he goes on to say, is a metaphorical image of Christ's passion, which people have contemplated, seeing in it Christ's love toward them. It lifts them up into ardent devotedness for the highest good, and Christ thereby grants that they may see his face in the saving work of their salvation.

William also here connects the vision of the linen sheet shown to Peter with his larger theme of ascension. A mental image of the passion opening into the truth that cleanses, he says, transforms one's conscience and consciousness into a well-disposed consciousness open to God. Such metaphorical images do not themselves provide understanding, but they transport one into an ardent devotedness through the experience they offer of love and sweetness coming from the person of Christ. Images, William suggests, lead one to look to what is beyond, lifting one into the vision that angels see in heaven. This cleansing by love, with insight into *your love*, conveys the idea of ascent proper to this form of meditation.

The Incarnate Christ as the Open Door to Eternal Life:
Meditation 10.9–12

William goes on to insist that Christ, wounded and crucified, is the door opening into the heavenly realm, and that one who strives to ascend into God by any other way endeavors worthlessly. Those who enter through Christ the door walk on level ground, toward one who has a human nature like their own, so offering them an easy ascent. They come to the Father, to whom no one comes unless through Christ, who says at the threshold of the entrance, *I and the Father are one* (John 10:30). Immediately the Holy Spirit conveys their ardent devotedness into God. Christ then comes and dwells with them not only spiritually but also corporeally, through the mystery, *mysterium* or sacrament, of Christ's holy and life-giving Body and Blood. So, William says, we ascend to God through the incarnation—human via human, because the incarnate one is one with the Father.

William's argument here is that one should not strive for understanding or intellectual grasp of divinity. Rather, real freedom results from the charm of a passionately devoted consciousness centering on Christ's love and on the Father with their mutual love, the Holy Spirit. A passionately devoted consciousness, apprehending the meaning of this mutual love, he says, embraces a divine tenderness: *For God so loved the world that he sent his only begotten Son* (John 3:16) so that we might have life. The cross itself becomes the face of a mind, both Christ's mind and the mind of a *concrucifixus*, bound in ardent devotedness to God. This is the vision to see God as God is.

William goes on to explain that in the sacrament of Christ's passion God is seen face to face, as the cross itself becomes for one meditating in this manner the face of one passionately devoted to the Father. This is the key element in understanding William's approach to meditative prayer, no longer laboring to reach a knowledge beyond the mind's ability, but striving to understand by the tenderness of a passionately devoted consciousness. So William insists that one should not strive to penetrate with human understanding the mystery of God, but to deepen one's ardent devotedness in order to receive the understanding that comes from above.

Images, as William explains, lead the seeker into to the sacrament of the passion, which opens onto the goodness of God—namely, what God has performed for our eternal happiness. When a person experiences that God is good, that is a vision of seeing God face to face. Goodness is the face of God revealed in Christ crucified. This mystery also becomes one's own face as one participates with Christ crucified in one's own way of life, which is the face of a person deeply and passionately in love with God. The cross is the face of Christ; the cross is the face of the person who ardently seeks Christ, so arriving at a face-to-face vision. William powerfully advocates that one sell all one has in order to find and possess God's face in one's heart, one's consciousness: "O, whoever you are! Go, and you will find this treasure hidden in the field of your heart. *Sell all that you have*, even your very self as a perpetual slave *[servum perpetuum]* so that you may possess it by the right of a hereditary possession. Yes, you will be happy, and *all will be well with you!*" (Med 10.12).

William's teaching here is a valuable explanation of the use of images in meditating, showing that the proper use of images of Christ's passion can lead to the experience of God's tender goodness. This, he says, is Christ's face, which becomes both the seeker's face and the face of Christ crucified: a contemplative union. This face of Christ crucified lifts one into an eternal trinitarian dimension of *your love*.

The Theme of Ascent: *Meditation 11.1–3*

William's declaration as he moves forward, "The treasure in your possession is Christ in your consciousness" (Med 10.12), is a far-reaching presentation of his understanding of Christ that leads to a more comprehensive experience of being face to face with God, the cross of Christ wherein is our salvation. He now prays, "God of heavenly powers, turn toward us and show your face, and we will be saved" (Med 11.1). In his reflection on this understanding, he sees that his life's fulfillment will be discovered in this face of God.

The following long portion of the *Meditations,* generally called Meditation 11, may be autobiographical in suggesting phases of William's exterior life. He certainly here presents as autobiographical his discernment of his desire to lay aside his pastoral duties in order to enter the Cistercian Order, his wish for release from abbatial responsibilities to pursue deeper intimacy and union with Christ crucified in his life as a Cistercian monk. We know, of course, that because William was hesitant about this desire, he sought counsel from Bernard, who advised against his desire and refused to accept him at Clairvaux. As a result, William eventually entered the Cistercian abbey of Signy. His inclusion at this point in the *Meditations* of his personal experience contains practical information for a discernment process: both the need to understand one's authentic desire and the power to accomplish it and flourish in it by personal fidelity.

William here records his prayer that God may manifest the divine face—divine selfless love—and that this manifestation will powerfully save him. He knows that he has seen this divine face in the risen Christ, who bears the glorious marks of his passion and death, and that his own heart with its ardent devotedness is properly oriented, yet he perceives himself as nonetheless estranged from the face of God. Of course this experience is normal: as he has written before, the human face has as many façades as it has desires, thoughts, and affections (Med 9.1). An experience of estrangement may arise from a lack of integrity and integration that emerges because of these various façades as one moves into intimacy with God. So William questions himself: is it that he is not genuinely turned to God, or that God simply remains turned away from him? Does God consider him his enemy because of his youthful sins? William is more than willing to do what God commands, he says, so he asks God for an understanding of the divine will and the power to accomplish it.

William here makes a fundamental distinction between the ability to understand and the ability to accomplish. He perceives the presence of a hidden place in the divine countenance, which is the divine goodness attracting him, and he knows that he does not deserve to enter into that hidden place. He declares his intense desire for intimacy with God, although he sees himself as undeserving of God's transforming his life. Nonetheless, he yearns to walk straightforwardly into God's hidden place. So he opens up a new dimension, a new horizon, in his intimacy with God.

The Scriptural Image of Bartimeus of Jericho (Mark 10:46): *Meditation 11.4–11*

Once again, William here employs an image he has used before (Med 3.3), but now with more detail. He continues to interpret his life, likening himself again to a blind person trying to walk straight forward with confidence. Unable to do so on his own because of his blindness, he is led hither and thither, this way and that. He does not know the way forward.

What is remarkable here is that William speaks of his walking forward as a process of ascent: "Wherever I put a foot forward for my ascent" (Med 11.4).[1] Here he echoes an understanding of

---

1. The Latin reads *quocumque assensus mei tendi pedem* (CCCM 89:62). Some thirty-seven times in his writings William uses *assensus*, "concurrence, agreement, approval, a going into, a process of ascent."

divine love that he earlier developed in *The Nature and Dignity of Love*, where he explained that one's love for God is a powerful driving force, giving a vision wherein all creation, all finite and limited creatures, appear as nothing in comparison to God. Accordingly, this vision empowers one to see that all things work together for one's good. Identifying the person in question with the soul, William describes its progress: "The soul . . . advances the more . . . now firmly, steadily, and prudently in her ways and in all her steps, for until now on all sides, prevented by ignorance, doubt, and wavering, she scarcely dared to put forward the foot of ascent to the good."[2] William pleads to the One who is the truth, the way, and the life to come to his support in this ascent into Good, and he records that the Lord does indeed reach out to him, sending an invitation.[3]

In these first paragraphs of Meditation 11 William reports that he now hears the Lord calling for a deeper intimacy. Already a monk, he has left everything because of that call. He has nothing to give to the poor in obedience to Christ's counsel to one who would follow him more intimately. The Lord has given himself in payment to William for his initial offering of himself, completing their mutual exchange. Nevertheless, William vows to investigate further by entering into the secret hiding place of his conscience, to search out any aspect of his life that he has not given to the Lord, and he pledges faithfully to offer whatever he finds to the Lord, because authentic intimacy requires total giving. Surprisingly, however, and possibly shockingly, it is here that William encounters his past sin: "But when I looked for payment from you, you imputed to me the sins of my youth, a long-ago debt. I implore you, Lord, *have patience with me,* for I have no means with which I may repay you" (Med 11.7).

2. *tendere pedem boni assensu* (CCCM 88:194; CF 30:79).

3. This divine assistance appears to be his vocational call to the Cistercian—that is, Benedictine—style of monastic life.

William's inner search causes him to stop, he says, and then to affirm his vision of himself, his face, which, because of his sin, he sees as one with the poor beggar in the Gospel. This vision of himself impels him to cry out to Jesus for mercy. But as he stands, unable to go further, he hears people tell him to be quiet, and Jesus himself seems to pass him by. Then Jesus stops; he asks what William wishes. William responds, *"Lord, that I may see!"* (Med 11.9).

Yet Jesus passes on, leaving William in his darkness and despondency: *"Woe to me that my sojourning is prolonged. My soul has been a sojourner* in the house of darkness too long" (Med 11.10).[4] He remains in the house of darkness, waiting for the Lord to return, attentive with his whole being. He knows that his destiny is in the Lord's hands. And now he recognizes that he must be gathered together, composed, and vigilant, for no understanding, no ability can accomplish God's will. William must remain in the silence of his blindness, waiting with peace for the Word of God to come.

Word of God, the Divine Protagonist: *Meditation 11.12*

Having reached the realization that he must simply wait for God to act for him, William declares that when the living and efficacious Word of God comes to save and transform, it is *"more piercing than a two-edged sword,"* dividing soul from spirit, even to the joints and marrow: *"It is the discerner of thoughts and intentions of the heart. No creature may be invisible in his sight."*[5] With this introduction, William continues to associate himself with the blind beggar sitting beside the road, waiting for Christ to respond. The pathos is powerful.

Everything about William is here nakedly exposed to his eyes, yet despite his sin and despondency, he is intensely aware of the power and role of the Word of God in his life. This self-knowledge,

---

4. Ps 119:5-6; William replaces *houses of cedar* with *house of darkness*.
5. This phrase echoes the opening paragraphs of the *Meditations*.

he understands, is fundamental to divine intimacy and essential to discovering the truth in his own life with its destiny. Nonetheless, he continues to question his own integrity, while the living and efficacious Word of God assists him, continuing to penetrate the depths of his conscience. He finds himself caught in the paradox that the Lord who grants him no response has passed him by, even while the Word works powerfully in his inner depths.

His Total Destiny, the Discovery of God's Truth, Is in God's Hands: *Meditation 11.13–14*

William acknowledges that what he must do to discover the Divine Truth is to reach self-knowledge, and he is determined to allow nothing to hinder his investigation. In his preliminary presentation of the *Meditations*, he had understood Divine Truth to be twofold, with truth embracing what God has predestined for each person, truth as the actual life that persons shape for themselves through their choices and the consequences of those choices (Med 1.7–8). It requires a humility of self-knowledge for people to know and embrace their own truth. This is the framework for William's discernment at this point in his search.

Still sitting quietly in his house of darkness, William questions whether he has done well in believing the Word of God. Reflecting on his monastic and abbatial vocation, he discerns his fidelity against the background of love and of Peter's profession of love for the Risen Lord, which resulted in responsibility to shepherd the Lord's flock. Proof of William's positive answer to his initial question is his certainty that he has manifested his love of the Lord as a good shepherd to his community. While his explicit concern here is his fidelity to his community as abbot, the underlying question is that of any person's fidelity in vocation or call from the Lord in the dimension of love. A fundamental element in this concern is the discernment of the quality of love required by one's vocation.

Scrutinizing Intention, Thoughts, Soul, and Spirit: *Meditation 11.15–33*

With his whole person dedicated to the love of Christ, William proceeds with his discernment of God's truth and of his own future, scrutinizing his intention, thoughts, soul, and spirit. He carries out a thorough and methodical review of his reason for wanting to embrace the contemplative life of Cistercians, asking himself why he wants to make this move if his life is going well as a Benedictine abbot.

Intention: *Meditation 11.15–20*

As demanding as it is to be a good superior of a monastic community, William recognizes it as still insufficient, because it is simply the superior's responsibility. As any superior is challenged in unexpected ways to provide for community members, he must do it well. As an abbot, William sees that he has done well and that he is still in sufficiently good health to continue in this service. At the same time, however, he understands that it is not enough to govern by word alone. Unsurprisingly, he sees that setting an example by behavior and way of life is most important. What has compromised his abbatial service and monastic life, he now sees, is the current level of exterior demands that he encounters in his ministry. These requirements draw him away from a balanced interior, from the ability to seek in the depths of his heart for the authentic truth about himself. He thus judges his intention to enter the Cistercian Order to be valid, in accord with his search for truth and intimacy with Christ.

William goes on to develop the details of what he is being required to do in response to the social demands of his life. While the Word of the Lord in the Scriptures demands that one seek first the kingdom of God, with everything else to be seen in its perspective, the practicality of daily life renders that impossible, he explains. Superiors must be skilled in worldly wisdom and elegance of manners rather than finding it sufficient to seek the things of God and care for the soul. Their culture imposes on them needs and demands that expose all kinds of openings for sin, not in accord or focus with the authentic monastic calling. The danger for superiors then is that they may become numbed and insensitive, if not hardened, by fascination with things of no importance, to be drawn out of themselves, and to find themselves involved in trivial matters. William employs several scriptural comparisons from both the Old and New Testaments to make his point that having served as an abbot, now in old age he should be allowed to enter into a life of contemplative prayer. He says that he considers the duration of his abbatial service as adequate, even ample, and that that duration alone ought to permit him as an emeritus to embrace a life with a singular demand of contemplation, being attentive to the Lord's Word.

William thus concludes that much more is now necessary if he is to reach intimacy with the Lord. An abbot's role in his time required that he go forth from himself, that he attend to worldly affairs for the needs of the community. He laments the requirements of this stage of his life, invokes the respect due to a superior (referring to his abbatial ministry as *militia*, a reference to the Roman military service), and declares himself now eager to be freed from the demands upon him so that he may be solely attentive to and enjoy the embraces of the Lord, the Word of God. He discerns his intention as valid and authentic, even citing an ancient Roman military custom as justifying his departure (Med 11.19).

Now William returns to Scripture as justification for his desire, first recalling that when Mary of Bethany sat at the feet of the Lord listening to his words, the Lord commended her for having chosen the better part (Luke 10:39). He invokes two other scriptural sisters in Leah and Rachel, Leah representing the active life and Rachel the contemplative. Jacob deeply loved Rachel and worked for many years to have her as his wife.[6] William, recalling his

6. Gen 30; Gregory, Mor 6.XXXVII.61 (CCSL 143:330–31; CS 257:86–88).

own long years of labor as an abbot, now views himself as entitled to the contemplative life. Additionally, like Jacob, he desires to be permitted to return to his father's house, that is, to the Cistercian contemplative life that he views as his true home.

Joints: *Meditation 11.21–24*

Now William returns from considering his life and choices to resume his discernment, returning to the physical body for his metaphor, using the Latin word *compages,* "joints," as well as "a framework or structure." A physical body cannot function properly if its joints, which are indispensable to its structure, are dislocated; similarly, a house deteriorates if its structure is not preserved, and a community will collapse if not properly sustained. William points to the essential responsibility of a doorkeeper to watch carefully over who goes in and who comes out, and what happens within the community. Otherwise, the community is like a public rest stop along an interstate highway. In that case, what good is its doorkeeper?

Building on these metaphors, William declares that a monastic community, the Body of Christ, has Christ himself as its door. To Christ is obedience due, to him who was obedient to the Father. He is the one who allows persons to enter and leave a community. The clear implication of this metaphor is that having set and maintained his monastic community in order, William must now discern his future in the context of obedience to Christ. His arrival at old age, which played a role in discerning his intention, and now at sickness, is not a reason for him either to remain or to transfer to Cistercian life. Rather, he has heard a call from Christ, and he desires to act in obedience to that call, for obedience is necessary. If the decision is to enter a Cistercian monastery, it is Christ who is opening the door for him and calling him to enter. He must obey that divine call and enter through the door.

Marrow: *Meditation 11.25–30*

William's discernment now engages the metaphor of marrow, the inner substance of bones, essential to producing blood cells and therefore, when healthy, epitomizing strength and vitality. William only rarely uses this metaphor—once each in *On Contemplating God* and *On the Soul*. *On Contemplating God* uses this metaphor more or less to point to the necessity of healthy marrow in supporting life, noting that those who savor the Holy Spirit will experience life in their veins and marrow, which will in turn give strength and vitality to their souls in relationship to God. In *On the Soul,* William uses the term in the context of his era's scientific knowledge, referring to the nourishment of trees when their marrow drinks in air, which in turn assimilates water, and water earth. Both usages situate the emphasis on marrow as essential to vitality and strength.

In the *Meditations,* however, having introduced marrow and joints in *Meditation* 11.12, with regard to the Word of God, which pierces so deeply into a person as to separate soul from spirit, marrow from joints, William approaches the subject from the perspective of Saint Ambrose and the New Testament letter to the Hebrews (Heb 4:12-13). In these works marrow represents the innermost places of the heart, where one's intimate thoughts dwell, what William refers to as one's center of truth. The Word of God, that is, Christ, in whom all things have been created, he who is their very life, reaches discerningly into these depths to bring strength and vitality to them.[7] No secret place can escape the Word of God. To descend into the inner depths of one's heart, one's conscience and consciousness, in order to discern who one is and what one's life is like is one phase of radical self-knowledge. William has reflected extensively on this center of truth to discern the quality of his life.

---

7. Boethius, *De consolation philosophiae* 3.9.

The other phase of radical self-knowledge is for one to ascend into the incomprehensibility of God's foreknowledge and predestination of oneself. This is also to discern one's vocation in Christ and the possibilities or horizons it creates in a perspective of new life. This feature of the center of truth opens up a bond between eternity and time. Thus the center of truth also reveals the profound meaning of what it means to exist in Christ, a phrase Paul uses repeatedly throughout his epistles. Discerning in one's daily life cultivates the stability and consistency one needs to live with strength and vitality. This is the process that William enters so as to discern the change he is contemplating. Unless one so discerns one's center of truth, one may continually walk around it in error, remaining on the circumference of life. William sincerely wants to be in Christ, his life-giving center, the marrow of his life.

What will stability and consistency produce in William's life? These concepts introduce another dimension of discernment: the interdependence between ardent devotedness and activity. Ardent devotedness is found in the center of truth, and exterior activity responds harmoniously to it, in a constant orbit around it. One's entire ardent devotedness is due to God. When God is adhered to faithfully, in whatever way the circle revolves, it cannot err in circling. Rather, it runs smoothly, so that every radius reaches equally to the center of truth. It is possible to have a point of reference without a circle, but a circle can never be drawn without a central point. William's use of this metaphor suggests that authentic discernment may not always lead to a clear decision about the way in which "the circle of movement is revolving" (Med 11.27), but whatever the decision is, it must be founded on ardent devotedness centered in God.

This metaphor demonstrates that stability and consistency is necessary to keep one's ardent devotedness and behavior balanced, and in constant consultation with truth. Cistercian writings use the Latin words *affectus* and *actus* to refer to ardent devotedness and activity in actions. Two other related phrases in Cistercian writing are *amor ueritatis,* the love of truth, and *ueritas amoris,* truth of love; these describe the balance and harmony necessary for an integrated life. Love of truth is consecration to truth, being face to face with God in authentic self-knowledge. Such consecration is one of many manifestations of God in a person's life, the *affectus* or ardent devotedness focused on God. Truth of love is doing one's duty, i.e., manifesting love for each person and fulfilling one's responsibility in service to others.

William uses these four terms in this section of his *Meditations* to integrate the various facets of discernment in which he is engaged. He knows that his ardent devotedness, *affectus,* is to be focused on God, and that his activity, *actus,* is to flow from this focus.[8] The integration between the two arises from his discernment of responsibilities to God and to others. Both are forms of charity, that is, selfless love, which is what God is. Which of these two forms of charity takes precedence depends on one's duties and vocational responsibilities. In the tribunal of truth, miscalculation of these matters has serious consequences. One consequence is knowingly to follow one's own will, which causes one to be opposed to neighbor and truth. It is an offense against ardent devotedness. To follow one's own will unknowingly is of lesser significance, but if one thinks that it doesn't matter, that is much worse. William thus speaks about clarifying one's life's circumstances.

William adds additional nuance to his prescription for an integrated life by introducing capability, the ability to perform the appropriate action. He exemplifies this concept through the image of a circle with truth as its center. To act, people must first discern whether they can perform the intended action. If they have the necessary capability, it will keep the circle round. Discerning with ardent devotedness to God and an authentic selflessness in all that one does and thinks is the essential test of one's commitment to the center of truth.

---

8. Bernard calls this integration between *affectus* and *actus* the ordering of charity (SC 50.2).

William defines one more necessary element in discerning God's will: not being so eager to accomplish God's will as to weaken one's ability to do it. The center of truth must be consulted to discover whether the one seeking to do God's will is capable of doing so. Those who presume capability but lack it do not cling to the center. So eagerness to act must not be confused with the necessary discernment that one is fit for fulfilling God's will. The objective is always to arrive as a truthful person before the tribunal of truth.

A Dialogue between William's Spirit and His Soul:
Meditation 11.31–33

William now reflects on the distinction between spirit and soul, seeking to discern his motivation for entering the Cistercian Order by clarifying the realm of the spirit—ardent devotedness (*affectus*)—and the realm of the soul, which is one's life's activity (*actus*), the actions that one performs. The spirit comprises the greater part of who a person is or could be. When a person's spirit enters a discernment process, it embraces a radically deep honesty, replacing self-flattery with profound humility. Presenting his struggle as a dialogue between soul and spirit, William concludes that his spirit now agrees that his decision to enter the Cistercians has emerged from the previous phases of his discernment.

The soul (*anima*) is the part of human life that vitalizes the body and is manifested in a person's activity and actions. Presenting his struggle to see his way forward as a dialogue between his soul and his spirit (*animus*),[9] William examines his earlier life's activity—as a Benedictine monk and abbot—rather than his intellectual development, distinguishing between his ardent devotedness (*affectus*), his activity (*actus*), and his loving care for his community

---

9. In the *Golden Epistle* William explains these aspects of the human soul more fully (Ep frat [CCCM 88; CF 12]). When referring to the rational and intellectual aspect of a person's life, that is, one's mind, reasoning, or cognitive abilities, William uses the Latin word *animus*.

(*affectio*).[10] In the process he recognizes the way he has changed over time, seeing that his age has led him away from the vigorous service he gave as a young abbot to a desire for a new way of life; his spirit acknowledges the change:

> Soul: Just as formerly I took delight in command, so now my will is to acquiesce. And my own choice brings about the welcome excuse of my own needs and does not allow me to attend to the needs of the brothers.
>
> Spirit: Although, O Soul, compassion for the needs of the brothers is not lacking, yet in this situation, as you say, your loving care is. (Med 11.32–33)

Spirit's acknowledgement here that William is now lacking in loving care for his community, though phrased gently, is a sharp reproach, pointing to a failure at the heart of his spirit, which is charity, ardent devotedness. In one of his first treatises, *The Nature and Dignity of Love,* William had succinctly explained why he held it as so important: "Yes, love enlightened is charity: a love from God, in God, for God is charity. Yet, charity is God. Scripture says: God is charity" (1 John 4:16). Brief praise, but it says everything: whatever can be said of God can also be said of charity. A few lines later in the treatise, William cites Saint Paul's famous words on charity:

> Charity is patient, it is kind; charity does not envy, does not deal perversely, is not puffed up, is not ambitious, does not seek its own, is not provoked to anger, thinks no evil, does not rejoice in iniquity, but rejoices in truth; it suffers all things, believes all things, hopes all things, bears all things. Charity never fails. (1 Cor 13:4-8; Nat am 12 [CCCM 88:186–88; CF 30:67–68])

Here charity opens out into action as the *spiritus* expresses itself through the *anima* or soul.

---

10. *Affectio* in this context does not imply an emotional love, the usual meaning given this Latin word (Med 11.33).

In the discernment process William dramatizes in *Meditation* 11, he has reviewed the choices his will has made. Having in the past taken delight in being a superior with the authority to rule, now his choice, his will,[11] is to live the monastic life of obedience rather than being a person in authority with the responsibility to be attentive to, serve, and govern others. The quality of his community service was the quality of his loving care for the brothers, which he understands as now being deficient. His ardent devotedness expressed in loving care for the community—the Body of Christ—did not vivify as he believes it could have the quality of his community service, because he made choices according to his personal desires rather than to ardent devotedness and loving care. So he distinguishes between exterior service and the interior duty of loving attentiveness or loving care.

Recognizing his inadequacy in that regard as a form of personal blindness, he shows himself as now struggling for a solid inner life through humble confession and quest for virtue. His proximity to his center of truth, whose role is to rectify, has at last given him deep insight, sufficient knowledge, and adequate understanding of his life and who he is. William is now asking himself a profound question about his motivation in life and his humility.

Spirit now advises Soul about what is necessary for William at this new moment in his life:

> nothing stands firm unless it is a humble confession and a striving for every virtue, so that howsoever we may appear unfruitful and useless externally, internally we may be found not entirely empty and sterile. And although the crowds may drown out our voice, let us cry out with our whole heart and entire mind, *Jesus, Son of David, have mercy on me!* (Med 11.33)

With this cry on his lips, William initiates the last major unit of the *Meditations*.

---

11. "Will" = *uoluntas,* distinct from "my personal choice," *propria uoluntas mea.*

Your Love: *Meditation 12.1*

In the first short paragraph introducing this final section of the *Meditations*, William six times refers to truth. As he has earlier made clear, he understands truth as radical honesty in one's self-evaluation in the presence of divine Truth. The opening words to this final portion of the work thus form the background for William's truth about himself standing face to face with divine Truth, re-visioning a new life by revealing his personal depths to the depth of *your love. Your love* is now transforming William as he creates his new beginning, and he cries out to God to hear him:

> *Lord, hear my prayer! Grasp with your ears my supplication! Hear me clearly in your truth and in your justice, Lord,* you who *are near to all calling upon you in truth.* Just as the Scripture of your truth promises us, just as truth is before you, it is my will to call upon you in truth today; so hear me, O Truth, *in the abundance of your mercy, and in the truth of your salvation. For I have said: Now I have begun! May this change be yours from the right hand of the Most High, O Right Hand of the Most High!* (Med 12.1)

William has held firm to his decision to enter the Cistercian Order at Signy. He thus makes a new beginning in both his exterior way of life and his inner commitment to relationship with Christ. He entreats God that this change may come from God's own right hand. The truth about himself, the thoughts and past experience of his sins, once again overpowers him. Being thus overpowered, he is deeply troubled by the fact he cannot undo this past, or forget it, or eradicate it. He has thus proceeded to recast his life and relationship with God on the model of the Hebrews in their exodus from Egypt. But the grid that underlies this journey, as it emerges, is Jesus' words promising that many sins may be forgiven when much love is present (Luke 7:47).

William Addresses His Past Life: *Meditation 12.2–8*

Having begun by calling passionately on God to hear him, William turns to revisiting his life and its ascent through his vision of the Face of God. Although he sees his past life as despicable and dead, vile and contemptible, the new beginning he has made, with its new perspective, is one of hope, for he stands anew in the presence of new life, yes, even in the presence of life itself, for truth about himself has brought him into the presence of the right hand of God.

As William sees himself and his life in the presence of truth, he entrusts all the good deeds he may have performed to the Lord. These deeds, he cries out, belong to the Lord: "If I have done any good things, they are yours! I consign them to you! You will return them to me *in time acceptable* to you" (Med 12.2). While acknowledging his sins as his own, however, he views them as his Egypt, where he had been held in bondage of slavery to sin. He knows that God is his salvation and that as the apple of God's eye, he has been led by God into the land of the living, though not without fear. If one sin on the part of Moses prevented him from entering the Promised Land, what, he asks, will happen to William with his numerous sins? There remains for him only one option: it will be the quality of his love that will lead him out of his Egypt.

As William understands himself to stand in the presence of God with an enormous bundle of sins, he brings forth the bundle to be burned, offering the sins to God: "Let them be brought forward as if gathered *into a little bundle* [*fasciculum*] *to be burned*—no, rather, in great bundle [*fascem*], enormous and unmovable *if there is no one present to help*. I don't sort them out. I don't count them out (nor am I able to)" (Med 12.5). So, admitting his guilt, he stands in sorrow in the presence of truth. His acknowledgment before God and his refusal to make excuses for his past sin highlight another aspect of what standing in the presence of God entails. The sinner's past evils are what they are and are not to be exaggerated or categorized. What they deserve is not past, for they are in the presence of truth. The sinner can now only wait! On the other hand, thoughts of what it means to love much lead William now to an insightful encomium of *your love*.

Your Love as an Advocate: *Meditation 12.9–10*

In *On Contemplating God*, possibly the first treatise William wrote, in around 1119 or 1120, William defined *your love* as the Holy Spirit, who is the love of the Father for the Son and the love of the Son for the Father, and he explained that this divine love of the Holy Spirit has been exquisitely bestowed in the depths of each person's heart and so can transform and sanctify each person's affections.[1]

William's stance in the presence of God brands people as their own adversary in God's presence, not as adversaries of God. Assuming personal responsibility, William acknowledges that no excuses can be admitted before God. He asks that God not turn his face and countenance from him, regardless of the punishment that might come. If God's face (what God is) and God's countenance (divine goodness, attracting William) are turned away from William, then he—he understands—has no hope. The judgment that he desires is God's countenance shining upon him, divine goodness drawing him into its presence. He will accept punishment, but as a friend of God and not an enemy: "Flog as much as you wish, while always *illuminating your countenance upon us. And may you be merciful to us*" (Med 12.7).

What is important here is the presence of a loving intimacy based on an authentic boldness and unadulterated trust in the

---

1. William, Contemp 1 (CCCM 88:165; CF 3:58).

presence of Truth. Truth's judgment does not admit excuses. The Lord can be a harsh and heavy judge. Nevertheless, William is sufficiently bold to request a judgment based on love:

> *You have deflected* our *evils to yourself,* and *paying* in your passion *for what you have not appropriated . . .* you yourself, having been judged unjustly, may in your justice acquit those who have been judged justly. Therefore, Lord, *your judgments will help me.* You will look on me *according to the judgment of those who love your name,* as on one occasion you judged the sinner who loved you: *Many sins are forgiven her, for she has loved much.* (Med 12.8)

Jesus' love for William is to be William's advocate. This insight is pivotal as William seeks an authentic evaluation of his own life. He needs to know God's love for him. Furthermore, the Lord's passion is the substance of the encomium on *your love* that William interweaves into this last section of the *Meditations.*

One indispensable element of William's new beginning is that the shame that he experiences arises not from his sins, but from the fact that in his life he has not loved the gift of *your love,* the very essence of the Trinity, as he should have. He certainly perceives the love the Lord has for him, and he loves that love, but has he been genuinely focused on it throughout his life? Has he been ardently devoted to this love throughout his life? Has he truly understood this love and drunk freely of it?

During the exodus, William reflects, the chosen people were nourished with manna—bread—and water from the rock. William requests that he too may be given the bread of understanding and refreshing drink by the light of truth, to dispel and scatter the dark fog in his life. He shows that one must labor to understand the divine mysteries of the Word and Spirit as one's food and nourishment. *Lectio divina* is a way to change one's life for the better, and the role of the liturgical and sacramental dimensions of one's life in Christ nurtures this understanding.

Your Love, an Experience of Love: *Meditation 12.11*

Another element of this new beginning is that William must experience *your love* as being at work in his life. "Experience of love" (*sensus amoris*) is a rather comprehensive expression, difficult to convey in a few words. *Experience* implies an awareness in one's consciousness, penetrating into the depths of conscience. Experiences can be recalled or remembered but not relived. Remembrance can thus be seen as a type of possession, something lodged in the memory. At the same time, experience conveys the idea of some degree of participation in what is experienced. So when William refers to the experience of love, he implies that he is participating in *your love*. This participation, a gracious gift from the Holy Spirit, is crucial to a life in Christ.

Conscious of his own past and present life, William now deliberates within himself about whether he has this divine love within himself, for it is the face of God. He is conscious of having a love for the divine love, for he has in the past written of the *love of your love*.[2] But is this divine love the sole dynamic energy in his life? If it were the one effective principle in his life, he would have no concern about how he would embrace it: "Deep down, I would not care how I spent myself for it, whether in death or in life, so that I might merit to look fully on its face and walk openly in its light and enjoy its delights" (Med 12.13).

The principal advantage to William's unfailing and constant recollection of his past life is that it opens up insight into his life in God. This recollection assists him to descend deeper into the house of his conscience, whose expansive consciousness encompasses his entire life. As his conscience is also the dwelling place of God in his life, the Spirit, which is still alive, he says, under all the ash (Med 12.30) and ember of his sins, bursts into a tiny flame questioning William: does he have a love for God's love dwelling

2. Med 3.12; 5.17; 12.9; Contemp 2; 5 (CCCM 88:154, 155–56; CF 3:37, 42–43).

within him? Does he have a sense or experience of this love, a significant relationship in his life in Christ?

To uncover in his inner depths an experience of *your love,* William again elaborates on the nourishment proper for an exodus journey: drink and bread. He views drink as a tasting of God's love—an ardent devotedness—and bread as understanding what one is tasting.[3] Both of these, tasting and understanding, are gifts from the Holy Spirit working within him.

The Life of the Trinity Working in William:
Meditation 12.12–13

William senses the consciousness that *your love* is working in him, so revealing another basic component of relationship. Thus his own love opens up possibilities of participating in what God is, for it bestows a mutual resemblance between William and God, a partaking in divinity. This teaching, as he wrote in his *Exposition on Romans,* is at the heart of the experience of love, the *sensus amoris:* "[God's] love for us is goodness. Our love for him is the Holy Spirit, whom he gives us, through whom the charity of God is poured forth in our hearts."[4] Love of this quality is an experience of God acting within a person, giving some intellectual grasp of what divinity is: "sometimes your *Spirit blows where it wills, and when it wills.* And it breathes on us the grace of your love. In fact, we hear its voice because we receive the experience of love" (Med 12.11). This is love's energy expanding consciousness. William continues, linking this idea briefly to the Body of Christ, the eucharistic bread, as the source of the "firmer and more solid understanding" (Med 12.12) that he requests as the sustenance proper to these two gifts. The Eucharist is the sacramental presence of *your love.*

3. In the context of technical terms found in Cistercian teaching, William is speaking about the interrelatedness of *affectus* and *intellectus.*
    4. CCCM 86:66; CF 27:98.

Your Love Expands Conscience: *Meditation 12.14–15*

William earlier distinguished between God's love—what God is—and his own love for God's love. He also distinguishes between conscience, understood in its contemporary meaning, and a broader concept of consciousness. It is God's love, he says, that calls forth this expansion into an expanded consciousness of God's activity in his life:

> This is my conscience, called forth and spread forth before you, in the light of your truth. It seems to me to respond without any anxiety about the love of your love. However, regarding you, whether it always loves you and loves you enough, it is disturbed in responding in the presence of your judgment. Yes, wherever and in whomever I see your love and its obvious signs, it makes me completely happy. And yet, since all things speak to me all the time of the presence of your goodness and power, I am sometimes scarcely moved by them. If then today you would ask me, as in time past you asked the blessed apostle, *Do you love me?* I answer hesitatingly, *You know that I love you.* Yet I respond with a joyful and carefree mind, "You know that I want to love you!" (Med 12.14)

Conscious of the marvelous and truly good things God has done for him, William is able to realize that in loving these manifestations of God's love, he arrives at a grasp of what God is. They send him directly to God. When he does not find God, however, he returns in his memory to these manifestations and realizes with penetrating insight his gift of having a love for God's love, *your love*, though only according to his capacity to understand imperfectly in this present life (Med 12.15).

In this section of the *Meditations* William writes of understanding as pure insight, separate from physical senses or mental concepts. His experience of love, he says, gives birth to this category of understanding:

For when I delightfully experience your love with ardent devotedness, then I seek you with an understanding of love itself. I love what I experience, I desire what I seek, and, languishing in desiring, I fail. For sometimes understanding itself is deeply affected by your gift, yet according to my capacity. Understanding is not allowed to swallow all the saliva contained in this good taste. (Med 12.15)[5]

William here speaks of seizing God's love for him, *your love*, present deep within his conscience and understanding, not yet to the degree he so intensely desires, but limited to his understanding's capacity.

Way of Ascent: A Will—Great, Enlightened, Ardent: *Meditation 12.16–20*

Now William again analyzes the will as a way of ascending (*ascendendi*) into the face of God. He enlarges upon his earlier realization that his will is capable of three dimensions—great, enlightened, and ardently devoted (*uoluntas magna, deinde illuminata, deinde affecta*)—to apprehend the fullness of love's experience, explaining to God the forms of this will as he understands it: "In everyone who is ascending the will is to be as great as it is able to be, enlightened according to your gift, and finally ardently devoted according to its own nature" (Med 12.16). These three dimensions establish the way of ascent. In other words, he understands *your love* as at work within the human will.

---

5. *intellectus non permittitur glutire totam saliuam gustus boni*; that is, William savors the taste but isn't able to swallow all of it and so to be satisfied. This language evokes Job 7:19 and what Gregory the Great says in his *Moralia* about this verse (Mor 8.XXX.50 [CCSL 143:421; CS 257:198]). William may have had in mind Gregory's line *saliuam itaque glutire non possumus*. Gregory says that in contemplation we taste God's goodness in the mouth but are unable to swallow it to the stomach, where it would satisfy us completely. Thus he implies that such satisfaction is left for heaven. I am indebted to Sr. Grace Remington for this reference.

In writing of these three dimensions William considers his natural limitations in considering what he has and what he does not have. He prays for a firmer and more solid understanding so as to encourage the flame of divine love within his will to burst forth. It is the property of the will to give assent and say yes so as to become love and to determine one's behavior.

Great Will

William has explained a great will in several of his treatises. In *The Nature and Dignity of Love* he explains it in terms of its being formed by divine love:

> The love that is God, your love, actually the Holy Spirit, is present within the depths of human life for the purpose of forming one's life. Naturally the human will, because of the beckoning of sin, is complex, continually reaching out toward many desires. Such ceaseless reaching towards the more and more is a false limitlessness. Nevertheless, the will becomes great to the degree that it allows itself to be formed by Divine Love, by sharing in the simplicity that is the form of God. For divine love, the form of divinity, is the very simplicity of the divine nature and substance. Divinity is the will's birthplace.[6]

Divinity is the will's birthplace! This is a formidable assertion. William proceeds to profess that since divinity is without form, it follows that *your love* cannot exist in any form. *Your love*, without form, has formed the human will to be without form, and to be love that has no form. A paradox, to say the least. William's word *formasti*, "you have formed," underlines this assertion:

> A will as great as you have created it, as enlightened as you have made it worthy, as ardently devoted as you have formed it.

6. William, Nat am 3 (CCCM 88:179–80; CF 30:53–55).

You have formed it, however, without form, since you are
neither form nor something that has been formed. Nor can
any form of your love be possible to exist so as to be formed
in anything, as something formed. (Med 12.16)[7]

William goes on in *The Nature and Dignity of Love* to describe
wisdom as a development of love,[8] a gift of grace bestowed upon
the will. It is, he powerfully says, the breath of God's power, the
splendor of God's omnipotence, the brilliance of God's majesty, and
the image of God's goodness. He goes on, citing Boethius, to explain
that what people owe to God is faith formed according to this vision of divine love: "For as a certain wise person[9] says concerning
faith properly due to you, 'We ought to strive so to form our faith
about a thing as that thing actually is'" (Med 12.18). By means of
one's effort to allow grace to transform the will, it becomes great,
enlightened, ardently devoted. Such a will ultimately participates
in divine wisdom. Formed by divine love, it shares in the simplicity
that is the form of God: for divine love, the form of divinity, is the
very simplicity of the divine nature and substance. Since divinity
is the will's birthplace, it is here that the human will is at home.
Unity of spirit becomes the will's ultimate participation in divinity.

Realizing the importance of simplicity, early Cistercians strove
to embrace simplicity in every aspect of their monastic life,[10] in

---

7. Verdeyen's text (CCCM 88:75), divides this passage into two paragraphs,
as is shown above: *affecta sicut eam formasti.* ¶ *Formasti autem sine forma.* Without this division the last word of the first sentence, *formasti,* would be immediately followed by the first word of the next sentence, *Formasti.* The emphasis,
then, would insist on the concept of forming, recalling the beginning of the
Meditations, where William emphasizes the intimacy between God, the potter,
and the human person, the vessel formed by God with ardent devotedness.

8. William, Nat am 3.5. For further consideration of this topic, see Bell, *Image
and Likeness,* 148.

9. Boethius, *De Trinitate 2.*

10. For a presentation of Cistercian simplicity and its major role in Cistercian
life and prayer, see Jean-Baptiste Chautard, *The Spirit of Simplicity,* trans. and
annot. Thomas Merton (Notre Dame, IN: Ave Maria Press, 2017). The challenge

order to participate in divine love and return to the will's birthplace, following the maxim of Saint Benedict: *truly to seek God* (RB 58). *Truly seeking God* is returning to one's birthplace.[11]

A great will, trained to a stable focus on the divine, brings consistency into one's life, counteracting the fluctuations of human nature. Because of these fluctuations, William wonders at times if his will is great enough to be called love, as he understands love as an intense will.[12] Yet an intense will does not determine the limits or boundaries of God's love, for the infusion of God's love overflows the boundary of created human will. But William continues to ask that his desire be limitless. Furthermore, since no limits can be placed on God's love, one's will can correspondingly be defined as desire, desire without limit and form, hungering more and more, moving forward into the mystery of divinity.[13]

A great will safeguards both its objective—that is, God—and its uncompromising focus on God. Shaped and trained in simplicity, a great will eradicates anything not leading to God. This gift of simplicity, God's abode within a person, opens the inner life of that person to a revelation of what God is, *your love.*

Enlightened and Ardent Will: *Meditation 12.20–21*

William explains that *Your love* creates an enlightened and ardent will that becomes the place of God's presence. Moreover, *your love* is present according to its own way in the will, providing the purpose to encourage and sharpen participation in the mystery of Christ. William's sins, he knows, weaken this process, dragging

---

that Cistercian simplicity aims at is to create a form of exterior life and inner personal life that allows one to participate in divinity, which neither has form nor can be expressed in any form. A veritable oxymoron.

11. This may be one dimension of William's intense desire to enter the Cistercian abbey at Signy.

12. See William, Nat am 4 (CCCM 88:180; CF 30:56).

13. This teaching is articulated in the opening paragraphs of William's *On Contemplating God* (Contemp 1 [CCCM 88:153; CF 3:36–37]).

his life after them. He longs for a full vision of this love, and he admits that he has a partial experience of it, or he would not love it.

Your Love Imparts Participation with the Saints:
Meditation 12.22

William views these two aspects of the will, being enlightened and being ardently devoted, as harmonizing with one another for the purpose of bonding with heavenly life. Some participation in this heavenly beatitude can be given to William even in this life by his reflecting on the saints' mutually enjoying and sharing the delights of eternal beatitude. For William vehemently loves God's love, that is, *your love,* in the saints, and affectionately embraces them in their loving God: "And in the depths of my heart I affectionately embrace those persons loving you. Also, I see them rejoicing in my joy that I have from their joy" (Med 12.22). Here he celebrates mutual participation, perceiving the saints' rejoicing in his joy, the joy that he has from theirs. In other words, in this life William's tender love for God is a participation in the saints' loving God. The bonding between earth and heaven is never far from William's thought. It is the motivation for his ascent, for he knows that the saints, having lived their lives in *your love,* are now immersed in this love, the life of the Triune God.

Your Love Reshaping Persons: *Meditation 12.23–24*

The reshaping[14] of one's life also results from bonding with or participating in eternal life. William explains that this participation

---

14. "Reshaping" = *reformare,* the etymon for English words such as *reform* and *reformation. Reformare* and thus *reshaping* echo William's opening metaphor of a potter affectionately shaping pots, now understood as necessary because sin has deformed them.

begins when one's life is reshaped by the image of the Trinity in which it was created, so coming to touch the Trinity's own happiness. For the blessedness of the Trinity is mirrored in human life when one understands what is loved and loves what is understood; this interchange empowers a person to rejoice. This triune dimension in human life is an enlightened will, an ardently devoted will that joins with the ability to rejoice (*voluntas illuminata, voluntas affecta, habitus fruendi* [Med 12.23]). The three graces rest in a great will, one totally devoted to Christ and to his resolve.

Your Love Forms Unpretentious Persons:
Meditation 12.25–27

Now William focuses on the reshaping effect of *your love* on the saints during their earthly life. The Holy Spirit, God's Love, dwells in those who can be rightly called the blessed meek ones of Christ,[15] namely, unpretentious persons. Gentleness and tenderness accompany meekness; together they enrich the grace of humility that forms people, making them unpretentious (*simplices*). William elaborates on this shaping of unpretentious persons in respect to their wisdom, a wisdom that is not from the spirit of this world, or from the prudence of this era. While they may not be well educated and knowledgeable, nonetheless they enter into the power of the Lord. Poor in spirit, they think only of God's justice. Therefore, William says, God taught them so that in their way of living they publicly declare God's marvelous deeds. They manifest their intense trust in the Lord through their way of life. As a result, divine wisdom has tenderly arranged all things for them, for divine wisdom formed them through their humility and unpretentiousness.

These persons, taught by God, William says, have a short ascent into the divine presence. For *your love* itself, having found in them

15. See Bernard of Clairvaux, OS I.9 (SBOp 5:334; CF 54:137).

unpretentiousness and genuineness, formed and conformed them to itself in both effect and ardent devotedness.[16] This reshaping of their conscience, and consequently of their consciousness, is visible in their lives:

> the inner life shines forth in their outer countenance to such an extent that from their countenance and behavior with its evident charm and simplicity, a kind of appeal comes forth from your charity. By its appearance alone, it challenges rude and sometimes barbarous souls toward your love. (Med 12.26)

The Holy Spirit, *your love,* further reshapes them:

> And when their spirits, *with the Holy Spirit helping their weakness,* pass over into divine affections, their bodily senses assume a definite spiritual discipline. Even their bodies put on an evident spiritual appearance, and their faces assume a more than human aspect, with a certain extraordinary grace. (Med 12.26)

Such people's entire behavior and their way of life are the consequence of wisdom, and a symbol of their ascent. The fullness of the human person that will be brought to completion in the final resurrection has already begun in this life. This teaching is William's notion of *eucrasis,* which he presents in several of his other treatises.

Eucrasis and the Saints

William understands the concept of *eucrasis* as a transformation denoting that the body, integrated with its soul, rejoices in the

---

16. "Effect" and "ardent devotedness" = *effectus* and *affectus.*

living God.[17] Such people manifest and live ardent devotedness, which is embedded in their consciousness and, consequently, in their appearance and behavior. Behavior and ardent devotedness thus reveal that *your love* has transformed such unpretentious persons. A bonding has taken place between God's working in who they are and how they live. This bonding is so dynamic as to bring about a transformation even in their physical bodies.

To Love Much: *Meditation 12.28–30*

William's understanding of *your love* as operative in the lives of the saints has had a profound effect on him. As lovers experience the love operative in their beloved and come to recognize the depths of their own love, so William realizes that *your love* in the saints' ardent devotedness is the divine presence in them, a presence that is also in William's ardent devotedness to God. Accordingly, he has come to understand that love belongs to human nature. *Your love*, that is, God dwelling in humankind, has ardent devotedness[18] as its manifestation. It belongs to grace, and it is

17. *Eucrasis* can be interpreted as meaning that a spiritually integrated soul or human life is clearly manifested in and determines one's behavior or, to use a monastic term, one's *conversatio*, manner of life. See for other examples of William's uses of this concept Nat am 43 (CCCM 88:209–10; CF 30:105–7); Spec fid 52–54 (CCCM 89A:101–3; CF 15:41–44). Nemesius, *Premnon phisicon* 2, may be William's source for this teaching. Nemesius was a fourth-century bishop of Emesa (present-day Homs, Syria). He wrote in Greek a work on human nature, which for its time was an anthropology based on Christian philosophy, with sources from Aristotle and Galen. Alfano I, archbishop of Salerno, translated this work into Latin under the title *Premnon phisicon*, sometime before 1085. The English translation of this work is titled, "On Human Nature," or more commonly, "The Nature of Man."

18. This is an important and major observation relative to ardent devotedness, *affectus*, in a person's life. Good zeal, with which Saint Benedict concludes the Rule (RB 72), is another manifestation of *affectus*.

a gift of grace. Previously William had questioned whether this divine love was in fact operative in himself, energizing who he was and how he lived. But now he has become aware that he does have *your love* in his own person. As he opens himself more and more to this gift of God within him, he sees that he can and does love much, for this inner love is nothing other than God's boundless, limitless love. Loving much thus brings about the forgiveness of sins he has so eloquently longed for in the *Meditations.*

Many vicissitudes press upon a person in this life, regardless of the quality of one's love, as William acknowledges when he writes, "There must be a regress [*defectus*] or progress of a soul, however loving it is" (Med 12.29). But at the same time there are advances in life's progress that lift a person upward, toward the ascent into contemplative intimacy with the triune divinity. Vital to this progress is discernment of the quality of understanding and authentic ardent devotedness, for ardent devotedness creates a happy balance to one's life, placing the ups and downs in a perspective of the understanding and love that is ever present in one's relations with God and other persons.

William concludes the *Meditations* with a remarkable metaphor underscoring what it is to love much: to understand, to love, and to enjoy. He compares this unfolding *your love* to a red-hot fire, quiescent under a cover of ash, associating that with human nature. Addressing the Holy Spirit, he implores the Spirit to be present in his depths, to purify them, to dig out material for humility so as to increase the divine flame, to make clear the glory and riches of his conscience, and, oddly, while acting carefully in all this work, to stay concealed lest the Spirit appear to scatter the riches of a good conscience. And so he ends his work:

> God, your love is always in the soul of your poor one, but hidden like fire under ashes, until *the Spirit, who blows where it wills,* pleases to manifest itself as and in the measure it wills for our usefulness [*ad utilitatem*]. Be present, therefore, be present, O Holy Love! Be present, Sacred Fire; *burn up* the

pleasures *of our inner depths and* the thoughts *of our hearts.* As extensively as you wish, bring forth a greater abundance of humble material for the flame of your appearance. As you please, appear to make clear *the glory* of a good conscience and *the riches* it possesses *in its house.* Make it clear that you act carefully to safeguard. Hide, lest you act thoughtlessly to scatter,[19] until God, *who has begun this good work,* brings it to completion, he who lives and reigns through all ages of ages. Amen. (Med 12.30)

19. *Manifesta, ut sollicitum facias ad custodiendum. Absconde, ne temerarium facias ad dissipandum.*

Meditation Thirteen[1]

J.-M. Déchanet has argued for accepting the document now known as Meditation Thirteen as authentic, with the contents coming from William, though written by someone today unknown.[2] This document is substantiated by its account of William's severe difficulties in adjusting to the more austere Cistercian manner of monastic life as they were recorded in *Vita Antiqua,* the earliest life of William, written sometime after his death in 1148 and probably before the 1200s.[3]

The *Vita Antiqua* reveals that several distinguished persons endeavored to persuade William to return to his former Benedictine abbey because he was needed there. In addition, the hard life he led at his new Cistercian abbey of Signy thoroughly shook him in his resolve to continue there. Temptations for him to return to Saint-Thierry were fierce. Having shared them with a brother monk who had become a close friend, William entered deeply into himself to reach accurate self-knowledge about his situation and what he should do. Whether he was aware of it or not, he was engaging in the proper techniques for finding the center of truth. Truth—his accurate self-evaluation—led him into his house of conscience and consciousness, causing him to acknowledge his feelings in both recognizing and accepting the absolute sovereignty of God

1. Verdeyen prints Meditation Thirteen at the end of his edition of *De contemplando Deo,* with the title "Meditatio: Seduxisti Me: Excerpta de Meditationibus domni Wilhermi," CCCM 88:171–73.

2. J.-M. Déchanet, introduction to "Meditation Thirteen," by William of Saint-Thierry, in *On Contemplating God, Prayer, Meditations,* trans. Sister Penelope [Lawson], 181–85.

3. For an analysis and translation of the *Vita Antiqua,* see David N. Bell, "The *Vita Antiqua* of William of St. Thierry," CSQ 11, no. 3 (1976): 246–55.

over him. At that point William's own inner voice and the voice of the Lord, always present in one's conscience, began an open and intimate dialogue, which constitutes Meditation Thirteen.

Meditation Thirteen shows that the dialogue that ensued between William's conscience and God gave William a sense of the right thing to do, so saving his integrity. His fierce temptations had dismantled his idealism, but the physical struggles he endured in his new life enabled him to understand and experience God's grace at work within him. So, as the meditation shows, an entirely new vision of God—a new face of God—came to birth in him. The dialogue reveals a new tender intimacy and affectionate care. In speaking to God, William begins by saying: "You have seduced me!" The Lord responds, simply and obliquely, "Do not disregard discipline" (Med 13.1).[4] Doubtlessly he is telling William not to fear the regulated strictness of the Cistercian life, while telling William that he has not been seduced into this way of life.

The Lord's words thus go to the core of William's problem. Cistercian life at Signy is hard, but it has a purpose, and it leads to a goal. William replies, "What I have been capable of, this I have done" (Med 13.3). The Lord replies again, "Take hold of discipline!" When William counters, "There is nothing hidden from you" (Med 13.5), he acknowledges God's sovereignty and all-encompassing knowledge. Now the Lord responds tenderly and affectionately, like an attentive potter: "I have made you and I will carry you" (Med 13.6). So William is able to declare, "You are made our refuge" (Med 13.7), proclaiming his total commitment to the Lord. These techniques of the center of truth open out into a quest for charity as William's ardent devotedness, present all along in his heart, has manifested itself in words. William will not reject the Lord's call.

4. Déchanet's edition of Meditation Thirteen has no paragraph numbering; I have added numbering for ease of reference.

I am including Meditation Thirteen here at the end of this commentary as an epilogue to William's *Meditations*. It presents a profound teaching of an integral aspect of a life that encapsulates a mystical ascent, a journey to participate in the triune divinity. Those who have professed a solemn monastic consecration according to the Rule of Saint Benedict no longer have their own bodies or wills in their control. Their radical detachment becomes more intense and is experienced in dimensions not previously known as old age and sickness approach. Meditation Thirteen reveals how William approached this last stage in his contemplative ascent.

After the discernment that William recorded in the *Meditations* about his own desire for a more focused monastic life, he did take up a more austere monastic life at Signy. This new life—*conversatio*—presented a final and unexpected challenge for him. He did not always find the peace and sweetness of a purely contemplative way of life that he had been expecting. The burden of obedience and absolute detachment seemed too much for his bodily ailments, the debility of old age, and other similar problems. It was easy for him to perceive himself as abandoned by God and humans. But the renovation of a person's expectations is part of the final movement into the divine presence. All one needs to do is recall the final cry of abandonment of Christ on the cross as presented in the Gospel of Mark: *My God, my God, why have you forsaken me?* (Mark 15:34). Christ's cry was an expression of profound intimacy with the Father. Similarly William's trials at Signy as expressed in Meditation Thirteen led him into a deeper intimacy with God as *concrucifixus,* as he entered the final phase of the contemplative life with its prayer.

William initially claims that God has seduced him when he followed the words of Christ to come to him and be refreshed. In his response to the divine call he seemed not to find refreshment, but instead to be so overburdened that he was collapsing under the burden of this new *conversatio.* He pleads for mercy, as there is no one to assist him. Is this burdening a form of judgment on his life? What is the meaning of this punishment? Is he being counted an illegitimate son of God? He places his questioning in the context of a favorite scriptural metaphor, the sinful woman doing her humble service to Christ. He quotes Jesus as saying, "*What she could do, this she has done*" (Mark 14:8). So William asks God, "Have I not also done everything I could? And, what is more, I seem to have done more than I appear to have been capable of doing" (Med 13.1). William has placed his new life in this context. As he speaks honestly and intimately with the Lord, he places the blame on God, making God responsible for all his difficulties and especially for his being so thoroughly disillusioned. Here William seems to return to the first phase of his mystical ascent, struggling not to surrender to the temptation to accuse God, and not to be oblivious of the magnitude of the call he has received to follow Christ.

Christ tenderly and graciously replies to William that he did not seduce him, that discipline is the sign of an authentic and healthy father-son relationship, that while the call to come and follow is given to all persons, only a few respond, and that William is one who has (Med 13.2). In itself, this response is a great gift, and Christ affirms William for making it. Finally, the fact that William is still able to stand and be viable in this new way of life is itself a sign of Christ's invigorating support. Nevertheless, William's groaning under Christ's yoke, his exhaustion in following Christ, indicates that his own charity, the selfless love that makes a burden light and charming, is somehow faulty. Charity will bring gentleness to his burdens and to the yoke of Christ that he has taken upon himself (Med 13.2).

Now William laments that if he had only had charity, he would have been perfect. Yet he does love; he has given his poor physical body over to Christ in the new *conversatio*. At least he can do this little service, so he asks Christ to accept it and grant him the perfect charity he so desires (Med 13.3).

Again, the Lord confronts William by asking if he is to make good where William is lacking and, on top of this, to give him the charity he is requesting. He reminds William that obedience is the way to charity. Obedience to the way of ascent, to the way of life that he has entered upon, is not to abandon it, but rather to cling to it and to be willing to suffer in imitation of the suffering Christ. Divine charity is a great thing, and worthy to be purchased at a price, though a great one. For God himself is charity. Once William has attained to this selfless charity, *your love*, he will no longer be weighed down (Med 13.4).

William reminds the Lord that he has opened himself entirely to the Lord, has thrown open all the dark corners of his conscience and consciousness. He has kept hidden absolutely nothing from the Lord. That is, he acknowledges and accepts all his faults, sins, and whatever else that he can conjure up in his conscience and consciousness. He now sets them before the Lord, but he continues to focus on his lack of charity. He questions who will work with him (Med 13.5).

Once more, the Lord graciously responds that he made William and will carry him. This is one of the first themes of the *Meditations*, the Lord's tender care for a person. Now the Lord recalls a further teaching, made, again, at the very beginning of these meditations: gratitude for what one has received will pave the way for greater gifts from God. The Lord reminds William that he has already received charity to a degree, but either he is not conscious of it, or he is ungrateful for it. Charity is proper to wisdom, and the beginning of wisdom is the fear of the Lord. Already the fear of God has escorted William to this point. At another time, fear established him in this point. If the end finds him there, he will come through this trial safely. Really, has he made so little progress? Is this something insignificant that he has received? (Med 13.6).

William confirms that he has responded to the call of his Lord to enter into more rigorous life of monastic living. This is God's gift. He invokes the image from the book of Exodus, where the Lord supports the chosen people with nourishment, and he himself requests from his Lord nourishment for this new way of living lest he faint and collapse. He pleads for help to advance according to his infirmities, and for patience, which will be a sign that the Lord is with him (Med 13.7–8). This is the noble dimension of his will, containing the good attitude or good zeal that he has confided into the Lord's hands. William asks for encouragement, consolation, illumination, and wisdom to do the right thing at all times, thereby remaining well integrated into the household of God: "Do not cast me out from your children, as I am your servant, and the servant of all your servants" (Med 13.8). Concerning his body, William asks only for mercy, and to know how to guide and guard it so he does not acquiesce in its pleasures or take away anything from its need. He is content to accept whatever God decides to give him for the body—sickness, health, even death (Med 13.8).

William has at last arrived at realizing that selfless love, charity, is the face of God. As an ending to this meditation, he prays for charity, so that he may love God more than himself, always be acceptable in God's presence, and remain his faithful servant, imitating the suffering, crucified servant, the Lamb of God:

> Father, grant that I may always be your faithful little servant and *a sheep of your pasture*, though I dare not say a son. Lord, speak sometimes to the heart of your servant. *May your consolations delight my soul*. Yes, teach me to speak to you more frequently, and to bring back to you, My Lord God and my Father, all my poverty and need. My Strength, have mercy on my weakness. Yes, may it be your great glory that my helplessness perseveres in your service. Amen. (Med 13.9)

✠

Bibliography

The Works of William of Saint-Thierry
Latin Editions and English Translations

Ænigma fidei (PL 180:397–440) (Ænig)
>   *Guillelmi a Sancto Theodorico Opera Omnia, V: Opuscula adversus Petrum Abaelardum et de Fide.* Ed. Paul Verdeyen. CCCM 89A. Turnhout: Brepols, 2007. 130–91.
>   *The Enigma of Faith.* Trans. John D. Anderson. CF 9. Kalamazoo, MI, and Spencer, MA: Cistercian Publications, 1973.

Brevis commentatio (PL 184:407–36) (Brev com)
>   *Guillelmi a Sancto Theodorico Opera Omnia, II: Brevis Commentatio.* Ed. Stanislaus Ceglar and Paul Verdeyen. CCCM 87. Turnhout: Brepols, 1997. 155–96.

De contemplando Deo (PL 184:365–80) (Contemp)
>   *Guillelmi a Sancto Theodorico Opera Omnia, III: De Contemplando Deo.* Ed. Paul Verdeyen. CCCM 88. Turnhout: Brepols, 2003. 153–73.
>   *On Contemplating God, Prayer, Meditations.* Trans. Sr. Penelope [Lawson]. Intro. Jacques Hourlier. The Works of William of St Thierry 1. CF 3. Kalamazoo, MI: Cistercian Publications, 1977. 36–64.

De natura corporis et animae (PL 180:695–726) (Nat corp)
>   *Guillelmi a Sancto Theodorico Opera Omnia, III: De Natura Corporis et Animae.* Ed. Paul Verdeyen. CCCM 88. Turnhout: Brepols, 2003. 101–46.
>   *The Nature of the Body and Soul.* In *Three Treatises on Man: A Cistercian Anthropology.* Ed. Bernard McGinn. Trans. Benjamin Clark. CF 24. Kalamazoo, MI: Cistercian Publications, 1977. 101–52.

De natura et dignitate amoris (PL 184:379–408) (Nat am)

> *Guillelmi a Sancto Theodorico Opera Omnia, III: De Natura et Dignitate Amoris.* Ed. Paul Verdeyen. CCCM 88. Turnhout: Brepols, 2003. 175–212.

> *The Nature and Dignity of Love.* Trans. Thomas X. Davis. Intro. David N. Bell. CF 30. Kalamazoo, MI: Cistercian Publications, 1981.

De sacramento altaris (PL 180:344–66) (Sac alt)

> *Guillelmi a Sancto Theodorico Opera Omnia, III: De sacramento altaris.* Ed. Stanislaus Ceglar and Paul Verdeyen. CCCM 88. Turnhout: Brepols, 2003. 53–91.

Disputatio adversus Petrum Abaelardum (PL 180:249–82) (Adv Abl)

> *Guillelmi a Sancto Theodorico Opera Omnia, V: Opuscula adversus Petrum Abaelardum et de fide.* Ed. Paul Verdeyen. CCCM 89A. Turnhout: Brepols, 2007. 17–59.

Epistola ad domnum Rupertum (to Rupert of Deutz) (PL 180:341–46) (Ep Rup)

> *Guillelmi a Sancto Theodorico Opera Omnia, III: Epistola Guillelmi ad Rupertum Tuitiensem.* Ed. Stanislaus Ceglar and Paul Verdeyen. CCCM 88. Turnhout: Brepols, 2003. 47–52.

Epistola ad fratres de Monte Dei (PL 184:307–64) (Ep frat)

> *Guillelmi a Sancto Theodorico Opera Omnia, III: Epistola ad fratres de Monte Dei.* Ed. Paul Verdeyen. CCCM 88. Turnhout: Brepols, 2003. 223–89.

> *The Golden Epistle: A Letter to the Brethren at Mont Dieu.* Trans. Theodore Berkeley. Intro. J.-M. Déchanet. The Works of William of St Thierry 4. CF 12. Kalamazoo, MI: Cistercian Publications, 1980.

Epistola ad Gaufridum Carnotensem episcopum et Bernardum abbatem Claraevallensem (Preface to Adv Abl) (PL 182:531–33)

> *Guillelmi a Sancto Theodorico Opera Omnia, V: Epistola Willelmi.* Ed. Paul Verdeyen. CCCM 89A. Turnhout: Brepols, 2007. 13–15.

Epistola de erroribus Guillelmi de Conchis (to Bernard of Clairvaux) (PL 180:333–40) (Er Guil)

> *Guillelmi a Sancto Theodorico Opera Omnia, V: De erroribus Guillelmi de Conchis.* Ed. Paul Verdeyen. CCCM 89A. Turnhout: Brepols, 2007. 61–71.

Excerpta de Libris Beati Ambrosii super Cantica Canticorum (PL 15:1851–1962) (Cant Amb)

Guillelmi a Sancto Theodorico Opera Omnia, II: Excerpta de libris beati Ambrosii super Cantica canticorum. Ed. Antony van Burink. CCCM 87. Turnhout: Brepols, 1997. 205–384.

Excerpta ex Libris Beati Gregorii super Cantica canticorum (PL 180:441–74) (Cant Greg)

Guillelmi a Sancto Theodorico Opera Omnia, II: Excerpta ex libris beati Gregorii super Cantica canticorum. Ed. Paul Verdeyen. CCCM 87. Turnhout: Brepols, 1997. 285–344.

"Excerpts from the Books of Blessed Gregory on the Song of Songs." In Gregory the Great, *On the Song of Songs*, translated by Mark DelCogliano. CS 244. Collegeville, MN: Cistercian Publications, 2012. 181–240.

Expositio super Cantica canticorum (PL 180:473–546) (Cant)

Guillelmi a Sancto Theodorico Opera Omnia, II: Expositio super Cantica canticorum. Ed. Paul Verdeyen. CCCM 87. Turnhout: Brepols, 1997. 17–133.

Exposition on the Song of Songs. Trans. Columba Hart. Intro. J.-M. Déchanet. CF 6. Kalamazoo, MI: Cistercian Publications, 1968.

Expositio super Epistolam ad Romanos (PL 180:547–694) (Exp Rom)

Guillelmi a Sancto Theodorico Opera Omnia, I: Expositio super Epistolam ad Romanos. Ed. Paul Verdeyen. CCCM 86. Turnhout: Brepols, 1989. 1–196.

Exposition on the Epistle to the Romans. Trans. John Baptist Hasbrouk. Ed. and intro. John D. Anderson. CF 27. Kalamazoo, MI: Cistercian Publications, 1980.

Meditatio: Seduxisti Me. (Med 13)

Guillelmi a Sancto Theodorico Opera Omnia, III: Meditatio: Seduxisti Me. Ed. Paul Verdeyen. CCCM 88. Turnhout: Brepols, 2003. 171–73.

"Meditation Thirteen." Intro. J.-M. Déchanet. In *On Contemplating God, Prayer, Meditations*, translated by Sr. Penelope [Lawson]. The Works of William of St Thierry 1. CF 3. Kalamazoo, MI: Cistercian Publications, 1977. 181–85.

Meditativæ orationes (PL 180:205–48) (Med)

Guillelmi a Sancto Theodorico Opera Omnia, IV: Meditationes Devotissimae. Ed. Paul Verdeyen. CCCM 89. Turnhout: Brepols, 2005. 1–80.

On Contemplating God, Prayer, Meditations. Trans. Sr. Penelope [Lawson]. Intro. Jacques Hourlier. The Works of William of St. Thierry 1. CF 3. Kalamazoo, MI: Cistercian Publications, 1977. 87–178.

Oratio domni Willelmi (Orat)

Guillelmi a Sancto Theodorico Opera Omnia, III: Oratio Domni Willelmi. Ed. Paul Verdeyen. CCCM 88. Turnhout: Brepols, 2003. 169–71.

On Contemplating God, Prayer, Meditations. Trans. Sr. Penelope [Lawson]. Intro. Jacques Hourlier. The Works of William of St Thierry 1. CF 3. Kalamazoo, MI: Cistercian Publications, 1977. 71–74.

"The Prayer of Dom William: A Study and New Translation." David N. Bell. In *Unity of Spirit: Studies on William of Saint-Thierry in Honor of E. Rozanne Elder,* edited by F. Tyler Sergent, Aage Rydstrøm-Poulsen, and Marsha L. Dutton. CS 268. Collegeville, MN: Cistercian Publications, 2015. 21–36.

Prologus ad Domnum Bernardum abbatem Claravallis (Prologue to Sac alt) (PL 180:344–45) (Sac alt)

Guillelmi a Sancto Theodorico Opera Omnia, III: Prologus [Ad Domnum Bernardum Abbatem Claravallis]. Ed. Stanislaus Ceglar and Paul Verdeyen. CCCM 88. Turnhout: Brepols, 2003. 53.

Responsio abbatum auctore Willelmo abbate Sancti Theodorici (to Cardinal Matthew) (Resp)

Guillelmi a Sancto Theodorico Opera Omnia, IV: Responsio Abbatum Auctore Willelmo Abbate Sancti Theodorici. Ed. Paul Verdeyen. CCCM 89. Turnhout: Brepols, 2005. 103–12.

Speculum fidei (PL 180:365–98) (Spec)

Guillelmi a Sancto Theodorico Opera Omnia, V: Speculum Fidei. Ed. Paul Verdeyen. CCCM 89A. Turnhout: Brepols, 2007. 81–127.

The Mirror of Faith. Trans. Thomas X. Davis. Intro. E. Rozanne Elder. CF 15. Kalamazoo, MI: Cistercian Publications, 1979.

Vita prima Sancti Bernardi, Liber Primus (PL 185:225–68) (Vita Bern)

Guillelmi a Sancto Theodorico Opera Omnia, VI: Vita Prima Sancti Bernardi – Liber primus. Ed. Paul Verdeyen. CCCM 89B. Turnhout: Brepols, 2011. 29–85.

William of Saint-Thierry, Arnold of Bonneval, and Geoffrey of Auxerre. *The First Life of Saint Bernard of Clairvaux.* Trans. Hilary Costello. CF 76. Collegeville, MN: Cistercian Publications, 2015.

Other Primary Sources

Augustine, *The Literal Meaning of Genesis*. Trans. John Hammond Taylor. Ancient Christian Writers Series 42. New York, and Ramsey, NJ: Newman, 1982.

Benedict. *The Rule of Saint Benedict 1980*. Ed. Timothy Fry. Collegeville, MN: Liturgical Press, 2019.

Tissier, Bertrand, Herbertus Claraevallensis, and Arnolfus de Boeriis. *Bibliotheca Patrum Cisterciensium: id est Opera abbatum et monachorum Ordinis Cisterciensis, qui saeculo S. Bernardi, aut paulò post ejus obitum floruerunt, in unum corpus aliquot tomis distinctum collecta.* 8 vols. Bonofonte: A. Renesson, 1660–1669. Vol. 4.

Studies

Baker, Timothy M. "'Be You as Living Stones Built Up, A Spiritual House, A Holy Priesthood': Cistercian Exegesis, Reform, and the Construction of Holy Architectures." PhD dissertation, Harvard University, 2015 (Baker-dissertation-2015.pdf.).

Bell, David N. *Image and Likeness: The Augustinian Spirituality of William of Saint Thierry*. CS 78. Kalamazoo, MI: Cistercian Publications, 1984.

Bell, David N. "*In manibus suis*: Guillaume de Saint-Thierry, les Pères du désert, et la spiritualité du travail manuel." In *Signy l'Abbaye, site cistercien enfoui, site de mémoire, et Guillaume de Saint-Thierry: Actes du Colloque international d'Études cisterciennes, 9, 10, 11 septembre 1998, Les Vieilles Forges (Ardennes)*, edited by Nicole Boucher. Signy l'Abbaye: Association des Amis de l'Abbaye de Signy, 2000. 475–85.

Bell, David N. "The Mystical Theology and Theological Mysticism of William of Saint-Thierry." In *A Companion to William of Saint-Thierry*, edited by F. Tyler Sergent. Brill's Companions to the Christian Tradition 87. Leiden-Boston: Brill, 2019. 67–92.

Bell, David N. "The Prayer of Dom William: A Study and New Translation." In *Unity of Spirit: Studies on William of Saint-Thierry in Honor of E. Rozanne Elder*, edited by F. Tyler Sergent, Aage Rydstrøm-

Poulsen, and Marsha L. Dutton. CS 268. Collegeville, MN: Cistercian Publications, 2015. 21–36.

Bell, David N. "The *Vita Antiqua* of William of St. Thierry." CSQ 11, no. 3 (1976): 246–55.

Boucher, Nicole, ed. *Signy l'Abbaye, site cistercien enfoui, site de mémoire, et Guillaume de Saint-Thierry: Actes du Colloque international d'Études cisterciennes, 9, 10, 11 septembre 1998, Les Vieilles Forges (Ardennes)*. Signy l'Abbaye: Association des Amis de l'Abbaye de Signy, 2000.

Carfantan, Jerry, ed. *William, Abbot of St. Thierry: A Colloquium at the Abbey of St. Thierry*. CS 94. Kalamazoo, MI: Cistercian Publications, 1987.

Catalogue general des manuscrits des bibliothèques publiques des départements. Vol. 5. Paris, 1879.

Catechism of the Catholic Church. Mahwah, NJ: Paulist Press, 1994.

Ceglar, Stanislaus. "William of Saint Thierry: The Chronology of His Life with a Study of His Treatise *On the Nature of Love*, His Authorship of the *Brevis Commentatio*, the *In Lacu*, and the *Reply to Cardinal Matthew*." PhD dissertation. Washington, DC: The Catholic University of America, 1971.

Chautard, Jean-Baptiste. *The Spirit of Simplicity*. Trans. and annot. by Thomas Merton. Notre Dame, IN: Ave Maria Press, 2017.

Déchanet, Jean-Marie. Introduction to "Meditation Thirteen," by William of Saint-Thierry. In *On Contemplating God, Prayer, Meditations*, translated by Sr. Penelope [Lawson]. The Works of William of St Thierry 1. CF 3. Kalamazoo, MI: Cistercian Publications, 1977. 181–85.

Déchanet, Jean-Marie. *Méditations et Prières*. Éditions Universitaires. Brussels: Les Presses de Belgique, 1945.

Déchanet, Jean-Marie. "Un recueil singulier d'opuscules de Guillaume de Saint-Thierry: Charleville 114." *Scriptorium* 6 (1952): 196–212.

Déchanet, Jean-Marie. *William of St Thierry: The Man and His Work*. Trans. Richard Strachan. CS 10. Kalamazoo, MI: Cistercian Publications, 1972.

Dutton, Marsha L. "The Cistercian Source: Aelred, Bonaventure, and Ignatius." In *Goad and Nail: Studies in Medieval Cistercian History, X*, edited by E. Rozanne Elder. CS 84. Kalamazoo, MI: Cistercian Publications, 1985. 151–78.

Elder, Rozanne E. "William of Saint Thierry and the Greek Fathers: Evidence from Christology." In *One Yet Two: Monastic Tradition East and West*, edited by M. Basil Pennington. CS 29. Kalamazoo, MI: Cistercian Publications, 1976. 254–66.

Garcia de Cisneros, Francisco. *Ejercitatorio de La Vida Espiritual.* Barcelona: Libreria Religioso, 1857.

Gilson, Étienne. *The Mystical Theology of Saint Bernard.* Trans. A. H. C. Downes. London and New York: Sheed and Ward, 1955. Repr. CS 120. Kalamazoo, MI: Cistercian Publications, 1990.

Hourlier, Jacques. Introduction to *Meditations*, by William of Saint-Thierry. In *On Contemplating God, Prayer, Meditations.* Trans. Sr. Penelope [Lawson]. The Works of William of St Thierry 1. CF 3. Kalamazoo, MI: Cistercian Publications, 1977. 75–86.

Klaas, Augustine. Review of Guillaume de Saint Thierry's *Méditations et Prières* and *La Miroir de La Foi. Theological Studies* 9, no. 1 (March 1948): 131–34.

Leclercq, Jean. *The Love of Learning and the Desire for God.* Trans. Catharine Misrahi. New York: Fordham University Press, 1961.

Leclercq, Jean. "Toward a Spiritual Portrait of William of Saint Thierry." Trans. Jerry Carfantan. In *William, Abbot of St. Thierry: A Colloquium at the Abbey of St. Thierry*, edited by Jerry Carfantan. CS 94. Kalamazoo, MI: Cistercian Publications, 1987. 204–24.

McGuire, Brian. *The Difficult Saint.* CS 126. Kalamazoo, MI: Cistercian Publications, 1991.

Sergent, F. Tyler, ed. *A Companion to William of Saint-Thierry.* Brill's Companions to the Christian Tradition 84. Leiden and Boston: Brill, 2019.

Sergent, F. Tyler. "*Unitas Spiritus* and the Originality of William of Saint-Thierry." In *Unity of Spirit: Studies on William of Saint-Thierry in Honor of E. Rozanne Elder*, edited by F. Tyler Sergent, Aage Rydstrøm-Poulsen, and Marsha L. Dutton. CS 268. Collegeville, MN: Cistercian Publications, 2015. 144–70.

Sergent, F. Tyler, Aage Rydstrøm-Poulsen, and Marsha L. Dutton, eds. *Unity of Spirit: Studies on William of Saint-Thierry in Honor of E. Rozanne Elder.* CS 268. Collegeville, MN: Cistercian Publications, 2015.